D0898980

The View from Apartment Four

On Loving and Leaving New York

SKIP ROZIN

The View from Apartment Four

Copyright © 2019 by Louis E. Rozin

Published by 77 Street Press

ISBN 978-1-7331563-0-1 (paperback)

ISBN 978-1-7331563-1-8 (e-book)

Cover Design: Tom Carling

Cover Illustration: Ian Dingman

Interior Design: GKS Creative, Nashville

All Rights Reserved. No part of this book may be reproduced or transmitted in any form or by any means, electronic or mechanical, including photocopying, recording, or by any information retrieval or storage system, without the prior written consent of the publisher.

For Rebecca, Alex, Matt, and Jake

Contents

Author's Note

More than any other city, New York attracts people from all over the world. Some are just passing through and move away for reasons personal and professional; others could not think of ever leaving. Nearly all are forever changed by their New York experience. I am one of those people. My story is intended to be a conduit to theirs.

All events described here are accurate to the best of my memory, the notes and journals I have kept, and what research I have conducted to support these sources. The people in it are real. Because of this, and to avoid being sued or having a lot of them pissed off at me, I have used full names only of family members and individuals whose identities are necessary for their inclusion to make sense. For most others no longer living, I've used only their first names; many individuals still with us appear with no identification at all.

Writer at work, circa 1979. Photo by Jerry Greenfield.

Oh no!

It was New York City in the 1960s: not the best or the worst of times but a time when theater was cheap and people in power generous, when drugs and crime were driving out the white middle class in search of the promise of the suburbs and an ambitious urban renewal project was turning the Upper West Side into the latest hot destination neighborhood.

Troublesome as the bad was, the good was really good. It drew gleeful throngs to the sidewalks bordering the Natural History Museum on the last Wednesday in November to marvel at giant cartoon characters taking shape, inflated from flat as chalk drawings on the street to become fifty-foot-tall balloons floating high above the Thanksgiving Day parade. Many of those same people crammed onto the West Side Highway blocked from traffic to oh and ah as July Fourth fireworks exploded over the Hudson River, the visual and audial spectacle spiced by clouds of marijuana wafting through the evening air.

These were the celebrity events. Out of sight were the gracious acts of established professionals extending their expertise and contacts to unproven newcomers, struggling

writers, and actors who fought long odds and rejection to practice their craft then comforted their battered egos with late nights of jazz at Count Basie's on 132nd Street and in the morning headed to Éclair on West 72nd Street for a cup of strong black coffee and a fresh-baked croissant so buttery that adding more constituted wretched excess.

My ticket to all of this—the good and the bad—was my residence in Apartment Four, 336 West 77th Street, granting easy and reliable access until it ended on that dark day in 2011.

The eviction notice taped to my apartment door was not a total surprise. I had known it was a possibility for months since I learned the building was being sold, a brownstone on Manhattan's Upper West Side just off Riverside Drive. Still, seeing it set my heart pounding. For forty-six years the little one-bedroom had been part of my life; that was a simple reality. What I had failed to understand was how integral a part it played and what losing it would mean—not until that moment.

I had moved there in November 1965, when I first came to the city. The Upper East Side was more popular in those days, the full impact of the Lincoln Square Urban Renewal Project having not yet spread that far west of Central Park and north of Columbus Circle. This was part of why I preferred the West Side; its low profile made it cheaper.

My other motivation had to do more with look and feel. The combination of modest brownstones, typically five-story

walk-ups, and majestic old buildings imbued the area with a sense of stability and elegance while permitting it to remain in human scale, distinctly different from the Upper East Side, where new high-rises dwarfed residents and seemed to sprout daily. Years later, the Landmark Preservation Commission would recognize its significance and declare much of the area officially historic, protecting its design features from change. But in 1965 it was just a neighborhood seeking positive affirmation, admittedly seedy in places, all of this ensuring that there were plenty of choices. From West 72nd Street to 86th, West End Avenue to Riverside Drive, at least a dozen "apartment for rent" signs beckoned from ground-floor windows. I settled on one on West 77th Street, second floor front.

Nomadic best describes my journey to New York. I graduated from college in 1963 and spent a year in Europe. Living abroad had been a plan of mine since my sophomore year, almost an obsession—odd because there was nothing I could identify behind it. None of my friends were leaving the country or ever had. No one in my family had ever ventured east of New York. Going to Europe had to do with me seeing myself as a writer; this was something writers did.

I had worked through four years of school to make my plan happen, refining all the early details: sail to England on an ocean liner (going by sea was important), buy an MG at the tax-free price of $1,800 (the color had to be British racing green), and live in Europe.

Looking back, I should have given more thought to the next portion of my plan. I arrived in London on a cold and

wet October evening and hit a wall. I was alone, forty-five hundred miles from home in a foreign country and had no idea what to do next. Confronting the unknown plagued me as I toured central and northern England, making stops purely on impulse: Scarborough to honor Simon & Garfunkel (nice beach but no fair), Newcastle looking for the coal (some four hundred years late), then to Scotland in search of any village resembling Brigadoon (just silly). Much of this was in the rain and not enjoyable. I could not shake the idea that I had made a mistake. Spending a year abroad was romantic, and starting in England was smart, but I was heading next for the continent and had conducted no research, had no contacts there, and spoke only English.

Anxiety about what lay ahead was probably too much on my mind that Saturday afternoon in Inverness when I crossed the street without looking and came so close to a passing car that I tasted the acrid exhaust from its tailpipe.

And the next day, too, a drizzly Sunday morning, when my car hit a slick patch crossing a bridge and crashed into one of the abutments. I remember sitting there thinking, *What am I going to do now? I am literally hung up here, stuck on part of this bridge, and have likely destroyed my new roadster. What a mess I've made!* Suddenly I was surrounded by six cyclists who treated my plight as routine. They blithely unstuck me by lifting the front of my car from the offending section of bridge, checked the undercarriage and declared it sound, wished me good day, and peddled off in the rain.

This was the rocky introduction to my personal version of Mark Twain's *The Innocents Abroad*. Improvement came slowly. Cold and wet as Britain was, France was colder and wetter, especially Paris. Being Paris, much was good—crepes fresh made by street vendors, student rates at the Jeu de Paume and Rodin museums, strolling through Luxembourg Gardens and Père-Lachaise, cheap seats at the symphony— and hiring myself out as a typist for an American writer helped defray costs. Friends and family sent letters to me at American Express. That famed Rue Scribe office, now closed, also served as a meeting place for fellow travelers. Because the basement mail desk was organized alphabetically in three sections (A–J, K–Q, and R–Z), I regularly lined up beside the same people and we shared news from home as if we actually knew each other.

But I found the winter oppressively dreary and bargain accommodations on the Left Bank—the only place for a writer to be—meant hotels that traded higher floors for lower rates and fewer amenities: little heat, little hot water, thin cotton blankets, and forsaking western-style commodes with one-ply paper for porcelain holes in the floor and strips of *Le Monde*.

As my money ran low and I sought cheaper hotels, the lack of comfort played on my psyche. I adjusted. I abandoned the hotel's barely acceptable general-use bath for one of the city's public showers, where two francs (forty cents then) bought twenty minutes of steaming-hot water in clean, private conditions. More and more of my afternoons were

spent in well-heated cafés, relying on the generous tradition
of the French to permit customers to sit as long as they wished
over a single cup of espresso.

The one thing I did not consider was going home; I'm
not sure why. I was unhappy, and as January gave way to
February, my prospects for a cheery April in Paris seemed as
realistic as encountering Ernest Hemingway or Gene Kelly
on Boulevard Saint-Michel. But somehow going home was
not an option. Call it pride, call it stubbornness, but a year
abroad was my plan and I would be damned if misery was
going to make me abandon it.

But I had to do something. So after four months,
and with my finances as depressed as my mental state,
I headed down the Mediterranean coast of Spain until
the rain stopped. On the Costa del Sol I dropped the top
on my MG for the first time. The town was Fuengirola,
then primarily a fishing village, far different from the
international resort it has become. What tourist trade it
enjoyed was brief, starting in late spring and lasting through
summer. I arrived toward the end of February, a time so
quiet that I could afford a four-room apartment two blocks
from the Mediterranean for less by the week than a night
in a two-star hotel.

A lack of cachet made the 1960s an ideal time to be
in southern Spain, not so different from how I imagine
the 1920s in Paris and the 1940s in Greenwich Village.
A sense of casualness permeated daily life. Fishermen sold
prawns from their boats before delivering to the market,

and bartenders filled customers' empty wine bottles for ten pesetas a liter, or about seventeen cents.

This low-key atmosphere also made for easy friendships with restaurant owners, regulars at local bars, and fellow expatriates, a term loosely floated among us with pride. It also led to my gaining full-time employment at a resort hotel in Torreblanca, one town away along the coast. Each morning I drove the hotel's owner as she inspected houses she was building. She talked enthusiastically about her dream to create an escape in the Iberian sun for families fleeing the harsh northern climates of England, Scandinavia, and Germany. "Look," she said to me one morning, pointing to a house nearly completed, "it's so Spanish." When not chauffeuring, I mixed drinks at the hotel's beach bar during the busy evening hours and by day operated the tiny rental fleet of pedal boats and sailfish, surfboards with a lateen sail. The tab for an hour was sixty pesetas—about a dollar—and guests unfamiliar with sailing could request me. (No extra charge; I worked for tips.)

Before long I was tanned, sported a beard, and even picked up a little job-specific Spanish. Beer and whiskey are pretty much beer and whiskey, but gin in Spanish is spelled *ginebra* and pronounced "henabra." I fell in with a little community of other staff from the local bars and restaurants and envisioned my ideal existence going on—well, I guess just going on and on.

Then midway through the summer I heard from my draft board. You know, one of those form letters that began with

"Greetings" and followed with the date I was to present myself for induction into the army. I drove to the American consulate in Malaga and requested a six-month postponement and was told no. I drove to the embassy in Madrid and requested a three-month postponement and was told no. I wrote to my draft board in the States, pleading geographic hardship and requesting the nearest Selective Service office to Torreblanca and was ordered to return immediately.

I wrote home for sympathy and the name of a lawyer and received a letter from my older brother warning me of the consequences of being labeled a draft dodger. Then came the telegram from my father:

> HAVE CHECKED WITH ATTORNEYS AND FEDERAL AUTHORITIES AND IT IS OF GREATEST URGENCY THAT YOU RETURN AT ONCE. PENALTIES ARE VERY SEVERE. THERE MUST BE NO DEVIATION FROM THIS REQUEST.

Their response should not have been a surprise. My brother, Lee, was then a lieutenant in the air force, and our father, Arthur, a staunch Republican who had prospered during World War II on the back of government contracts. I shipped my MG to the States with the help of bar regulars—sailors stationed at the US Navy base in Rota—rode trains to Paris for a French farewell to civilian life, and prepared to face two years in the army.

This was October of 1964. I remember sitting in one of the cafés where I had sought heated comfort just eight

months before, this time outside in the afternoon sunshine, drinking a glass of Muscadet and perusing a copy of the *International Herald Tribune*. There was some coverage of Vietnam but nothing that hinted that I was heading into physical danger; the war did not garner major attention by American media until after we began committing substantial numbers of combat troops the following year. I saw the future as blank, not in a negative way but open, less with apprehension than curiosity; millions of men had survived two years in the army and so could I. Had I understood what was already percolating thirty-eight hundred miles away in Washington, DC, I would not have been so blasé.

Two months earlier reports had surfaced that three North Vietnamese torpedo boats attacked the USS *Maddox* off the coast of northern Vietnam. The reports—which may or may not have been accurate—led to passage of the Gulf of Tonkin Resolution, granting President Lyndon Johnson authorization without a formal declaration of war by Congress to escalate military action against North Vietnam. Johnson took full advantage of that authority and in the process made history.

I never became part of that history—at least, not directly. Why and especially how are best told later in this book; I promise to do that.

It took me thirteen months to get from the Left Bank to my apartment in New York City, but in the fall of 1965, I was establishing residency on West 77th Street. Even when 31.9 cents bought a gallon of regular gasoline and mailing a letter cost a nickel, my apartment was a bargain: $110 a

month, furnished with utilities extra. I soon learned it was even cheaper than that. Within a month of my moving in, a neighbor introduced me to the magic of rent control, enacted during World War II to guard against rent gouging and still in effect. This, he said, was a rent controlled building. I applied to the City Rent and Rehabilitation Administration for "relief" and found the legal rent for my apartment was $68.85 a month.

The Upper West Side in those days combined urban sophistication with a kind of intimacy in everyday services usually associated with small-town life. Just up the street was the Collegiate School, whose founding date of 1628 made it the oldest school in the United States. We were only twelve blocks from the newly created Lincoln Center of Performing Arts, where limousines nightly squired the rich and famous but five dollars bought a decent seat at a concert for the rest of us. Two blocks to the east, Broadway offered shoe repair, hardware stores, Woolworths five-and-dime, and G&S Linens, a holdover from another era; its wood-and-glass display drawers contained high-quality Egyptian cotton, fine linen for bed and table, and women's handkerchiefs exquisitely embroidered in Madera.

A block more to Amsterdam was Osner Business Machines, a hospital for ailing typewriters and much more. When business was slow, owner Stanley Adelman shared stories of how he and his father survived five concentration camps during World War II, including macabre accounts of children staging corpses for amusement. "Toys were in short

supply," said Stanley. Good timing might reward visitors with a glimpse of Stanley's more illustrious typists—Tom Wolfe, Alfred Kazin, Philip Roth, or David Mamet, none willing to trust his machine to anyone else.

There were fancy restaurants like Fleur de Lis on 65th Street off Broadway and Café des Artistes on 67th, and also establishments to serve the frugal but discerning: narrow little Daitch Dairy with tub butter and a wide variety of cheeses, Horn & Hardart with prepared foods and great tapioca pudding, supermarkets on 74th and 72nd, Gitlitz Kosher Deli right on the corner of 77th and Broadway, and four bakeries, including Éclair on 72nd where an afternoon's coffee and pastry break in its dining area was like a trip to Vienna, every table featuring conversation in a different language.

A block north of 79th Street was Zabar's, just then building its reputation as a world-class delicatessen and already endearing itself to locals who knew near closing to ask for cold cuts and smoked salmon ends at half off. Across the street was the less obvious but equally amazing Broadway Nut Shop, famous not only for the fruits and seeds of its name but chocolates and the city's best assortment of licorice; if not shopping, the fragrance of roasting nuts was reason enough for a visit.

That relatively small area also offered a strong sample of classic New York architecture. We were bordered by two block-dominating apartment buildings, the Dakota on 72nd and Central Park West and the Apthorp on 79th and

Broadway. Known for their grandeur, they attracted the rich prior to World War I when the Upper West Side was considered remote compared to addresses farther downtown. In between was the Central Savings Bank on Broadway and 73rd, its ironwork ceiling reaching sixty-five feet above the bank floor, the posted list of directors in 1949 including Dwight David Eisenhower. Across the street, the Ansonia, that beaux arts–style residential hotel that at its height was home to Babe Ruth, Theodore Dreiser, Arturo Toscanini, and Enrico Caruso.

Soon after I arrived, the Ansonia took on the identity of its basement tenant, the Continental Baths, a gay bathhouse where Bette Midler sang early in her career. In the late 1970s it became Plato's Retreat, the very private and infamous sex club. On the east side of Broadway, the Beacon Theatre posed a secret of its own. It looked prosaic from the outside, but the price of a movie ticket unveiled an ornate neo-Grecian interior that boasted thirty-foot-tall Greek goddesses and spectacular murals flanking the stage, all under a ceiling covered by enough gold leaf to wrest one's attention from anything on the screen—this years before it became a concert hotspot for the Allman Brothers, the Grateful Dead, Cirque du Soleil, and Paul Simon.

It was in every sense a neighborhood, and because it was New York, it attracted a broad spectrum of humanity. Those stately apartment buildings along West End Avenue were home to some of the city's oldest and most dignified residents. They seemed to be defiantly clinging to their independence as

they negotiated the traffic and weather to shop, attend church or synagogue, or catch subways and buses on Broadway. I never ceased to be touched by the sight of old couples, usually nicely dressed, gingerly helping one another over the banks of snow left by plows that cleared the streets but created perilous barriers at every crosswalk.

And especially in those early stages of evolution, we had junkies and drug pushers, their choice of Verdi Square— actually a triangle formed by 72nd and 73rd Streets, Broadway, and Amsterdam Avenue—as a place to conduct business earning it the label Needle Park.

They were all parts of a disparate population, comfortably including the likes of writers Isaac Bashevis Singer and Joseph Heller, actors Melvyn Douglas and Tony Randall. Did we interact with them? Not really. I was in the crowd when Shelley Winters, who lived in the co-op across from 336, picked the winning raffle ticket at our street fair, and occasionally saw Miles Davis on one of his late-night walks to relax after performing; he lived a few doors east on 77th Street. But this was New York, a place we all called home, where common folk encountering celebrities made no fuss; that was the pledge we made to share this space.

Also inhabiting those late-night hours were prostitutes, a holdover from the era of single room occupancy hotels, often referred to disparagingly as SROs, that gentrification was slowly eradicating. I learned of them during an awkward encounter within months of moving in. While taking a late-night walk, I noticed a young woman crossing

13

Riverside Drive and heading into the park. It was nearly 3:00 a.m.; I figured she was in trouble so followed at a respectful distance. When she continued through the passageway that led under the West Side Highway and to the Hudson River, I was convinced that trouble was serious. I'm from Ohio; I assumed she was going to jump. I thought, I obsessed, and then I intervened, albeit timidly. I asked if I could offer assistance. She politely thanked me, explained she had been "working Broadway" and was "taking some air," as she put it.

I was puzzled. Working? On Broadway? Then I got it. "Oh, working Broadway," I said hesitantly.

She smiled sweetly. "Yes."

"So you don't need help?"

"No, but thanks."

What, you ask, was I doing on the street at three in the morning? Walking—just walking. I had moved to New York to write but never seemed to get down to work until very late, my days mostly filled with staring at my typewriter. Evenings often found me in Greenwich Village, at the Lion's Head or the White Horse—only bars claiming a literary reputation would do—drinking and empathizing with others who, if not able to actually write, could at least talk about writing. Saturday night was the Limelight, not the disco club of the 1980s but a coffeehouse on Seventh Avenue where in the mid-'60s Jean Shepherd broadcast his radio show, a mixture of Americana, homespun philosophy, and stories about writing. By midnight or one o'clock I would take the

Number One subway uptown; it was then that I actually got down to writing, mostly short stories in those early years.

It was a struggle. I had worked as a newspaper reporter and I liked it. Writing was the closest I had come to being attracted to a profession, and I figured, hey, I can do this. And where does one go to write? New York. Why New York? That was the city most associated with writers, where they lived and set their stories. In Henry James's "Washington Square" and Stephen Crane's "Maggie: A Girl of the Streets," from Edith Wharton and F. Scott Fitzgerald to J. D. Salinger and Truman Capote, the grit and charm of New York came through and drew us. Reporters and novelists and playwrights traveled there to test themselves. Whatever their dreams, New York was where they came to play them out.

Yes, a cliché, something writers did, but one deeply embedded in the national consciousness. Two years after moving to the city, I visited my brother in Ohio and we adjourned to a bar for an after-dinner drink and a little local interaction. After some general conversation, the question arose, "So what do you guys do?" I said that he ran a paper mill (the family business); he added that I was a writer living in New York. One of the young women seated at the bar said, "A writer, in New York!" She didn't say "Wow," but she might as well have; it was all over her face. That's what being a writer in New York meant, at least in the rural Midwest in the mid-1960s.

The reality was less glamorous. It was my first time creating my own subjects and trying to sell the result, and I

had trouble setting a schedule and sticking to it. Most nights I walked around the neighborhood, trying to figure out the story I wanted to write, the details of the plot, and sometimes simply what words to put in what order.

We formed an odd little group during those late-night hours: people returning from evenings out, the occasional prostitute, and once in a while Miles Davis. And oh yes, the young woman standing on the southwest corner of West End and 77th; she was always there. This was when state psychiatric hospitals released thousands of patients into residential communities—the popular word was "dumping." She was our most visible dumpee, probably in her midtwenties, medium height, straight brown hair, and always wearing the same soiled whitish chubby coat over what appeared to be a housedress and short boots—all seasons, the same outfit. I do not know where she was during the day; I never saw her then. But she was there every night, for what seemed to be years. I often said hello but she never answered. In fact we were mostly a group of nonverbal communicators, just a nod here and a smile there—simple gestures that nonetheless transmitted friendship.

My nightly walks included Broadway for the last edition of the *New York Times*. In those days my local newsstand sold three versions each day: the bulldog or street edition came out about 7:00 p.m., a second arrived about 1:00 a.m., and the late final at 3:00 a.m. I liked getting the late edition. I have no idea why, except that I had no television in those early New York years—something about avoiding distractions so I

could spend more time writing, well-intentioned but flawed logic—and I wanted the latest news before going to bed.

Perhaps you have guessed by now that I did not get much written that first year. I did have a plan—always a plan—and it was quite different. I came to New York with $2,900 in savings—enough, I assumed, to support myself until I began selling. (This couldn't take more than eight months, a year at the most, I was sure.) But in my first ten months I sold not one of the dozen or so short stories that I finished. I submitted to periodicals from *The Atlantic* and *Playboy* to the women's magazines, and every story was rejected. The established practice was for writers to send a stamped, self-addressed envelope with their stories and I complied, and every one came back. I began to dread the arrival of the mail each afternoon.

All this failure made a cheap apartment essential; in fact, it spelled my survival in the city. I lived frugally, my apartment serving as not only a place to live and write but also entertain: cheap wine, music from my KLH record player—LPs and 45s saved from my teenage years, ranging from the Mills Brothers and the Four Freshmen to Della Reese and Bob Dylan—and meals built around chopped chuck. Before the year was up I was waylaid by a gimpy transmission in my MG. Suddenly my economic plan imploded. I needed money and my only marketable skill was journalism.

Fortunately this was New York, then the newspaper capital of the world. When I arrived there were ten dailies competing for readers in Manhattan; papers also served

Long Island, Queens, Staten Island, and Brooklyn, across the Hudson in New Jersey, and in nearly every town upstate. In September of 1966 I hired on with the Mount Vernon *Daily Argus*, one of the Gannett newspapers that served Westchester County, just north of the city.

My mornings started early, at the police station, where I checked for any newsworthy events of the previous afternoon and night then drove to the paper to write articles based on those events and anything else listed beside my name on the assignment sheet.

I found a home on the police beat just as I had in Miami and in Bethlehem, Pennsylvania, where I worked after returning from Europe, though the situations were different. I was twenty when I started at the *Miami Herald*; editors called me a sub-cub reporter and stuck me wherever I was needed. The major part of my cop house job was to monitor police and fire department radios for breaking stories to be passed on to veteran reporters, but I also culled through the handwritten reports of uniformed officers for little stories the paper's more experienced staff was too busy to cover.

In Mount Vernon and earlier Bethlehem, real news was scarce. The result was that I became skilled at making something out of very little: the parents who advised their restless eight-year-old to walk off his excess energy and then in alarm called police to track him down four miles away, and the eighty-year-old derelict found dead of natural causes, an unused one-way first-class air ticket to Buenos Aires in his pocket. Occasionally the sixty-seven thousand citizens of

Mount Vernon produced real news, like the federal investigation into charges that town hall was in bed with organized crime; I covered that too. But most days it was up to me to dig for those golden little nuggets filled with the flavor of small-town life.

Police was one of the underappreciated beats on a newspaper, not unlike obituaries. I wrote those, too, and found them equally satisfying but with a philosophical twist. Everybody dies, and it is the local newspaper where these passings have traditionally been recorded, especially small papers like the *Argus*. Not so much with big papers like the *New York Times*. Alden Whitman, the renowned *Times* obit editor, wrote in 1970 that 146,000 people died every day in the world, 250 just in New York. Only a tiny fraction of the most "unassailably famous or utterly infamous," as he put it, were covered in the *Times*. Small papers back then reported the death of every local resident or at least everyone who made it to a funeral home; that is where most reports of deaths originated. I liked to think we added a little dignity to the people's lives.

Taken together, obituaries and reports from the police presented a clear, uncompromising picture of a community. Transgressions of all kinds, from vandalism to murder, got reported to the police; everybody who died ended up at the morgue or a funeral home. From my perspective as a reporter covering obits and police, most of whatever else appeared in the average local newspaper was tangential.

Of course, that was back then, when I was younger—the world too. Since then we have had gasoline shortages, men

walking on the moon, a president resigning in disgrace, and terrorist attacks of horrific proportions. The *Daily Argus*, in business since 1892, ceased publishing in 1994, joining a lot of other newspapers, my *Bethlehem Globe-Times* among them. Most of those that have survived print only local obituaries paid for and written by the families. I cannot begin to guess what now constitutes crime to the police in Mount Vernon or Bethlehem, or where it is reported.

Within a year I had saved enough to quit the *Argus* and return full-time to 77th Street. By then I had learned a lot about surviving as a writer in New York. To stem the flow of money out, I picked up freelance publishing assignments, first retyping manuscripts too heavily edited to go into production. Publishers farmed out the work instead of handling it in-house, preferring to pay an hourly wage to hiring staff with benefits. Women in the 1960s complained that their typing skills shunted them off to menial jobs, but I value that one class I took in high school that taught me the touch system. It served me well as a reporter, earned me a job in Paris, and with the knack of deciphering editors' scribbles, sped me through eight severely marked-up pages an hour at a dollar a page.

Typing was good, but a better discovery was creating an index, that section at the end of nonfiction books that tells the reader where to find names and subjects in the text. It seemed simple: just read the uncorrected proof provided by the publisher, mark every proper name and subject or topic as it appears, then compile a list with the appropriate page

or pages. Names were easy but subjects tricky. If the subject were "global warming," the index should not reference the first page where "global warming" appeared but back where the discussion about it began, and then where it finished. This was, of course, before computers. I do not know what magic compiles a good index today.

I committed my early hours to publishing work then wrote well into the night. When I couldn't write, immobilized by writers' issues, I walked. And while I walked, block after block through those urban canyons, I gained comfort from knowing this was New York City, the Upper West Side, home to scores of writers; Isaac Singer and Joseph Heller were practically neighbors. At the same time, this realization was troubling because I clearly was not keeping up my end, not with Isaac or Joe or with any of them. The city continually reminded me of the gap between us. It actually taunted me. As I walked I swear I could hear the sound of typewriter keys striking sheets of paper, other writers producing feverishly behind drawn shades while I just walked.

Every night it was the same: write until the words no longer came, walk the streets of my neighborhood, then return to my apartment to try again to write. Ideally I would quit by five or five thirty and go to sleep. Much longer and the morning traffic—cabs and school buses and garbage trucks and the incessant horn blowing of drivers stopped when cabs and buses and trucks paused to conduct their business—impeded my falling asleep until the midmorning lull.

Beating that deadline was critical. I needed to get up by 11:00 a.m.; I had a plan and a schedule to keep.

All of it, from my work at the *Argus* to the bars where I spent my time getting down to write, the freelance publishing jobs typing and indexing, even my crazy schedule necessitating me getting to sleep before the city came to life, were a product of living in New York, the place I felt certain I absolutely had to be.

The key during all my time in New York was that apartment, the converging point where unlikely forces met that permitted me to remain there for all those years and, just as important, helped form me as a person and a writer. This was true from the day I moved in until the day I found that eviction notice affixed to my door. That was the beginning of the end.

People

In 1972 I read Stephen Longstreet's book *We All Went to Paris* chronicling Americans' then 195-year love affair with the French capital. I respected Longstreet's decision to ignore my time there in favor of the exploits of Benjamin Franklin, Isadora Duncan, Gertrude Stein, and Jackie Onassis, but I took umbrage with his premise as stated in his title. While many of us did go to Paris, where we all went was New York City.

We may have had different reasons, but we went. Not just the prospective professionals, drawn because New York is the center of everything from business and sports to fashion and the arts. They had to go; they still do. New York is *the* place to prove yourself. But it also attracts those outcasts shunned at home. Blacks from the South and gays from the Midwest, Jews from North Dakota, atheists from Mormon families in Salt Lake City and Luddites cast out of Silicon Valley, they all come to New York and feel at home because that is the one city certain to have others similar to them. And for those few who see yourselves as unique, unlike anybody else and

therefore alien, that's OK too; New York welcomes you. And probably more important, it will not harass you, because in New York nobody cares what you are.

Somewhere in at least one of these groups I fit right in, along with the rest of those strangers looking for someplace other than where they were from. Most of us were not born in New York, and fewer would die there, but for some part of our lives more of us came to live in New York than any other place. And New York accepted us. This is rare. Xenophobia is rampant in the world and in America. Island and coastal communities even have a name for nonnatives, "washashores," and it's not a term of endearment. But New York natives are themselves a rarity. It is a city of strangers and proud of it. I joined that diverse group when I moved into 336.

Five floors, two apartments on each floor, seven of them occupied in that fall of 1965. First floor front, one room and the building's smallest apartment, was understandably vacant then and in years to come showed the greatest turnover. First floor rear, with access to the backyard, was occupied by the owner, Florence Lescot, a woman in her sixties from someplace in central Europe—I guessed from her accent, Germany or Austria, maybe Poland—and her very frail father.

Maintaining a brownstone was hard work and for our landlord a hassle. She cut costs by depriving us of adequate heat in the winter, especially unpleasant for a building near Riverside Drive, the howling winds off the Hudson so strong that they literally wiped the painted information off

the parking regulations sign closest to the corner. She also saved money by making what repairs she could herself. Only when absolutely necessary did she call in help, and then usually some friend with skills only slightly more advanced than her own. As for routine maintenance, washing the hallway floors or changing overhead light bulbs, they mostly did not happen, at least in anything resembling a timely manner. And the state-required painting every three years? Forget it.

The result was perpetual friction between Florence and the tenants. I admit to being as impatient as the others— even at $68.85 a month—at least initially. Then came the weekend afternoon during my first spring, while I was visiting my neighbor across the hall in Apartment Three. I happened to look out his window and saw our landlady in the backyard with her father. He was thin and pale, sitting in a chaise, a blanket drawn up to his neck; she was in the chair beside him, chewing food in her mouth and then feeding it to him, similar to a mother bird feeding her chick. I found it endearing and had greater patience for her thereafter. This is a New York pattern: while preserving a comfortable distance often promotes indifference, tiny insights can inch strangers closer. Florence noticed the change. She did not keep the floor outside my door any cleaner, but she did occasionally invite me in for tea when entertaining friends, often artists visiting from Europe.

The man in Apartment Three was about fifty; he ran a lighting business in one of the other boroughs. Short, stocky,

and without any obvious interest in exercise, he did enjoy riding his bike made to order for him by the famous Alvin Drysdale: frame of 531 Reynolds aluminum, all Campagnolo components. We greeted each other regularly, engaged in innocuous conversations about his work and mine. Then on the morning when I finally completed my first novel, a three-year effort, I opened my apartment door to find a cake. I was delighted and surprised. I guess in those fragmented exchanges in the hall I had said that I was close to finishing, mostly in explanation for my not surfacing in recent days. Perhaps that was followed by, "Yes, soon." And then, I suppose—I swear I don't remember—"Tonight." And there it was on my doorstep, this obviously homemade cake, all frosted and with the piped message, "Congratulation on your creation."

Third floor front, in Apartment Six, was a musician who played the oboe. I did not know him. We were on different schedules, but I did hear him practice, that haunting, lovely sound, dry and clear, easing between the floors and into my apartment.

As this was my introduction to apartment living in a city, it was also my first exposure to the variety of peripheral noise generated by five floors of mortals with little in common except an address. Over the years I became accustomed to different sounds from different sources: the restaurant worker later in Apartment Six who returned home each night late, his dog barking happily as they headed out for their midnight walk; loud conversation and for a period of

three years screaming fights between the tenant and various guests transmitted through the walls from Apartment Seven, fourth floor rear.

And all kinds of music, some through the ventilation shaft and directly into my kitchen from Apartment Nine, top floor rear, but most from Apartment Six. At least three different musicians followed the oboist, the last being a frequently out-of-work actress who helped support herself by giving piano lessons. This all started before I arrived, I eventually learned. One summer afternoon, while standing outside waiting for the postman to deliver the day's mail, I was approached by a woman who had lived in the building during the 1950s. She asked about the current tenants, and when I got to the piano-playing actress, she said, "That was always the musical apartment."

I have no memory of the person in Apartment Five, third floor rear, when I arrived, but I shall never forget the couple in Eight, fourth floor front. He was a film writer in his forties, a native New Yorker living with a very attractive and much younger woman—tall with long blond hair, from California. At the time they were the only couple in the building and, for a twenty-four-year-old from Cincinnati, exotic and very New York: older man, younger woman, unmarried. Apartment Seven initially was a quiet widow from New Jersey in her late sixties with a daughter and her family living a few blocks away. When she moved, the tenants seemed to change every few years.

The top floor rear, Apartment Nine, was vacant when I moved in; I rejected it mostly because of all those stairs,

opting for the second floor front. Apartment Ten in the front belonged to a single man about thirty from Philadelphia who worked in the textile business and attended school at night, first to buck up his undergraduate degree and then to attend graduate school to become a psychotherapist.

Interaction with my neighbors was as different as they were. I rarely spoke to the woman in Apartment Seven except to say hello and occasionally offer to carry packages up those steps. Top floor front was my first new friend in the city—it was he who introduced me to rent control—and we forged a close friendship. When he received news that he had been rejected from the first graduate school to which he applied, the phone call was brief: "You'd better come up." We spent that night railing against the forces of injustice and remain friends to this day. We celebrated when he was awarded his PhD; I was an usher at his wedding. The film writer and his girlfriend, together and then apart, would remain friends during most of my time in the city. When I wanted a break from writing—or not writing—I would push their buzzer three times; they'd respond with one buzz if they wanted company and silence if not.

Other relationships were hit and miss, often with surprising results. Years after moving in, a man then in Apartment Seven, fourth floor rear, knocked on my door late one evening, obviously distraught. I invited him in, offered him coffee, a glass of wine. He only wanted to talk, so I listened. All he kept saying was, "You know about me, don't you?"

I told him that I did not; I guessed he was gay but was uncomfortable saying so.

"You must know," he said.

I paused and finally ventured, "You mean you're gay?" He nodded, and I shrugged. "I've got to go," he said, left, and never approached the subject again.

Our building was like the city, strangers keeping our distance or inching toward becoming friends, with most relationships falling somewhere in between. The encounters that initiated those relationships were part of the jumble of circumstances that prevail in New York. Some were predictable. I contacted two high school buddies of my brother and several of my classmates from college. Results were mixed. One of my brother's friends, although eight years my senior, has remained close to my family and me, while the other and I soon drifted apart. Some of my old classmates remained close for years; with others, I never really connected. One friend from college, Jerry, was my best friend in the city until he died in 1995.

Some encounters were truly random, and some that appeared random had near-magical links, part of a strange selection process that characterizes life in New York.

While drinking an espresso at the Café Tel Aviv on 72nd Street, I noticed something familiar about the waitress. I was not a regular, drawn by the menu of Israeli specialties or to catch "singing rabbi" Shlomo Carlebach or comic Gabe Kaplan—this was ten years before his *Welcome Back Kotter* television fame—so I did not know her from that setting. But

she looked so familiar, and it seemed as if she briefly lingered after taking my order, suggesting that she recognized me.

When she returned with my coffee, she stopped and stared at me. And I stared at her. I did know her, but from where? Suddenly she smiled and pointed at me. "R to Z," she said, and immediately I knew.

"R to Z," I responded and we both laughed. She had staffed the mail desk at American Express in Paris and for all those months had handed me my mail from the last section of boxes. She didn't remember my name, but she did recall that my letters were stored in the R–Z section—amazing as that desk daily handled between eight thousand and ten thousand pieces of mail.

These unlikely little dramas happen because New York attracts so many people who, for one reason or another, prefer not to remain in their hometowns and feel a connection with others who have followed the same path. And also because New York—and when I say New York, I'm primarily talking about Manhattan—is a relatively small place.

Add to this mixture of ordinary people all those elite individuals drawn to this capital of so much, and a normal Midtown outing becomes an adventure of celebrity watching. I was on the second floor of Abercrombie & Fitch one afternoon in the late 1960s, back when A&F stocked merchandise capable of equipping safaris and not upscale casual wear. There was Danny Kaye entertaining the sales staff with that charisma that turned *The Court Jester* and *The Inspector General* into movie classics, his exotic hand gestures and

facial contortions keeping them and me enthralled. I saw Liv Ullmann getting out of a taxi on 58th Street east of Madison Avenue, saw a remarkably thin Dick Van Dyke walking down Fifth Avenue near Saks, and shared a subway for three stops with Marian Seldes.

Even while respecting their privacy, occasionally interaction occurred. I once entered the Scribner Book Store on Fifth Avenue and asked the saleswoman if she had a copy of Loren Eiseley's *The Night Country*. Scribner's—famous for its Beaux arts design—was the appropriate place to shop for Eiseley, as Charles Scribner's Sons was his publisher. "No," she said, "but we do have Loren Eiseley," and turned with a dramatic flourish to reveal the brilliant naturalist. We talked for a few minutes, and when we parted and I told him how pleased I was to meet him, he responded with: "I'm always concerned when meeting someone who likes my writing, fearful that he'll discover I have feet of clay."

Sometimes these brushes with celebrity lasted longer than a few minutes. A friend happened to be the stepson of Jacques Lipchitz, the Cubist sculptor and part of the Paris artist community that included Pablo Picasso in the early twentieth century. Another friend ended up marrying the son of couturier Pauline Trigère, who counted among her clientele Grace Kelly and Elizabeth Taylor.

Jacques and Pauline never became my friends, but over time I saw enough of them to gain a sense of who they were. Ms. Trigère, one hell of a dresser, was abrupt and often forbidding but not on the night her only grandchild

was born, when she turned into a typical *bubala*, worried and proud. Mr. Lipchitz, not such a good dresser, was warm and generous, and even at eighty, overtly sensual. He once allowed me to spend a morning with him at his Hastings-on-Hudson studio, and during lunch at his favorite delicatessen he surreptitiously assessed every woman entering or leaving, often speculating on how they might appear naked. "You must remember," he said, almost apologizing but not really, "I am by profession a student of the female form."

Social connectivity thrives in New York. An urban phenomenon postulated in the mid-twentieth century and popularized in John Guare's play *Six Degrees of Separation*, it is characterized by a friend-of-a-friend chain of interactions that makes unlikely chemistry almost common. I am a believer. It led me to most of my friendships, to the woman I married, and to many of my chances for work.

Nothing more actively impacted my personal chemistry in New York than enrolling in a writing class at Columbia University's School of General Studies. The decision came to me gradually over my first four months in the city and with some pain. Every day I woke up, went to my typewriter, inserted a fresh piece of paper, and stared at it for the rest of the morning, afternoon, and well into the night. I took breaks to walk, occasionally to go down to the Village for a drink or two; I took a break to buy a newspaper. And after each break I returned to that piece of blank paper. It was terrible.

I should not have been surprised. The only writing I had done until that time was for newspapers, a kind of forced

labor. I would enter the city room, read the assignment sheet to discover what was expected of me, then go on to report and write the articles. A simple cause and effect was involved: if I did not file my articles by the deadline, I would get fired. There was no such urgency on West 77th Street other than what I created myself, and I responded by writing very little. I do not recall who suggested the writing class, probably somebody in one of those Village bars.

Regardless, it worked. I began writing more, if only to satisfy assignments that would be read and discussed in class. I ended up taking classes for three years, first with Dick Humphreys, who originated the writing program as part of the General Studies curriculum, and then with Robert Gorham Davis, the literary critic. For many of us, those classes were a substitute for the critical interaction that successful writers get from dealing with an editor. But because they were at Columbia, in New York City, the value went much further.

It was a girl I met there who worked as an editor at Random House and secured for me my first job retyping manuscripts for publication and then introduced me to indexing. It was in one of those classes that I met Joanna Steichen, who was then married to the photographer Edward Steichen; she became a close friend, and it was in her apartment where my former wife Julie and I were married. And it was at a party given by Dick Humphreys that I met James Oliver Brown, who became my agent for more than twenty years.

This is what living in New York does: creates an environment of opportunity to experience interesting situations. At Joanna Steichen's apartment I met playwright Edward Albee, who at one of her parties moderated a discussion about the difference between an incubus (male demon in a sexual fantasy) and a succubus (female version). His mother, Frances, was at one of those gatherings; she explained to me that the artistic design of the Albee movie theater in Cincinnati was an example of her late father-in-law's commitment to decorate his chain of theaters with real art.

At Jim Brown's apartment in 1968 I met the writer Jean Stafford, and later in a restaurant she became so enraged at my supporting the students in the ongoing Columbia protests that she threw down twenty dollars to cover her portion of the bill and stormed out. At another of those parties I met writer Herb Gold, who forty-four years later encouraged me to write this book.

Perhaps most amazing about these encounters is how random, routine, and especially common they are. Nearly all New Yorkers experience them, have a set of stories that begin with the line, "You'll never guess who I saw today!"

These dynamics do not exist in Pocatello or Dubuque, but they do in New York, or at least they did then, a time when paparazzi were still more common to Hollywood and the Riviera than New York, when famous people still felt comfortable and safe appearing in public and even interacting with strangers. In that everyday environment, opportunities happened.

You did not have to be special for them to happen; you just had to be there. And it didn't need to involve celebrities to be memorable. Daily, casual interaction yielded a richer, more interesting life. Even at a bar or restaurant, or ice skating at the Wollman Rink in Central Park, the chances were better of striking up an interesting conversation than at a similar location elsewhere.

From early on, some opportunities for me included work, and not just typing and indexing. The editor of my first published book, Jonathan Segal, had worked on the *New York Times* travel section; his introduction there led to ten years of articles in the *Times*. The attractive young woman in Apartment Eight at 336 eventually broke up with that older man and began dating an editor at *BusinessWeek* who hired me to write a piece about anabolic steroids, which led to my writing off and on for *BusinessWeek* for eleven years.

It is hard to explain to a non-New Yorker how these things happen; there is no one pattern, no single scenario. When a woman I was dating and I met one day for lunch near her job at the Time, Inc. Building—then at 51st Street and Avenue of the Americas—we were joined by five other *Time* magazine staffers; I knew two of them besides my friend.

It was crowded and noisy, typical of Midtown restaurants on a weekday, and the conversation was typical as well. "So," said one man I did not know, "I understand you're a writer. What do you write?"

"I consider myself primarily a reporter, so pretty much anything," I said.

He introduced himself as head of *Time*'s New York bureau. "I need reporters who can cover anything," he said. "You need work?" That was the beginning of four years reporting for *Time*, for him and the two bureau chiefs who followed him.

Not all of these encounters bore fruit. During my first weeks in the city, when I was just settling in and worried about making my way, money was ever on my mind. I made no secret of this, and an acquaintance put me in touch with a furrier who ran a fancy store on 57th Street off Fifth Avenue. He needed someone to handle his correspondences for a few hours a week—perfect for me.

The first week of the new year, the furrier told me that some of his coats were going to be used on *The Tonight Show*; he wanted me to take them down to Rockefeller Center, home of the NBC studios. My instructions were to remain with the coats until the show finished taping and then return them to the store. Regular *Tonight* host Johnny Carson was off, replaced by Woody Allen. I ended up assisting him during the rehearsal as he clowned with the furs, even tossing them on the floor; mostly I retrieved the coats that he tossed, but it was all in good fun. (The furrier watched the show that night and was not amused, I heard the next day.)

Later that week, a friend or perhaps an associate of Allen—I don't recall Marilyn's actual position—called to ask if I would be interested in working for Allen as an assistant; apparently he felt that I handled the horseplay of the rehearsal well. This was 1966, and I was a New Yorker for

all of three months. Woody Allen had just made *What's New Pussycat?* Such Allen classics films as *Annie Hall* and *Hannah and Her Sisters* were years away, and I had no knowledge of his time writing for Sid Caesar. I knew him as a comic, and I had come to New York to write.

I said no but thank you—probably in retrospect a mistake. Working for Woody Allen would have been a good thing, even if I started off running errands. I might have ended up writing for movies or learning to play the clarinet. If I hung around long enough, I might have met Mariel Hemingway.

Or maybe not. But at least there was a chance, which is part of the appeal of New York. In New York you can encounter just about anybody at any time, and once you do, almost anything can happen. Once you leave, these chances vanish.

THREE

Writing–Part One: Pain

Short fiction was not my only class at Columbia that first year. I also registered for a nonfiction workshop taught by Harry Nickles. Nickles was an editor at *Holiday*, a glossy, upscale travel magazine known for publishing famous writers such as Graham Greene, William Faulkner, and Saul Bellow.

Nonfiction was an afterthought, a skill worth sharpening in class but not my primary interest. I had come to New York to write, and by that I mean fiction. Short or long, it had to be fiction. That is what being a writer meant to me. I had worked as a reporter on two newspapers—three counting the *Daily Argus* after moving to the city—and had written and published dozens of news and feature articles, hundreds if you include obituaries. I liked nonfiction, but fiction was where I would make my way.

I started writing short stories and testing them in Dick Humphreys's class, reading them aloud and listening as the

other students commented. Ideally I had someone else read; since this was New York there was no shortage of theatrical experience or at least ambition. Listening gave me an additional perspective beyond hearing my own voice; I also gained from watching the class's reaction.

It went well. Humphreys was a good critic, and I quickly learned which students had something valuable to say and which were more interested in criticism as performance. The class was probably more valuable for me than some of the other students, primarily because I was actively writing and so always provided something to be discussed; many of them soon withered from the harsh reactions and were slow to turn in their assignments. (There were exceptions. One woman who had lived in India wrote haunting and highly sensual stories, and a tall, skinny young man had an energetic—almost exhausting—but impressive writing style. A later class included Robert Deane Pharr, who went on to publish *The Book of Numbers* and *S.R.O.*, well-received autobiographical novels.)

I accepted the criticism I thought was valid and ignored the rest, retyped final versions, and sent them off to magazines, always with a stamped, self-addressed envelope as custom dictated. These were all unsolicited, cold submissions, known in publishing as "over the transom." Transom in architecture is the crosspiece that separates the door—usually the front door—from the shallow glass window above it; it's also the nautical term for the surface that forms the stern or back of a boat. Publishing combines these. "Over the transom"

describes a manuscript submitted unceremoniously through the back door; picture it being thrown, rarely an advantageous introduction.

Whether because of the means of submission or the quality of my work, the results were the same: every story was rejected. The only difference was how. Most common were preprinted rejection notes, usually on little pieces of paper, four-by-six inches or smaller.

Rejection came from major literary magazines like the *New Yorker* and *The Atlantic*; less major ones like the *Paris Review* and *Evergreen Review*; women's magazines like *Harper's Bazaar*, *Redbook*, *Cosmopolitan*, and *Mademoiselle*; men's magazines like *Playboy* and *Cavalier*; general readership magazines like the *Saturday Evening Post* and *Esquire*. I tried all levels and types of magazines, any that published short fiction, and they all said the same thing: no. The wording was different, but only slightly. "Thank you for submitting this material. After careful consideration, we regret that it doesn't suit our present needs." Or "Thank you for showing us your manuscript. At the present time it doesn't fit in with our editorial needs and we must regretfully return it."

Slightly worse and highly insulting were form letters that contained an introductory paragraph followed by multiple choices of rejection; that's right, a list from which the very busy editor selected the most appropriate. "Dear Contributor," one began. "Since we receive a number of unsolicited manuscripts every week, it is not possible to send an

individual letter with each one that is returned. However, your contribution was given a careful reading and we are unable to use it because:

- o It does not fit into our present feature needs.
- o We have duplicate material already on hand.
- o Material and style not suitable for our use."

According to "The Editors," my submission fell into the last category.

A surprising number of editors, even while rejecting a story, showed that they were engaged in the action or the characters, a primary goal in writing and so a victory for me. One of my favorite short stories, "To a Fine Cocktail Party," was about a young couple going to a party in southern Spain, proceeding up the Mediterranean coast through a dense fog in a pedal boat but so involved in their personal argument that they got lost. I'd like to say the fog symbolized their inability to recognize each other's needs but I probably just fell in love with the imagery. This particular editor was taken with neither.

"I found it absolutely impossible to believe that even a heedless young man would continue in a peasoup fog being absolutely certain that he knew where he was going. My husband and I have a summer place on an island off the Maine coast and although we knew the shape of every rock and every tree between the mainland and our cove, we have turned back to pick up a forgotten compass when we have seen the fog roll in far out at sea."

In those days, when nobody bought anything, I counted this as a victory. Admittedly, not a big victory, and my so elevating it indicates my state of mind at that time—very dark.

It was all part of a new kind of education. I was learning how to deal with frustration. Months and months of rejection took a heavy toll. Every story required hours of writing and rewriting—often days—to get it to the point where I risked exposing it in class, where I listened to criticism and then went back for more rewriting before selecting which magazine might make a good match. And the result: more rejection. It plagued me. Filling a blank page with words worth someone else's reading takes a healthy ego; the constant battering of my ego made writing all the more difficult. And that looming rejection took much of the joy that came from writing a good story or even a good sentence.

Sources of my anxiety and depression often work their way into my dreams. In the case of rejected stories, my recurring nightmare involved the mailbox in the foyer of my apartment building, one of the old brass models with cutouts in the center of each little door revealing the presence or absence of mail. In my dream I was maybe ten yards from the box—much farther away than the actual foyer permitted—struggling to reach my mail. I struggled because I seemed to be knee-deep in some gook that was inhibiting my progress; maybe quicksand or just mud, the dream wasn't specific. At the same time the mailbox was inexplicably moving away, always remaining just out

of reach as I tried to inch closer. And through that little cutout in the brass door, I could just make out that there was mail and it was one of my own envelopes, coming back to me. In those days, the rejection of my stories was never far from my mind.

When I first arrived in New York and began submitting stories, I expected to meet some opposition. I was prepared for months of failure, and so I saved every rejection letter and note. My plan, once I began publishing, was to frame them and hang them on my wall. *Look,* I would say to guests, *this is how I started, and look where I am today.* I never did buy that frame. I first kept the rejections in an envelope, and then a second envelope. Eventually, I bought a file cabinet.

Hard times. But because it was New York, a city with all those people, a shocking number of whom knew each other, there were tantalizing connections: somebody who knew somebody who knew somebody else. And even more shocking—or not, depending on one's view of the human condition—was the number of these people willing to help a young writer to whom they had only the most tangential connection. One of these was J. M. Flagler, an editor at *Look.*

Look was a general interest, large-format magazine patterned after *Life,* in existence from 1937 until 1971. It published photographs and nonfiction articles in its biweekly issues and also a two-page humor section featuring mostly cartoons but also some very short fiction. For a time in the 1960s, Jack Flagler was the section's editor, relevant for me because he was also a friend of Dick Humphreys. When I

turned in something Humphreys liked, he sent it to Flagler, less as a submission to *Look* and more to get it before an established editor.

I never met him, never spoke to him on the phone, but he took an interest in my work, and in the midst of all that rejection, his interest was a life preserver. Yes, nobody liked what I was writing enough to publish it, but here was this editor who thought enough of my stories to recommend them to his friends at other magazines. And when they rejected a piece—as they invariably did—he sent me letters of encouragement. One of these stories was about a young man desperately looking for a parking space before picking up his very important date. Flagler sent the following letter along with the rejection note that he was careful to interpret for me; while they said no, it was no with a caveat.

"I enjoyed your parking story very much, so much that, though I couldn't see any way to cut it to our length without serious mutilation, I took the liberty of referring it to a former colleague of mine in the fiction department at the *New Yorker*.

"I attach his note, even though it's a turndown, because it actually should encourage you. When 'they all like' an idea over there, it means you got fairly serious consideration . . . I hope you continue working in this vein."

I did continue, at least partly because of the encouragement of Jack Flagler and the others who understood the difficulty of getting published and took the time and energy to help lower those odds.

This is not to suggest that failure didn't test my resolve to stay put and keep writing. It did, but New York is a great place to salve frustration. I sought a good dose. In addition to the city's many distractions, I relied on the support of friends, many of them frustrated painters and writers who could identify and empathize with turning a blank canvas or page into something that not only satisfied them but a critic or editor. Talking with them—bitching really, about one condition or another—helped, knowing I was not the only poor schmuck slogging through all that failure.

But it was still a test, and no event was a greater test of my resolve than the fate of one of my favorite stories, "The Coffee Break." It was a simple piece, very short, about a man trying to get his chosen beverage from a vending machine and repeatedly failing. I wrote it for Dick Humphreys's class; in fact, the vending machine was the very one in the basement of Lewisohn Hall, the building where the class was held.

Humphreys sent it to Flagler, who sent it to an editor friend, and when it was rejected he encouraged me to keep it moving. I did, and every time it came back I sent it out again. This was before photocopy machines became standard in every office; to save myself the task of retyping page after page, I ironed rejected stories before resubmitting them, making them crisp and fresh looking.

So it went, out with a new cover letter, on to its next magazine, and back it came. It was a good little story, and those editors who bothered to write often said nice things along with their rejection. Until the day I opened my returned

envelope to read the handwritten note with just three words: "Not funny—yuck."

I was furious and embarrassed. I have successfully blanked out the editor's name and the magazine, but my feelings as I read that note remain with me. I was mortified. While I knew I was alone, I looked around the apartment to make sure there were no witnesses to my shame. I ripped the note into little pieces and flushed it down the toilet. I wasn't very happy with the story either. I threw it in the very back of my special file cabinet for rejections, vowing never again to look at it or show it to another person, and never, NEVER to recount the incident.

I tell it now because "The Coffee Break" resurfaced, but it took nearly five years. More on this later.

Me and Uncle Sam

Writing or not writing, and coping with the rejection of what I did manage to get down on paper, were not my biggest problems during those early New York years. That distinction belonged to the army. During two months in 1968, I could think of nothing else; for the rest of that year, it was never far from my mind.

You may recall the subject of the army and me; we last visited it in Paris, 1964, just before I boarded a plane to return to the United States. My army career was supposed to begin at the end of that flight. New York was the first point of induction; I was to report there. And I was ready, more or less; at least I was resigned to serving. It was one of those writerly things I pictured myself doing, a well-trodden path with a rich tradition; I had read James Jones (*The Thin Red Line*) and Norman Mailer (*The Naked and The Dead*).

My military adventure was set to begin early on a chilly October morning at the Army Induction Center on White-hall Street in Lower Manhattan. This was before the center's famous years—1967 when Allen Ginsberg and Susan Sontag

protested the Vietnam War there and Woody Guthrie's son Arlo sang about it in "Alice's Restaurant," and then 1969 when it was bombed. Back in 1964 the center was pretty innocuous except for the millions of young men who passed through as they bade farewell to civilian life for their foreseeable futures.

I sensed a kinship with these men as I climbed the stairs leading to the entrance—something about brothers in arms, foxhole buddies. This was a very American experience, I reasoned, shared by a certain percentage of able-bodied males once they reached the age of eighteen and a half. Weren't we all there because of the Universal Military Training and Service Act? Universal, as in all of us together. I felt it.

But once inside the big, steam-heated room, one of fifty or sixty future inductees, that vision began to fade. Clearly, they were of one group and I was not, and it wasn't just that at twenty-three I appeared to be older than any of them. More than those few years separated us.

They lounged on long wood benches, joked with friends, tapped their feet to music whining from little portable radios held close to their ears, this before the ubiquity of personal stereos and earphones. They seemed so at ease, as if being inducted into the army were a natural stage of life, the next step after going from grammar school to junior high to high school. Not for me. This was new and foreign.

I never knew anyone else who had ever been drafted. All of my group had received college deferments, and most went on to preserve their precious I-S status through some

form of advanced study—med school or law school or just plain graduate school. When I say "my group," I use the term loosely. I was part of a group only in the broadest sense: male, white, middle class, Jewish. I joined no college fraternity, was a member of no clubs. I did not even live in the dorm. Initially I lived at home. When I moved, it was into an off-campus apartment; I had no roommate.

Suddenly, looking around the room, I realized that I was going to be living in a barracks filled with roommates. I know—it was the army. You must be asking, "What did you expect?" I didn't. Odd as it sounds, being in the army had never entered the reality portion of my mind until that draft letter reached me in Spain, and that had been only months before. Everything had moved so quickly since then. On that morning in 1964 it became very real and not very comfortable.

The longer I sat there, the more isolated I felt. These young men were city-tough, reared on the streets of the five boroughs, and I suspected more the South Bronx than the Upper East Side of Manhattan. Their quips and horseplay made me realize that they had lived a life far different from mine. This did not make me want to jump in and bond; it intimidated me. The bravado of their manner—real or manufactured for the day—made it clear how much I did not belong.

This was not a Vietnam thing; Vietnam in 1964 was just beginning to heat up. This was about alienation. Minute by minute I felt less and less like joining up, less and less eager to begin serving my two years in the army. Whatever I had

been thinking hours before, some connection with my inner warrior, was delusional. I was out of place here as I had never been before and ill-equipped to survive what lay ahead. All the while, time was passing.

My internal struggle was interrupted when a portly sergeant, barely constrained by his khaki uniform, walked to the front of the room and called for order.

"Awright, youse guys," he said with some difficulty, having to talk around several pieces of gum he was chewing. "Let's knock it off. I'm gonna call off names and I want youse to come up here, pick up your files, and then sit back down."

He approximated each of the names—some Hispanic, others Polish, Italian, and Russian, with one or two Johnsons, Williamses, and Browns thrown in, an accurate representation of New York's ethnicity but not a single Goldstein, Cohen, or Levy—in a steady cadence without apparent concern for accuracy. Then he shifted the wad of gum far to the left side of his mouth, giving notice that what came next was important.

"Now," he said and paused for more emphasis, "I gotta know if any youse ever had trouble with the cops."

The room fell into silence. Every individual looked straight ahead, pictures of innocence. *Can't be,* I thought. None of these rough-and-tumble guys has ever been arrested? REALLY!

The sergeant was waiting. Suddenly, and quite surprisingly, I had an epiphany. In that entire room, only I raised my hand.

It was true. While working for the *Miami Herald* during my senior year in college, I was assigned to write a story about the city jail from the inside. I got myself arrested for vagrancy—a catchall charge used against undesirables until it was ruled too vague but still on the books in 1962—and served three days in jail. It wasn't much, but it was all I had.

"What exactly do you consider trouble?" I asked.

"What exactly did YOU have in mind?"

"Arrest and conviction before a criminal court and three days in jail?"

This, he seemed to feel, would qualify. He told me to take my file and report to a room one flight up. I was asked the circumstances of my "legal issues," and I laid out the details of the assignment, my arrest and time in jail, and the story I wrote. After several minutes of conversation among the officers there and some literal head scratching, my name was placed on a standby list and I was told to go home while they could investigate, maybe six weeks.

Their inquiry would undoubtedly uncover the true nature of my incarceration: that I was a reporter acting on assignment and not a criminal, a distinction too nuanced for these men but perhaps discernible at a higher level and therefore qualifying me for duty. Or not—I could not know. But as I left 39 Whitehall Street that morning, I knew it was a good place for me not to be six weeks later. My problem was how to make this happen.

The extreme choices were out of the question. I was not moving to Canada, declaring for Consciousness Objector

status, or shooting off one of my toes. I saw myself less a draft dodger than a draft objector, newly minted. The obvious place for me was the Army Reserve, that haven for like-minded young men during those early years of Vietnam; the first reserve units would not be sent to Southeast Asia until 1968. The operative word was obvious. I quickly discovered how many other draftable men had the same idea. Reserve units in New York City had a two-year waiting list. In nearby New Jersey, the wait was twenty months; Connecticut, eighteen months.

The message was clear: Move away from New York City and improve your chances. So I did. A mere 536 miles west lay Lancaster, Ohio, a town important in my youth and where by 1964 my brother ran the family's paper mill. The reserve unit there had no waiting list and no problem with the fact that I had already been drafted. All I needed was a signed release from my draft board. "These," said the clerk of the unit, holding up an official request form, "are never refused."

Perhaps, but mine was ignored. Three weeks of silence led me to call my draft board in Miami, asking about the delay. "Rozin, the smart guy who wrote from Spain," demanded the woman on the phone, more a statement than a question. "Out of my hands," she snapped and hung up. It took nearly three more weeks for my appeal to the regional office in St. Augustine to be denied.

By then it was late November. I could hear the military wheels of investigation grinding through my records, envisioned the long arm of induction reaching out from Whitehall Street; I could wait no longer. I drove to Washington to plead

my case at the very top of the Selective Service System, to the office of General Lewis Hershey. He was out. They told me his assistant, Colonel Dee Ingold, would see me. He did not but an assistant did. He was brief and efficient: "Son, if you don't want to be in this man's army then we don't want you. Good luck in the reserves."

My initial experience as a reservist was passable. The meetings were painless, and while basic training at Fort Dix, New Jersey, and advanced infantry training at Fort Polk, Louisiana, included very early mornings and lots of marching, running, and what the army called humping—which had nothing to do with sex and everything to do with hiking burdened by a full pack—my reporter's experience as a typist freed me from arduous activity; apparently the army needed someone to type reports more than another fighter.

Time in uniform proved to be surprisingly congenial. There was general sympathy for my swapping training for what my fellow soldiers considered torturous hours of typing, and even moments of individual closeness. I became friends with a former gang member who, while freely sharing accounts of confrontations on the streets of the Bronx, took pride in displaying his portfolio of art that he worked on in time off; I have a pastel of a woman's partial profile in my living room. One barracks mate from the south waited till after lights out to ask what it meant to be a Jew.

Once training ended, a little miracle occurred. In one of Defense Secretary Robert McNamara's moves to improve our military, several reserve units were beefed up to combat

readiness and others were disbanded. The Lancaster unit was dumped, and my records ended up in a filing cabinet in the National Personnel Records Center in St. Louis, Missouri. This was late in 1965, and that file cabinet was where I planned to spend the rest of my military career.

For a while it looked that way. Then on a cool May afternoon in 1968—at a time when I still considered difficulty filling blank pages with my own words to be a crisis—I received an "Involuntary Order to Active Duty." In forty-five days I was to get myself to Fort Knox, Kentucky, then to be transported at government expense to the Army Replacement Station in Oakland, California, and then on to the United States Army installation center at Schofield Barracks in Wahiawa, Hawaii. While the orders did not say as much, I could fill in the rest: to be sent to Vietnam to die.

How could I be so sure? Combat preparedness for me consisted of fourteen weeks in the wilds of New Jersey and Louisiana, perfecting my typing skills and trying to learn to march in step. (The words of my drill sergeant still ring in my ears: "Your other left, soldier, your other left.") There was no chance I could survive a shooting war, and by 1968 Vietnam was all of that.

The nature of the war changed radically between 1965 and 1968. The summer of 1965 saw a series of defeats of South Vietnamese forces followed by a buildup of US troops and skyrocketing causalities, up from 206 in 1964 to 1,863 in '65, rising steadily to 1968, the war's bloodiest year, when 16,589 Americans were killed.

These were not numbers hidden away in some top secret document. Night after night the public watched as all three networks broadcast gruesome images of American soldiers being killed and maimed. "Television brought the brutality of war into the comfort of the living room," media guru Marshall McLuhan would later say. "Vietnam was lost in the living rooms of America—not on the battlefields of Vietnam." Not until 1971 would the Pentagon Papers disclose that the Johnson Administration had withheld that US forces were bombing Cambodia and Laos—out and out lied to the public and Congress about covertly expanding the war—and massively misrepresented the chances for a victory that would never come. But even the sanitized coverage played poorly.

What had been isolated resistance became a national referendum. Such figures as Walter Cronkite, Robert Kennedy, and Martin Luther King Jr. condemned our involvement. Protests broke out on college campuses here and at US embassies abroad; the turning in and burning of draft cards were reported across the country. A Gallup poll in August 1968 showed that only 35 percent of Americans agreed with the war, down from a high of 59 percent in March 1966. Among those in opposition were groups claiming to represent students, women, black women, mothers, and teachers, and also individuals including Senator J. William Fulbright, Joan Baez, and Yale chaplain William Sloane Coffin.

Nearer to home, my college friend Bob Simon took time off from his studies at the New School of Social Research in New York to demonstrate against the war; in November 1967

he and three other protesters burned their draft cards in front of the federal courthouse in Foley Square. He was arrested and convicted under the federal law providing penalties for any person who "knowingly destroys, knowingly mutilates" a draft card. Bob served two years of probation; he died in a car crash in August 1969 while returning home from a protest.

We were close when we were both new to New York but saw less of each other as our views on dealing with the war diverged. I cautioned him against running afoul of the law; he saw the war drawing America into an immoral conflict and warned that when conventional resistance failed, more radical avenues were called for. His fear was for the soul of the nation; mine, for my personal safety.

Looking back, I question my taking the low road, unwilling to stand beside my friend protesting the war or to join the thousands of men my age in battle. I was incapable of either, consumed instead with my own vulnerability. Sadly, I was immobilized by it.

For that first month I did little more than remain in my apartment and watch *General Hospital* on daytime television and *The Smothers Brothers* and baseball at night. Call it depression; call it denial. Whatever the cause, I could do nothing. Then early in May news broke about the calling up of additional troops. Within those first two weeks some five thousand reservists were ordered to report to their home units, soon to be sent to active duty. I had to do something, so I prepared to again take my case to Washington.

I knew I was on shaky ground; my fear of death would

gain little sympathy among members of the military. One of the advantages of living in New York is the access it grants. I needed a new plan, and friends who sympathized with my efforts to avoid Nam were happy to oblige. Two tax lawyers and a specialist in corporate law listened as I proposed what I thought was the simplest course of action—the truth. While I had completed advanced infantry training at Fort Polk—so jungle-like, it was known as Little Vietnam—I rarely saw the outside of the company clerk's office, not so different from my experience in basic training at Fort Dix. Nearly five months of active duty and I knew nothing about fighting. None of my advisers liked my idea. The army would consider me a challenge and take pride in turning me into a battle-ready soldier, they argued.

They asked if I had had any childhood diseases like rheumatic fever or suffered from asthma or had flat feet, a time-tested road to a medical deferment. No, no, and no. Finally I recounted being rear-ended in a car accident during my freshman year in college; I had to wear a neck brace for months.

Their glee was instant. Three days later, after they had secured for me an appointment with an orthopedic surgeon, we met to examine my X-rays. And there it was, a still-broken bone just below the place where my spine met my skull, protruding from one of my vertebrae.

Back I went to DC. On the first Monday in June, I carried my X-rays to an appointment with Ohio Congressman Clarence Miller, a Lancaster native. He looked at my films,

nodded in sympathy, acknowledged that combat might not be the best place for me, and promised to do what he could. I left his office practically ebullient and that night expressed my confidence to friends over takeout Chinese food.

These were savvy Washingtonians, wise in the workings of the federal government. They listened patiently while we waited for our food to be delivered and shook their heads in concern. I was adamant; I had the support of my congressman. They suggested I was foolish to waste precious time on "the hill"; one called me callow. I needed a lawyer, and not just any lawyer, not even a member of my New York legal brain trust but a specialist experienced in dealing with the military. We debated until our food arrived. I remained confident, and then I unwrapped the little flag that came with my meal, that restaurant's version of a fortune cookie. "Live it up before it's too late," it read.

I am a sucker for omens. "I get it," I confessed. "Find me a lawyer." And they did. A quick survey of their collective resources led me back to New York to a recommendation from a friend of a friend. Two days later I sat in the office of Joan Goldberg, a bulldog of an attorney with Rabinowitz, Boudin & Standard, a firm specializing in the defense of civil rights and individual liberties and in the 1960s an impressive list of famous draft resisters and war protesters. Two years later she would become a partner of the flamboyant William Kunstler, the champion of left-of-center causes and such clients as Martin Luther King Jr., Abbie Hoffman, and the Black Panthers.

Joan in 1968 prepped for her time with William and his brother Michael Kunstler by representing—among others—me. Her first question upon reading my orders was, "Cutting this a little close, aren't we?" We were meeting on Thursday afternoon, June 6; I was to report to Fort Knox on Saturday morning, June 22. That was the closest she came to uttering a discouraging word. Whatever kind of appeal she filed with the army, what kind of legal action, I never knew. Her only instruction to me was, "Don't worry." But I did. From the following Monday on I called the office every day to ask for new developments in my case—any progress, any response, anything. "Not yet, don't worry." Every day I called, that week and into the next. For years I could remember the firm's phone number, and can recall it now with a little effort: 697-8640.

Finally came Friday, June 21, the day before I was to report to Fort Knox, and we had still heard nothing. I was a wreck, and Joan could tell. "Why don't you come in this afternoon," she said. "We'll wait together."

As I sat in her office, she put in a call to the army. I don't remember what part of the army or where, but she knew the number and she got through. By then it was four thirty, close to the end of the workweek. She covered the phone with her hand. "Sounds like they're having a party," she said. "I can hear laughter . . . and ice in glasses." Finally, she got someone's attention.

"You have the X-ray I sent?" By the nodding of her head, I could tell the response was yes. "You see that chip fracture

of the C5 vertebrae?" Again, the nodding of her head. "You want to send a man into combat with that on his record? He could be crippled for life, and you'll be paying for life."

Again she covered the phone. "They're talking," she said, and then: "OK." And: "OK. By when?" Silence. "And if he doesn't receive it?" More silence. "OK."

And that was it. I was told to go home; I would receive new orders countermanding my orders to report while the army figured out what to do. No, they would not arrive by Saturday—this was pre-email—but sometime during the week. When I pointed out that when I did not report to Fort Knox on Saturday, I would be officially AWOL, Joan gave me that same reassuring smile. "Don't worry," she said. "Go home."

I did, but I continued to worry until the following Monday, when the new orders arrived in a telegram:

PRIVATE ROZINS ORDERS HAVE BEEN REVOKED IN VIEW OF HIS QUESTIONABLE PHYSICAL QUALIFICATIONS FOR ACTIVE DUTY.

I was assigned to an army reserve unit on 42nd Street, where I served out the remainder of my six-year commitment, attending weekly meetings and once-a-year summer camp. Mostly I typed reports, just as I had at Fort Dix and Fort Polk, exactly what I was trained to do.

The events in my military melodrama had moved quickly from the initial meeting that led to my getting my neck X-rayed till that last phone call late on June 21. By the time

I got around to seeing a lawyer I, had just fourteen days to stave off reporting for active duty—eleven if you eliminate weekends. There was no time for even a really good lawyer to gain the necessary experience to deal efficiently with the US military establishment.

But that friend-of-a-friend chain that so effectively characterizes social and professional interaction in New York led me to the right lawyer to keep me out of Vietnam. This is the magic of the city: whatever your needs, somewhere on that little island you'll find it.

Thank you, Joan Goldberg. Thank you, New York.

Parking

Did I mention that I kept a car in New York? Of course I did, but briefly. The details are too embarrassing and cast decisions made while living there in a negative light. But that in part is what this book is about—the positive and the negative.

Few things make less sense for anyone living in New York on a tight budget than owning a car. Free on-street parking is scarce and risky, and the city has an excellent public transit system. Yet New York is filled with these idiots. Regrettably, I was one. And I had lots of company. There are between 3.4 and 4.4 million on-street parking spaces in the five boroughs, according to parking experts, and on any given day every one is occupied.

Most of us competing for these spaces are not native New Yorkers. They grew up without a car and know the hazards of keeping one are the stuff of legend. But this is a hard lesson for newcomers, the vast majority of whom came to the city with a car in our history. And that car is not a fixed image; it comes with deep-seated associations.

My most vivid memories of being young in Cincinnati are not of family gatherings at Thanksgiving or Chanukah but of car rides. Sunday mornings my father took me with him when he drove his dark-green Buick sedan downtown to the Fountain News to purchase copies of the *Cincinnati Enquirer* and *Chicago Tribune*. These were the only times I was ever alone with my father, and I treasured them. Every Sunday? Probably not even most; this is just how I remember it, with such reverence.

While these outings eventually stopped—I don't remember when or why—cars continued to take on an inordinate importance. I read *Motor Trend* magazine and Henry Gregor Felsen's teen novel *Street Rod* and eagerly awaited the annual unveiling of the new models.

Midway through my sixteenth year, I took all of my $550 savings and bought my first car, a five-year-old Ford convertible with a flathead V-8 and standard transmission. I proceeded to customize it to 1950s tastes: remove the hood ornaments and have the holes filled by welding (we called it "wiping"), replace the taillights with the bullet style of a '54 Oldsmobile, and install glasspack dual exhausts. I mark this as my entrée into teenage maturity, much of it centered on pursuing teenage girls.

From that day on I have never been without a car. To be otherwise was unthinkable, even in New York. This was especially foolish as I rarely drove any distance: back and forth to Mount Vernon while working for the *Argus*, home to Ohio twice a year, and occasionally for important errands.

I would have used it more if every trip did not necessitate breaking my parking routine, which was not done lightly.

Motorists in New York are confronted with the demonic alternate side rules, city-wide regulations that prevent drivers from leaving their cars in one spot for as long as they want. That's right, even when you find a legal parking spot, you cannot keep it. The result forces us to participate in a bizarre version of musical chairs.

When my car and I arrived on the Upper West Side, alternate side parking was enforced from Monday through Saturday; only Sunday was excluded, along with holidays. Parking was forbidden on the north side of the street from 11:00 a.m. till 2:00 p.m. on Monday, Wednesday, and Friday and on the south side on Tuesday, Thursday, and Saturday so that street-cleaning machines and garbage trucks could operate uninhibited. Similar regulations applied to avenues, restricting parking on first the east side of the street and then the west.

These rules instituted a ritualistic behavior by drivers. Each day we moved our cars from one side of the street to the other, ideally parking as close to our apartments as possible. My routine began at 1:15 and entailed taking a copy of the *Times* to my car, legally parked on one side, moving it to the other side before the spaces filled up, sitting there reading the paper until 2:00 p.m., then locking and leaving my car. Police allowed this obvious violation of the letter of no-parking rules, ticketing only those cars left unattended.

Easy enough, so long as I carved out those forty-five minutes to sacrifice to the parking god six days a week. Most days I did, but it required commitment, especially if I dared use the car. For even an extensive series of errands, I had to rush back to 77th Street by 1:15. Travel required more planning. When visiting family back in Ohio, I had to depart at three in the morning to arrive on 77th Street close to 1:15. At least this was under my control; I simply scheduled my driving to arrive home on time. I could never leave work in Mount Vernon early, which always landed me on 77th Street late.

Showing up after two o'clock put me at risk of finding not a single available spot. Nothing! Believe me; it happened.

What ensued was an ordeal common to all New Yorkers who hazarded keeping a car on the street. It involved a slow, methodical canvas of the area, looking for an open spot. Even today the experience haunts me, a scene from a bad movie looping over and over.

I see it now in my mind as I drive down 77th Street to Riverside Drive, turn right on Riverside to 78th, up 78th to West End, looking. I turn right on West End and drive downtown, checking carefully for a spot on those three blocks till 75th, the next westbound street, drive down 75th to Riverside, right on Riverside and back up to 78th. I look not only for an open spot but anticipate one about to become available, the indicators being someone walking with keys handy and ready to unlock a car or taillights in a parked car suddenly flashing red, the sign that a car is about to pull out.

Perhaps you think I am making too much of this, you who live in the civility of St. Louis, Missouri, or Rapid City, South Dakota, who without an ounce of appreciation routinely park in front of your own house. Wrong! Police blotters are filled with proof of how serious New York parking is, many misadventures ending up as headlines: "13-Year-Old Boy Shot Over Parking Space in Harlem," or "Thug Gets 1 Year for Punching Out Woman Over Parking Spot." It should surprise nobody that the hero of one of my early short stories was trapped in parking hell.

Of course not every car owner goes through this. In one of the richest cities in America, no Mercedes, Porsche, or Cadillac is ever parked overnight on the streets. They are ensconced in safe car homes, which at $8,000 a year are beyond consideration for anyone who remains in the city by counting pennies. In part because of this exclusion, we who parked on the street constituted a family. We greeted each other at the bank, inched our cars up or back to make room for one another to park, and chatted on the sidewalk as the clock ticked down to 2:00 p.m. and it was safe to leave.

The shadow hanging over this abysmal expenditure of time and energy was that army of New York City Transit Authority police who scour the streets in search of cars illegally parked. The penalty is not just a ticket but getting your car towed. (The total bill, even back in the '60s, approached $150—as much at $370 in 2019.)

But getting ticketed and towed were just the opening act of this psychodrama. More personal was common,

everyday vandalism. Offenses included broken windows, slashed tires, bent radio antennae, and a key dug along a door, a practice so popular it earned its own term, "car keying." And there were more unique indignities. A neighbor with an eight-year-old Dodge convertible found that someone had not only slit the top and spent the night in his back seat but defecated there.

While windows were frequently smashed for the fun of it, profit was often the goal. Radios and tape decks were an obvious temptation; a common sight was a handwritten sign affixed to a window or dashboard: "No radio—already stolen." I cannot imagine the allure provided by today's array of technological gadgetry, including global positioning systems and, perhaps most strange, airbags.

The ultimate loss was the entire car. This was the mid-1960s, before stealing cars in New York City became epidemic. The official total in New York state in 1965 was 58,452 thefts, 75 percent stolen in the five boroughs. By 1987 that had more than doubled to 125,329 thefts (numbers from autothefts.com). This was about when ads first appeared for The CLUB, that red bar that locks across the steering wheel, invented by James Winner Jr., supposedly after his Cadillac was stolen. According to the *New York Times*, the city led the nation in 1991—my last year as a full-time resident—with 139,977 vehicles stolen, twice the number reported by second-place Los Angeles. Back in 1965, it was more paranoia pushing us than reality.

But that fear was palpable. Every time someone smashed a window to steal a coat or slashed a top to take a dump

was a reminder that those cars could as easily been stolen. This threat was exacerbated by experience. I was not that concerned when I arrived in the city, until the morning of January 4, 1970, a Sunday.

It was about 11:30 and I was on my way to Broadway to buy a couple of croissants for breakfast when, halfway up 77th, I came upon a parking space on the south side of the street. I stopped and looked at that lovely void, knowing that I was parked nearby. Very soon it was clear: not nearby—right here! The moment is stuck in my mind; I suspect it always will be. I remember embarking on a little vacation from reality. *OK*, I reasoned, *my car appears to be gone. I'll just go pick up my croissants, come back, and see if it materializes.* I did; it didn't.

If I had not been aware of my car being vulnerable before that Sunday, I was thereafter. And this wasn't just another car, but the sports car I had saved for and purchased in London: my British racing green MG that I had parked for five months in Paris, driven through Europe, and shipped back to the United States, now gone.

I replaced it with a used Ford Mustang—a gift from my brother in Ohio—and while it wasn't an MG, it was my car and this was New York, and so the parking routine continued, except with the added anxiety of theft. Years before the CLUB became ubiquitous on cars parked on city streets, I improvised with a chain and padlock from steering wheel to brake pedal. Cumbersome and a pain to lock and unlock each day but a precaution I had to employ. And it worked; the car was never stolen.

The thought, however, was by then firmly planted in my mind. Security became paramount. Any legal parking spot was no longer enough; I wanted a spot under a streetlight, ideally in front of a building with a fulltime doorman and visible from one of my apartment windows so that I could periodically check on its safety. Extreme? Yep, and this obsession did not exist only while awake; it permeated my subconscious as I slept. Over and over, a new dream haunted me: I go to my car to move it and it isn't where I left it. I search up 77th and over to 78th—up and down—and then back over to 76th. Nothing!

My dreams got inventive: The Mustang that my brother gave me to replace my stolen MG is within a week stolen. It was infuriating and infantilizing. And on it went: I get another car from my family and it gets stolen, this time, bizarrely, even before I leave Ohio. The frustration builds. Reality blends with the fantasy: I couldn't sell a story and I couldn't keep a car. It was maddening.

Writing–Part Two: Pleasure

I realize that I have spent a lot of time complaining about the act of writing. Permit me to explain: Maybe it is not as hard as portrayed by sportswriter Red Smith—"There's nothing to writing. All you do is sit down at a typewriter and open a vein."—but it has its bad moments . . . and days and weeks and often months.

The hard part is getting it right, and the first step along that road is understanding what "it" is. Writing for me is taking an idea—or an event or feeling or scene—that the writer has experienced or envisioned and recreating it for the reader and doing it so effectively that the reader experiences what the writer intends. Figuring out for yourself what that thing is can be difficult; understanding it well enough to describe to someone else, often agonizing. This is the really hard part, what those painful hours spent in front of a typewriter—or a pad of paper or a computer

monitor—are about. When I complained about writing, this was the source.

But when the process works, when the right words in the right order recreate that original idea or scene, the result is exhilaration. In a quiet room, alone at two in the morning, I can feel myself smiling. It is not so different from what I imagine a gymnast feels when nailing that perfect maneuver. Getting it right is that good, except at that instant when it happens only you know about it, and so it is very private. And then, of course, if writing is your profession, it must happen over and over again.

For me, this happened first, and continues to happen most, when I am working as a reporter, when I can take a jumble of facts, quotes, and background information and use them to tell a complex story. But it has been more than a cerebral pleasure; it was a lifesaver during those early years in New York. Without that ability, I could never have landed that job on the *Argus* or picked up part-time editorial jobs, including six months writing for a newsletter about the printing industry, both before selling my first freelance article. Looking back, reporting has always been something in my back pocket I could rely on, a skill I purely stumbled into.

My high school years were so empty that out of desperation I presented myself to the University of Miami freshman football coach days before classes began, intending to make a place for myself as an athlete, this having never played football or any other sport. (No comments, please.) The coach was Whitey Campbell, a former UM star who had lettered

in baseball, basketball, and football in the late 1940s. He assessed my five-foot ten, 144-lb. frame, and my absence of history in sports and suggested I try cheerleading or maybe the student newspaper, which is how I ended up writing for the *Miami Hurricane* as a freshman and early in my junior year for the *Miami Herald*.

Time on the *Hurricane* was good, but it was at the *Herald* that I got hooked. For a twenty-year-old who had grown up on films like *His Girl Friday* with Cary Grant and Rosalind Russell and *Deadline–USA* with Humphrey Bogart, it offered genuine adventure into which I leapt each afternoon at three o'clock when my shift started and 9:00 a.m. on Saturdays. This was 1961, before the *Herald* moved to its own street—One Herald Plaza—into a building that one report called "the boxy behemoth on Biscayne Bay." Perhaps the new facility was not elegant or classy but it was clean and modern, or as modern as a newspaper could be in those pre-computer days; reporters used electric typewriters, an upgrade over the Royal manuals we used at the old building.

That once noble structure in the heart of downtown was by then seriously outdated but with a proud facade that dominated the corner of Southwest Second Street and South Miami Avenue and with a city room straight out of Hollywood. The chita-chat-chat of typewriter keys striking paper intensified with the approach of deadlines, unfiltered cigarettes laid on the edge of desks left burn marks and filled the air with smoke, articles were sent from the copy editors' desk to the back shop through a pneumatic tube, and when

the presses began rolling, they shook the building. The only thing missing was Bogie, necktie pulled to one side at his open collar, fighting to break one more big story before his crusading paper, *The Day*, was sold to a weak rival more interested in profit than news.

The *Herald* did not need his ghost haunting the city room; the staff was redolent of newspaper authenticity. We had a slot man who issued commentaries on the day's endeavors from the hub of the copy desk with the vigor of a carnival barker, a one-armed columnist and war hero who championed the building of South Florida's only licensed specialty hospital exclusively for children, a police reporter whose friendship with judges reduced staff speeding tickets ten to twenty miles per hour, reporters who valued equally the facts of a story and the truth behind them, and assistant city editors so known for holding editorial meetings that a reporter desperate for a response once sent a memo addressed to "any city editor not currently in a meeting."

And while editors and reporters pursued their jobs with serious determination, they always had time to help those less experienced, turning that city room into a classroom. I learned to start assignments by checking the library—traditionally referred to as "the morgue"—for any previous articles on the same subject, even for beats as routine as obituary writing, searching for facts that could turn a one-graph story into a full feature. I learned to look for patterns: two cars with slashed tires were a coincidence; four, a case of malicious mischief; and eight, a mini crime wave. From the pressroom

at the police station, I learned to seek out potential stories from police and fire monitors, from the handwritten reports of uniformed officers, and quickly break away every hour to scan check-ins at the jail upstairs.

And I learned to respect details. While writing about a young man who chased down his mother's stolen car, my editor—a gruff but soft-hearted veteran named Rose Allegato—asked me how the son knew that was his mother's car and not just another six-year-old Chevrolet heading down the street. "He recognized it," I said defensively, not really knowing the answer.

"One black Chevy out of all those black Chevys on that busy street, and you said he was driving in the opposite direction?" Rose was not letting me off the hook. "Unlikely!"

I called the son back and found that his mother's car had a broken muffler that sounded like a hot rod. He hadn't seen that it was his mother's car; he heard it. Details, an important link to credibility.

Some lessons were taught in direct exchanges while others came in the normal course of the day. As the youngest reporter, I was the one sent to cover spot local news: the service station attendant who set himself afire by accidentally combining a leaky gasoline hose with lighting his cigarette and the mother who fell asleep by a pool and woke to find her infant had fallen in and drowned. I was always in a hurry and always running: running out to cover the incident, running back to the office to file my story. The executive city editor—Larry Jinks, whose desk was strategically positioned between

the elevator and the city room—stopped me one afternoon as I raced to start writing. "What happened out there?" asked Jinks, who would go on to be editor. Annoyed that he was holding me up, I gave him the fastest and most concise of responses, which apparently was just what he wanted. "Good," he said, "now write it that way."

Quick and concise were watchwords, but accuracy was the glue that held the operation together. One afternoon while writing "cutlines only"—a caption for a photo without an article—I labored to achieve the right feel for the image of police officers in a funeral procession honoring their fallen comrade. Finally I decided that "gunned down in the line of duty" conveyed the drama of the moment. It survived through the city desk, but when it reached the copy editor he held it high over his head and yelled in the room filled with reporters working to meet the deadline. "Rozin," he bellowed, not really looking for me and not waiting for a response, "the cop hit a grease patch and crashed his motorcycle."

Thereafter, whenever I am tempted to place mood over facts, I hear those words.

Valuable as these lessons were, it was the daily experience of being a reporter that lifted me out of the pristine and theoretical existence of a college student and thrust me into the gritty real world of covering the news. My mornings were occupied with lectures on twentieth century European history and romantic literature as represented in textbooks. Afternoons and evenings were filled with the tangible acts

of life and death on the streets of Miami and Dade County and occasionally the world beyond.

Late in September 1962, while President John F. Kennedy weighed his decision to send thirty thousand troops to force the University of Mississippi to admit James Meredith, its first black student, *Herald* reporter Rick Tuttle was barricaded with federal marshals inside the administration building in Oxford. Outside, an armed and angry mob was just as committed to defend the segregationist policies of Governor Ross Barnett. Once the action quieted down, Tuttle got to a phone and dictated his story to me, safe at the *Herald*, 961 miles away, seated at my desk and typing as fast as I could. Somewhere I have a copy of Tuttle's front-page story, but I need nothing to recall the headline: "It Was War—and Marshals Were Losing." By the time Meredith enrolled and calm was restored, two people were dead and more than three hundred injured. One historian called the integration of Ole Miss the last battle of the Civil War.

Three weeks later, at the height of the Cuban Missile Crisis, with troops and antiaircraft equipment deployed from Fort Lauderdale to Key West, the city room was focused on the desk of Lee Winfrey, the *Herald*'s rewrite man, also considered one of the paper's fastest writers. He would need to be that day. With President Kennedy set to address the nation at 7:00 p.m., the threat of a nuclear confrontation in the air, and no advance to the media on whether we were going to war or not, the presses were to be held as Lee listened to the speech on the portable radio positioned on his desk, set to type as the president spoke.

"This is exciting," I said to Lee as we waited.

"Yea," he said in his southern accent, "and hard."

The government ended up releasing thirty minutes early that Kennedy was declaring "a strict quarantine on all offensive military equipment under shipment to Cuba," a story we in the city room knew before the people of Miami.

These were major stories, and to be there while they were reported, in some cases being part of the process that brought the facts to the reading public, made working on a newspaper in those pre-internet days fascinating. When not actively involved I slipped into the wire room—more of a big glassed-in box than a room—and scanned the teleprinters spewing forth copy from the Associated Press, United Press International, and the other news services to which the *Herald* subscribed in a cacophony of automatic typing, some destined to be the next day's headlines but most of it less important, train derailments and bank holdups and building fires, relatively minor in terms of world-shaping news but still fragments of the chronology of the day. This close proximity to events big and small was physically exhilarating—if not heart-pounding, at least increasing my pulse rate.

Newspapers were important back then. While radio and television also delivered the news, for a large percentage of the public it wasn't real until they could read it in black type. Major metropolitan newspapers still came out with special editions for breaking news. Newsboys—and they were mostly boys back then—flogged copies to cars caught in traffic by

barking out key headlines, on special occasions sparked by that most revered of newspaper phrases, "Extra! Extra! Read all about it!"

To be part of that little club of gatherers and documenters was fulfilling, and it happened every day, routinely and without ceremony. When I secured a quote at the police station from a man who, while trying to stop a robber, accidently shot and killed an innocent motorist—"What'd you want me to do? The guy was trying to rob me."—the reporter writing the story handed me one of his carbons to show me how he used the quotes. No need for thanks; we were just getting the job done. Everybody worked that way, to get the paper out, every day.

At any moment in any one of those days, the most ordinary story could become extraordinary. One afternoon I was told to take a call from the police reporter, a seriously rumpled veteran who was also my mentor for my stints in the pressroom of the police station. A man repairing his boat docked on the Miami River had been killed while using a faulty electric drill, one of those little tragedies that just happens. I copied down the facts from the police report—the man's name, time and details of the incident—called the morgue to check for any past articles involving the victim, and began writing. As far as its news value, this was routine; sad, tragic in human terms, but minor in the scope of daily news. With nearly an hour to deadline, I had plenty of time.

And then word came back to me—from the morgue or the police, I don't recall—that the dead man had been one

of Fidel Castro's top lieutenants, active in the revolution but mysteriously gone for more than two years. This was early 1963, four years after Castro drove Fulgencio Batista from power and months after the Cuban Missile Crisis; everything related to Castro was news, especially in Miami.

Within those few minutes I had a new story and there was no longer plenty of time. *Get a grip*, I told myself and heard my city editor's words echo in my ears: "What happened out there?" A former lieutenant of Fidel Castro, missing from Cuban politics for more than two years, was killed today while using a faulty power drill to repair his boat, according to Miami police. I banged out the lead, rethought it, and tried it again. Suddenly there was Rose Allegato at my side, performing her assistant city editor job of keeping me on course. "No time," she said. "Write it straight."

As she issued her command, calmly but firmly, she lit a cigarette and placed it in my mouth. I rarely smoked in those days, but that image of a seasoned newspaper man with a cigarette dangling from his lips was so seductive that I took a drag, fought to keep the smoke out of my eyes, and went back to typing. Rose hung over my shoulder, reading as I typed. Every few graphs she pulled the copy out of my machine, edited it, and turned it in to the desk while I went onto the next paragraph, rushing to meet the deadline.

Was this guy so important? Probably not, even with his true identity, not by national journalistic standards. It didn't make the front page, but did run on the first page of the local section, along with a photograph of that hand drill.

But the event was one I shall never forget: that moment of discovery, the Castro connection turning three graphs with a one-column headline buried inside the paper into a substantial article warranting a two-column head and art on page one of local, above the fold; that was a big deal for me in those days. And mostly the excitement: editor Allegato, hanging over my shoulder, ripping out pages as I typed, and that cigarette—all so real, so much a part of newspaper lore.

I did not fully realize at the time how the *Herald* experience was shaping me as a writer. Not just the direct intervention of editors but the daily association with other reporters. In seemingly casual conversations around the water fountain or waiting for that first edition of the paper—it was everybody's responsibility to scan for mistakes—they taught lessons that remain with me today, broad concepts like the ability to spot a story by digging below the surface and assessing all the information, a process that began by treating every story as important, even though not every one turned out to be.

I wrote my last article for the *Herald* in 1970, but I still hear the voices of reporters Lee Winfrey, Juanita Greene, Henry Reno, and Gene Miller, of editors Larry Jinks, Al Burt, and Rose Allegato, raised in support and correction, offered gently and sometimes not so gently. While this is primarily a book about what I gained from my time in New York, it was the *Miami Herald* that equipped me to take what New York had to offer and use it well. That education covered more than any journalism class.

Among my duties early in my *Herald* tenure, in addition to contacting every funeral home for news of reported deaths, was rewriting handouts from the various clubs and civic organizations, news of their upcoming events, meetings, and the names of new officers. There were dozens of these every day. On one of these days, I dutifully reported that this particular club had just elected six new board members. I listed their names in what I thought was a nicely written two paragraphs, turned them in to the city desk, and went on to the next release. "Rozin!" came the summons from the desk. "You say six new board members but you include only five. Did one die?"

I offered no response, just quietly retrieved my copy and set about the task of correcting my mistake, hoping that the incident would go unnoticed. I assumed it had, until, from somewhere in the city room, came: "Is this mystery to be continued on the obit page?" I swear I could hear the guffaws above the rattle of the typewriters, or maybe it was just the sound of my ego deflating.

Detour, or On to a Better Road

So, you ask, if I loved reporting so much, and I even got paid for it, why did I not immediately pursue nonfiction in New York? It was that old prejudice of mine. Being a writer meant fiction. Reporting and writing nonfiction were another craft and, yes, less romantic. I know—dumb. But I am a slow learner, and I continued to write fiction, short stories and novels, hundreds and even thousands of pages. But while continuing to write and to collect rejection letters for my fiction, I began considering my old trade as a reporter. My question was how to do it.

Once again, it was New York to the rescue, and while this officially began in 1972 with my first published article in *Audubon*, the journey starts earlier and includes many twists and turns.

By 1969 I was represented by James Oliver Brown, an agent whose clients included Louis Auchincloss, Herb Gold, Erskine Caldwell, Dominick Dunne, Jessica Mitford, and

Katherine Anne Porter. Neither Jim nor his list helped my writing, but he was incredibly supportive and always invited me to his parties, where I ate and drank well. At one of these parties, quite indirectly, I received a boost to my struggling career, which at this point consisted of several dozen unpublished short stories. Enter the lost boy.

We met at one of those parties. He was the scion of a literary family who had just finished a book. Both of us being young and lacking star power, we fell into conversation. He had graduated from Columbia School of Journalism and had just landed a job on an English language newspaper in Lima, Peru. (I never did learn how; I suspected some family connection.) He was set to leave in a few weeks and expressed anxiety. Throughout the party he quizzed me about my time in Miami, Bethlehem, and Mount Vernon. Then he asked if he might call with more questions and I agreed. After two or three phone conversations, I was invited to dinner with his mother.

A month or so after he left for Lima, I got a call from the mother. Her son was having difficulty with the job, she said. Would I mind if he called me from South America to talk over some of his issues, collect? They would reimburse me for the calls. I agreed.

That began a series of long-distance telephone conversations, at least once a week, often lasting an hour or more. We talked about his assignments and how he prepared for them, discussed which interviews he would schedule and even some of the questions he might ask. This went on for months, and he seemed to be fitting in nicely. He was handling his assignments well and

even managing to deal with an editor he found unreasonable, a problem I assured him was a common part of being a reporter.

Calls grew briefer and less frequent and stopped when he took time off to travel in Bolivia. This seemed to be a good sign. Then I got another call from his mother. Her son, she said, was stuck, as in immobilized. He had gone to a place called Cochabamba, a relatively large city in central Bolivia, midway between the mountains and rainforest; for work or vacation, I did not at the time understand his motivation. But he had been there for weeks and didn't seem to be leaving, either returning to Lima or New York.

I was sympathetic but didn't know what I could do. "Would you go to Bolivia?" And do what? "Talk to him. He says he would like that." Just talk? I waited, and then it came: "Well, get him to come home." I was not sure I could do this and I told her so. "Would you try?"

In essence, I reasoned, this was not so different from all that telephoning, except this would be face to face and in Bolivia. The idea was intriguing. This was early 1970 and Bolivia, normally obscure to most of us, was suddenly in play. The previous year's hit movie, *Butch Cassidy and the Sundance Kid*, with Paul Newman and Robert Redford hunted down by Bolivian soldiers, was being touted for several Oscars. Che Guevara, executed by government forces in Bolivia's Yuro ravine in 1967, was catching fire as an antiestablishment hero. I said yes but with conditions.

We laid out the details over dinner with her husband present but mostly quiet; I think he was not the father. I

would fly to Cochabamba, seek out her son, and assess his situation. If I found it to be as untenable as she posed, I would try to point out the wisdom of his returning to Lima and perhaps even New York. I made it clear that I would rely on logic; I would not push him to leave or use his family's concern as coercion.

They agreed to my terms and also to cover my expenses. The husband's only question was what fee I could charge for these services. I assured him that I was acting as a friend of the family and not a bounty hunter. Finally, I said that if her son was simply taking time off and living the good life in Cochabamba—even if this involved some questionable judgment—it was not my place to point out the error of his choice. He was by my loose calculations about twenty-nine and in charge of his own life.

My travel connections permitted me an overnight in Miami, and I used the time to visit old friends at the *Herald*. I had remained close with several staff members and had written a few travel articles while in Europe. Jay Clarke, the paper's longtime travel editor, suggested that I look for possible stories in Bolivia. The *Herald* had a strong interest in Latin America and since 1946 had published its Clipper edition, named for Pan American's Clipper seaplanes that delivered it daily to tourist areas in the Caribbean and Central and South America. Since then large seaplanes have become obsolete, Pan Am's gone out of business, and the *Herald*'s Clipper is called the International Edition, but the *Herald* still covers the Latin world and did actively in 1970.

During my stopover I agreed to consider contributing to that coverage.

Cochabamba proved to be rich in material. Music at the folklorica introduced me to the haunting, multi-tubed pan flutes. Street carts sold anticuchos, chunks of heart and other organ meat cooked on an open grill, while restaurants served more complicated local dishes like silpancho, rice layered with potatoes and meat pounded thin and fried.

La Cancha was the central market, blocks of capitalism that functioned daily but was at full force on Wednesdays and Saturdays. It attracted resident Spanish-speaking vendors but also descendants of Bolivia's native Quechua population who traveled twice a week from the altiplano and the jungle to sell fruits and vegetables, slabs of beef, goat and lamb, alpaca ponchos and sheepskin rugs, and an assortment of pottery and baskets.

But travel research was not the reason for my trip. My friend was pleased to see me and quickly launched into the quandary that, as his mother suggested, had him stuck. He wanted to interview the mayor for an article and every morning presented himself at the mayor's office, where he waited for an audience. All day he waited, until the secretary informed him that the office was closing. Back he came the next morning to the office, where he waited—all day, every day. One week eased into a second. "Did you ever have a situation like this one?" he asked me over dinner one night. Not really, I said, but added that this was Bolivia and I had never worked in Bolivia. I could think of nothing else to say.

"What can I take away from this?" he asked. All I could think of was that the mayor did not want to talk.

I suggested that he give up on the mayor and take advantage of being in exotic Bolivia. This was, after all, the land of Che Guevara, Butch Cassidy and The Sundance Kid; I avoided the fact that they had all died there and stressed the romance. More convincing proved unnecessary; he just needed a little push. He even had an idea. He had met a man in the mayor's office who operated trucks that ran back and forth between Cochabamba and the river village of Porto San Francisco on the Beni, an essential cargo link as Bolivia had lost its last ocean outlet in the 1879 war against Chile. We could catch a ride on one of the man's trucks, negotiate at the port for a boat ride up the Beni—he even offered the name of a captain—and have a genuine Bolivian adventure through the Amazon rain forest.

The man from the mayor's office was true to his word; we left Cochabamba three days later, about sundown. The truck, loaded with produce, first headed out of town along a narrow road then dived down to a jungle thick with huge trees and dangling vines, plants with great deep-green leaves illuminated by the truck's headlights. After eleven hours we fell in line behind other trucks waiting to enter the port.

Porto San Francisco presented a scene from a movie depicting late-nineteenth-century Africa. A handful of one-story shacks—walls of wooden planks so loosely connected that the morning light shown through, roofs of palm fronds laid on bamboo frames—functioned as a

bar, the port office, and some outbuildings. Their reason for being was the Beni, emerging from a jungle still black from night, forming a big "U" at the village edge. Six boats jammed into that bend could have been transplanted from Mark Twain's Mississippi, the only obvious difference being means of propulsion, diesel-powered propellers replacing steam-driven paddlewheels.

We sought the captain who was our contact and asked for news of our departure. He assessed the number of trucks to be unloaded and boats waiting for cargo and explained that he had to be fully loaded before leaving; this could take days. So we waited all day as the trucks unloaded beer from Cochabamba and crops from the surrounding farms and filled their bays with cattle, wood, and raw rubber from the boats then headed out to make room for more trucks to fill the greater-capacity boats. Day gave way to night, and we waited. We drank warm beer and ate greasy chicken in the bar and swatted at the fat, black mosquitos drawn by the room's lanterns.

At some point the lack of urgency of the operation became clear. Loading and unloading seemed casual, with crews more interested in their games of dominoes, slapping tiles down on the crude wooden table and with dice thrown from a leather cup. Suddenly my friend's waiting for an appointment with the mayor for weeks was less unreasonable and our exotic trip up the Beni more in doubt.

He and I held a quick conversation and reached agreement: our plan was better in theory than reality; this could go

on for days. I approached one of the truckers and confirmed that he was headed for Cochabamba at sunrise. "Room for two passengers?" I asked in my limited Spanish, making the universal gesture with my thumb. He responded with his own thumb, pointing over his shoulder to the rear of his truck.

"With the cargo."

"Cattle?" I asked with dread.

"Wood!" We had a deal.

By sundown we were back in Cochabamba and planning more conventional adventures—this time in neighboring Peru, a weekend in Cusco, and three days at Machu Picchu—in the process making our way back to Lima. And while we traveled we talked about his job on the paper and what options were available back in the States. He agreed that perhaps he had made the most of this experience and he would consider returning. I left that weekend; he followed me a week later.

En route to New York I stopped in again at the *Herald*. I filed stories about the market at Cochabamba, how climbing Huayna Picchu afforded the best view of neighboring Machu Picchu, about our misadventure in Porto San Francisco, and something I labeled local high, about the day I spent with two Peace Corps workers who introduced me to the method used by native Bolivians to work long hours in the cold at the elevated altitude of the altiplano: they chewed the green leaves of the coca plant, speeding the effect of the extracted cocaine by biting off pieces of potato-mash-and-ash cake. (My guides just did it to get stoned.)

Those South America articles reconnected me with that element of writing that drew me to reporting in the first place: the pleasure of watching a story develop, turning it over in my mind, and then making it happen just that way for the reader. Not that I had completely lost touch with this joyful chemistry during my time in New York, but it was dampened by falling into a deep write-and-wait-for-rejection hole. Writing—even when it was difficult—was the best part of my work; trying to sell that work, the worst.

Back in the city I continued to write fiction, but nonfiction was now a consideration, hanging at the edge of my business plan. And because it was New York, with that friend-of-a-friend action always present, September found me in Greenwich Village at a going-away party for a recent college graduate whom I did not know. He was leaving the following Monday for Labrador, teaching in a one-room schoolhouse in a remote fishing village with no running water, generator-provided electricity four hours each evening, and heat only from the woodburning kitchen stove.

"Hey," he pled to anyone who listened, "if you're in the neighborhood, stop in for a visit." To him and most of his guests it was a joke, but I was listening. Two months later I was aboard a freighter that serviced the rocky Labrador coast, headed for Rexon's Cove, thanks to one of those chance meetings that helps define life in New York City.

The tiny village, fewer than a dozen wooden houses perched on the edge of a fjord, constituted half of a two-site community. Residents split their time with William's Harbor,

a twenty-minute boat ride closer to the North Atlantic but without sufficient trees to feed the stoves that supported life in winter. The families spent five months fishing from William's Harbor before retreating to Rexon's Cove for seven months of short, cold days and long nights that in February reached twenty below. The Canadian government added to their hard times by pressuring residents to relocate to a larger town in an effort to save the expense of supplying educational and medical services.

What I found were forty-nine distant relatives of the English who had settled in the region in the early 1800s, trying to hang on. Women filled their days with cooking, cleaning, caring for their children, washing clothes by hand in water carried from the lake in buckets, hanging them outside in the winter sun to freeze solid as boards, then bringing them inside to thaw. Men hauled the water, mended boats, and hunted for fresh meat, game birds, and ducks when they were available then toward the end of winter for seals, their dark oily meat a sign that times were indeed tough.

Recreation was nearly nonexistent. There was no interest in whittling; only the young read and then only assignments from school. What spare time there was went to maintain boats and houses. Even the large table-model radios, given a prominent place in every kitchen, were used only for steamer reports and church music on Sundays.

Harsh as it was, the people seemed happy with a life filled with work but free of many of the concerns of a more urban setting. Residents did not lock their doors, and an ax

or gun left outside overnight was simply a cold ax or gun in the morning. They appreciated that, and resisted efforts of the government to make them move three hours away by boat to Port Hope Simpson, a town with nearly three hundred people, full-time electricity, telephone service, a post office, three general stores, and even a few cars but also drunkenness and enough crime that all doors were kept locked.

I pitched the story of Rexon's Cove and its people even before I returned to 77th Street in late November, sending a query letter to *National Geographic* from Gander, the first post office I encountered. They liked the piece but kept asking for more of me in it. "I want to see you reaching for that cod," said the editor, "you hauling water from the lake." I maintained that the story was them and not me, but he was insistent.

After several more tries, maybe to the *Smithsonian* or *Natural History,* I do not recall—only that it took six months—an editor who rejected the story liked it enough to suggest that I call a friend at *Audubon* magazine. I did and dropped off my article and slides at their offices. A couple of weeks later the editor called back and said yes. In January my first magazine article was published, six years and two months after I arrived in New York City.

Before that story ran I accepted my first assignment for *Audubon* and traveled to the Gulf of Alaska and then Loggerhead Key in the Dry Tortugas to write about lighthouses. Over the next nineteen years I went to Greenland to write about icebergs, Eastern Kentucky for strip mining,

Michigan's Keweenaw Peninsula for ghost towns, and lots of other places for research. Nearly every assignment provided material for a travel story, first for the *New York Times* and then for the *Washington Post*.

Not every trip. Letcher County, Kentucky, did not welcome strangers, especially those reporting on its streams fouled by years of removing coal from the top down. When my motel discovered I was working for *Audubon*—I suspect but had no proof that the office listened to my phone calls—I returned from a day's research to find a note stating that I was being "permitted to check out," written on the stationery of a local coal company. Letcher County may have been unfit for travel readers of the *Times* or the *Post*, but my motel experience provided good cocktail party conversation back in Manhattan.

I continued to write for *Audubon* until 1991, when long-time editor Les Line was fired in a power struggle with the society that published the magazine. This is one of the unfortunate realities of freelance: connections often last only as long as your editor remains in place. But that's the nature of the business; one learns to move on. In the twenty-two years to follow, at *BusinessWeek* and then the *Wall Street Journal*, I pursued the kind of nonfiction writing that I so blithely dismissed when I arrived in New York and has helped me survive as a writer.

Of course I still wrote novels but apparently only for my own amusement—and frustration—as none ever sold. Why did I continue? I'm not sure. I guess because I liked the work

despite the risk and inevitable pain of rejection. There was with each book a joy in creating a world and then stepping into it, wholly and completely, each day, a safe and wonderful place to go, even if when finished, nobody else wished to join me there.

Either way, good and bad as writing fiction was, it was nonfiction that kept me alive and publishing. And in truth, my passion for fiction waned as my file of rejections grew. I said I was a slow learner, not an idiot.

Home Safe Home (and Other Fantasies)

Returning home from an assignment, I invariably experienced a feeling of comfort as the taxi turned onto West 77th Street. There was stability to a block with some buildings dating back to 1890, no new construction, and not many changes among the residents, especially through the 1970s. Even the businesses on nearby Broadway were constant: Fairway market down on 74th Street, Zabar's up on 80th, and scattered between them the ever-present hardware store, shoe repair, H&H Bagels, and Osner over on Amsterdam.

While the neighborhood remained steady, I worked to turn my apartment into more of a home base. At first there was space only to write in one room and sleep in the other. Both were small but with high ceilings typical of second-floor apartments in those nineteenth-century brownstones built for one family. So I improvised. A platform six feet above the floor and big enough for a desk and a chair—with a wooden

railing to keep me from falling—became my work space, an office floating over my living room; another platform in the second room big enough for a mattress was my sleep space with a television room below. Voilà: four rooms.

With this combination of a stable community outside and the odd configuration of multilevels creating an efficient space to live and work inside, I had the makings of an anxiety-free environment, leaving me with the sole responsibility to block out all those negative emotional forces—you know, like failure—so I could write.

Part of this comfort came from the sense of security that the apartment would be there upon my return, just as I left it. I really felt this, deeply, but I confess that my confidence stood in contrast to the prevailing attitude of the time.

According to popular views expressed in conversation and print, crime in those years was rampant on the Upper West Side. West 84th Street between Amsterdam and Columbus was described in the *New York Times* in 1961 as "a block of decaying tenements packed with poor Puerto Ricans and Negro families and the gathering place of drunks, narcotics addicts and sexual perverts." The perilous quality of life in that very neighborhood was a terrifying presence in Saul Bellow's novel *Mr. Sammler's Planet*, published in 1970. As one character says, "New York makes one think about the collapse of civilization, about Sodom and Gomorrah, the end of the world."

Only blocks away, West 77th off Riverside was safer but still not actually safe. It was not just our cars in jeopardy, defenseless out there on the street; our homes were also at

risk, and ourselves. One of my neighbors was mugged in the foyer, robbed of her purse and knocked down when she resisted; the couple in Apartment Eight returned home one afternoon to find their stereo gone.

The young woman then living in Apartment Nine called me in a panic one night; someone was at her door, trying to get in. I grabbed my baseball bat—we all had some kind of weapon handy—and proceeded with considerable trepidation to her fifth floor rear apartment. By then the intruder had fled but left what appeared to be a deposit of semen on the door, starting with a plop about crotch high and descending in a downward stream.

The very nature of a brownstone residence, generally without a doorman, adds a level of danger. Buildings with doormen are obviously safer, regardless of the neighborhood; a uniformed person manning the entrance tends to deter evildoers.

Adding to our risk, 336 had no working intercom linking the outside to the apartments, only rudimentary signaling and unlocking devices. Visitors could buzz to notify tenants of their arrival and tenants could buzz back to allow entrance to the building, but there was no way to communicate who was visiting. Instead of walking down to check, the pattern was to push the buzzer and open the door, a security violation most often committed by tenants of the upper floors.

This abuse of apartment protocol was common; welcomed guests and deliveries from neighborhood restaurants arrived

well into the night, every night. But also strangers. The results were predictably mixed. Blithely admitting an order of General Tso's chicken was not the issue, nor a visiting date or relative. Thieves were the threat, and we had thieves in many forms, from those with a simple approach—pushing the buzzer for each apartment to see which lazy soul granted access—to the more sophisticated. Some of these were quite inventive; few of us were immune.

One evening around six o'clock, my buzzer sounded. By then a street-smart city dweller, I walked downstairs before opening the door. It turned out to be a nicely dressed young man who greeted me by name. Did I not remember him from school? he asked. I did not. "Sure," he said, "we met and talked about your photography."

I really did not remember him, but I had been attending classes at Columbia and I did take pictures. And he was quite insistent and did know my name.

While I tried to place this guy, he kept talking, going on about how he remembered my enthusiasm about my photography, working on it and wanting to get better. And then somewhere in that fog of his verbiage, I heard the magic word: NIKON. Suddenly he had my full attention. He said he'd "come into possession" of some F2s. F2 was the professional Nikon Single Lens Reflex; "come into possession" was a phrase like "fallen off a truck," code for stolen. I could almost see him wink.

"Nikkor lens?" I asked.

"F/1.4," he answered.

I was about to express my approval but he had already moved on, talking about how he immediately thought of me, how much I would appreciate such a fine camera. And I would. I had bought a Pentax tax free in Panama on the way back from Lima, but a Nikon F2, well, that was THE camera. Even if I couldn't shoot like a pro, I could at least shoot with a pro's camera.

How much? "Two hundred dollars." I thought an F2 with a Nikkor lens sold for over $600. I couldn't resist. I did not have $200 cash; no, he wouldn't take a check. I thought of the man in Apartment Eight, whom I considered an adult with resources. I quickly went upstairs to borrow $120; I had the rest.

My visitor—I do not recall his name or whether he offered one—counted the money and said the camera was in his car and I could go with him to pick it up; I felt secure with this arrangement. He said he was parked at the garage on West 76th Street, just east of Broadway, and as we headed there he kept talking about how great this camera was and how using it would make me a better photographer.

He kept this up until we arrived at the garage. "Wait here," he said. "I'll get the camera." I wasn't born yesterday; I balked. He looked hurt. I immediately felt bad about not trusting my new/old friend. "Look," he said, "you hold half the money. I'll be right back; I swear." He pulled the money out of his pocket, showed me what he said was half, slipped it into my shirt pocket, and disappeared into the garage. I took a quick look at the bills and settled in to wait.

And I did wait, and wait. After about ten minutes I began to get what is commonly called a sinking feeling. Ten minutes more and I knew I'd been scammed. But where could he have gone? I got my answer when I walked into the garage and found that while the entrance was on 76th Street, the exit was around the corner on Amsterdam. He had taken my money and walked out the other door. An expensive New York lesson, but at least I'd only lost half the money.

I pulled the folded bills out of my pocket and discovered that he had wrapped a twenty around four singles. Fucked! I lost my money and still owned my neighbor $120. What I fool. I ran over what had happened while walking back to my apartment as if I could correct my mistake, ending up brooding. He was so smooth, so confident; I guessed that's why they're called confidence men. But he knew my name and that I attended Columbia and liked photography.

When I reached 336 and unlocked the front door, my attention caught on my mailbox, which bore my name. I got it. But Columbia—what about Columbia? He did say Columbia, didn't he? Or was it just classes? Classes were everywhere, uptown at City College of New York and downtown at Pace, in the middle at New York University and the New School. But there was all that shit about photography? How did he know about the photography? I didn't know then and I still don't.

What I do know is that we had thieves, thieves of all types. Like most New Yorkers, I learned of their risk through experience and adjusted along the way. Some lessons took

a little longer to register. Thankfully, scam detection took affect quickly; never again did I purchase anything "off a truck." I proceeded through the other stages of my education more gradually.

My apartment came equipped with a police lock, that essence of New York apartment security created by Emiel Fox around 1910 and consisting of a solid iron rod that ran diagonally from a little steel-enforced slot in the floor to a metal box attached to the inside of the door. When the rod was shifted to the closed position, it became encased in the box and rendered the door pretty much immoveable, the apartment impregnable to violation. In the open position, the bar slid easily along a track and permitted the door to grant access.

When I moved to the city, I assumed it was what all New Yorkers had. I later learned that employing police locks was need-specific and that need had a strong geographic component. Residents of the Upper West Side and Lower East Side installed police locks; residents of Park Avenue did not.

As I heard reports of break-ins and muggings from neighbors, I fortified the good work of Mr. Fox, adding two deadbolts and equipping all three locks with Medeco cylinders, the most secure then available, protected by brass-plated guards. And while I felt comfortable with my choice of locks, the door was still made of wood, and so I implored the machine shop at the family's paper mill in Ohio to cut a steel panel that I screwed onto the inner side of the apartment door, making it virtually invulnerable to

a thief though he be equipped with a saw or a heavy pair of boots and a strong leg.

My obsession with security went beyond a fortified entrance. In an effort to mystify would-be burglars about my comings and goings, I connected a timer to a lamp in my living room set to go on each evening at six o'clock for five hours and another to a radio positioned by the door set to turn on at 10:00 a.m. for six hours.

It does not escape me that on the subject of the inviolate nature of my apartment, I embraced two separate and distinctively different attitudes. While busily fortifying it with every device I could find to ward off the evil forces of the city, I simultaneously waxed poetically about the security of my home, my castle, my "safest refuge." Not only did I champion these seventeenth-century words of Sir Edward Coke but I expressed them—no, vigorously proclaimed them—to East Side snobs who insisted the Upper West Side was crime-ridden.

The reason goes to the nature of my early years in New York. Part of my survival technique was to create a fantasy for me and anyone willing to listen. This approach was multifaceted. In addition to deluding myself that my apartment was a bastion of safety, I convinced myself that every story I wrote would sell and every article I pitched would find an editor eager to commission it.

In both cases, I simply had to. If I accepted the real danger of living in a war zone, I could never leave town for a week and expect to return to property unravaged by thieves;

certainly my stolen MG was proof of that. And if I accepted the unlikely chance of selling even a single article, especially in light of all those other writers in New York and throughout the country and the world—all of them submitting to those same publications—I could never have completed a single article, never finish a single proposal.

So I denied both conditions and while existing in that fantasy world, I happily occupied my apartment for forty-six years without a single break-in and balanced all that rejection by publishing in some of the best newspapers and magazines in the country.

To hell with reality!

NINE

A Sense of the City

Part of Manhattan's appeal—beyond the obvious, culture and excitement and job opportunities—has to do with the sheer presence of the metropolis and its physical diversity, how the scale shifts from towering glass and steel canyons in Midtown and Lower Manhattan to charming brownstones in Greenwich Village to pastoral Central Park, itself a separate city of trees and lakes surrounded by a forest of huge buildings.

All this is packed into 22.82 square miles, smallest of the five boroughs and the one exuding the most energy. New York is the original city that never sleeps. And not just the obvious parts, like Times Square and the Village. Walking to the newsstand as part of my nightly ritual to buy a late *Times*, often at 3:30 in the morning, I marveled at the activity at 79th Street and Broadway: people entering and leaving the subway and waiting for the crosstown bus, returning from a night out or going to work.

That appeal helps explain why New York has been used by writers from Henry James and F. Scott Fitzgerald to J. D. Salinger and E. L. Doctorow; why when radio

was our primary source of home entertainment, we had *Broadway Is My Beat* and *Grand Central Station*; why early television gave us *Amos and Andy* and *The Naked City*, and later *Friends, Seinfeld,* and *Blue Bloods,* all set in New York, along with hundreds of movies from the silent era through today.

It is why Andrew Carnegie eschewed his hometown of Pittsburgh and built what would become the most famous of all concert halls in New York; why the United Nations, after the failure of the League of Nations in Geneva, took its shot at saving the world to New York; and why Thomas Edison chose an area adjacent to Wall Street in Lower Manhattan to launch the modern era of illumination by installing electric lighting.

Ever since Admiral George Dewey's triumphant return from Manila in 1899, heroes have been fêted with parades not on State Street in Chicago or Hollywood Boulevard in Los Angeles but on lower Broadway in New York. Edward Eisenstaedt's iconic photo of a sailor kissing that woman in a white dress on V-J Day depicts action in Times Square. Even *Sesame Street*, that most beloved of children's television shows, is located in Manhattan: 110th Street, according to one cast member. While other things that are good and important and fun happen in other places, more of them happen in New York.

Perhaps most amazing, it does not take being Salinger, Dewey, or Big Bird to connect with what the city offers. It takes only being there. This is because the best of New York is so accessible, so familiar.

One has a sense, just walking down the street, that New York is the one place we all have a piece of; everywhere you look, there is something you know. Mostly it is the big stuff that no one can ignore: the Empire State Building on 34th Street, Lincoln Center from 62nd Street to 66th, horse-drawn carriages in Central Park, and Times Square—which, if nothing else, is where they drop the big ball on New Year's Eve. Who hasn't seen that on television?

But unlike the Super Bowl or the Oscars, events attended by only the privileged and rich, New York offers experiences available to everyone: watching Mickey Mouse and Superman being inflated on West 77th Street off Central Park the day before Macy's Thanksgiving Day Parade; walking up Fifth Avenue in the Easter Parade (not really a parade at all but a great stroll); and yes, if you are brave enough these days, going to Times Square on New Year's Eve to watch that giant light fixture drop. They are all free and accessible, these symbols of America.

A little social networking can gain entrance to more specialty events. I once joined guests at the annual meeting of the New York Zoological Society—the Bronx Zoo—to mingle among an alligator, an iguana, and four baby gorillas at Lincoln Center. While dating a former waitress at Le Figaro Café, I enjoyed the closed party celebrating the anniversary of that famed hangout of counterculture figures.

New York is also filled with secret treasures, quite public but requiring a little work to enjoy. The payoff for expending that effort is an elevated appreciation of the experience of

living in the city. You walk along 42nd Street past Times Square and come upon the New York Public Library on Fifth Avenue. The largest marble structure in the United States when it opened in 1911, it is now appreciated by the average New Yorker for the two marble stone lions that guard the entrance—named Patience and Fortitude by Mayor Fiorello La Guardia—for being a good place in Midtown to use a free and clean toilet and for its little metal tables and chairs, snapped up by office workers eager for an al fresco lunch. When the tables fill, there's always room on the wide flight of steps leading to the entrance.

Continue up those stairs and head inside—no admission charge—and walk to the Rose Main Reading Room on the third floor, big as a football field with a fifty-foot-high ceiling and cathedral-style windows, walls lined with books, the floor filled with massive solid oak tables and comfortable chairs. It takes your breath away, and that is before you learn you're sharing space once used by Norman Mailer, Ed Doctorow, and Alfred Kazin.

Visually exciting as the reading room is, I am drawn to the periodical room on the first floor, filled with magazines still being published and defunct but also newspapers on microfilm from every major city in America and many from around the world. You can read coverage of the San Francisco earthquake directly from the *Chronicle*, the Chicago fire from the *Tribune*, and the hoopla surrounding the Jack Dempsey–Georges Carpentier prizefight of 1921—one of the great nonevents in sports—in newspapers from coast to coast.

Continue east along 42nd Street past Grand Central Terminal—certainly worth a look inside but hardly a surprise—and you might notice a stunning Art Deco office tower on the south side of the street between Third and Second Avenues. Inside is this really big globe, twelve feet in diameter, housed in a mirrored pit beneath a black glass dome and lit from below. Go on in and look; it, too, is free. You'll quickly realize it's the same globe that Clark Kent and Lois Lane walked by every time they entered or left the *Daily Planet* when Superman graduated to the big screen. The globe occupied the lobby of the Daily News Building, home of that tabloid until it moved to West 33rd Street in 1995 then further downtown to New York Plaza in 2011.

This, too, is part of the city's personality—change. Change, for better and for worse, is an inescapable reality in New York, a city constantly in motion. The Waldorf-Astoria on Park Avenue between 50th and 51st Streets is the second incarnation of that stately hotel; the first, located on Fifth Avenue, was demolished to make way for the Empire State Building. Today's Madison Square Garden, recognized as the most famous sports arena in the world, stands at its fourth location; sadly, old Penn Station was destroyed in its favor.

Few decades were more costly to New York's great buildings than the 1960s. There was the destruction of the three Brokaw mansions on 79th Street overlooking Central Park—torn down when workers came in clandestinely over a weekend in 1965 to avoid efforts to save them—the Hotel Astor and the Metropolitan Opera House, both gone in 1967;

and especially Penn Station, its vaulted glass ceiling 150 feet above the main concourse, considered the ultimate tribute to rail travel. Their loss diminished the city's architectural status but also spurred the creation of the landmarks commission, which continues to at least slow the process.

To live in the city during that period was to witness first-hand major forces working in conflict: politicians and developers pushing against architectural critics and historians, a battle that continues today but with the preservationists being better organized. If not for these efforts, much of the best of New York could be found only in photographs, records of men like Peter Moore, who documented the dramatic end of Penn Station from that day in 1963 when destruction began until the wrecking balls completed their work in 1965. And of course we have movies, scenes of people arriving and leaving through Penn Station, meeting under the clock at the Astor, and frolicking in nearly a hundred short and feature films set in the original Coney Island, all now in our past.

Movies are a big part of why New York lives in the memory banks of so many of us. It is, simply, the most duplicated-on-film city in the world. Dustin Hoffman in *Midnight Cowboy*, stopped in the middle of 58th Street by an advancing cab, yelling, "Hey, I'm walking here!"; Audrey Hepburn on Fifth Avenue, posing before that window in *Breakfast at Tiffany's*; any part of the city in many of Woody Allen's movies, including *Bananas* with Woody masquerading in that ridiculous red beard as president of the fictional South American country of San Marcos, arriving at the very real

Hotel Belleclaire, right up 77th Street from my apartment. Sometimes you are there before movies become movies. Production crews shoot in New York all the time—forty films in 2014, its latest big year. You know it is a set when the sidewalk is blocked by big gray sawhorses and instead of a street filled with parked Toyotas, Hyundais, and the occasional Ford, you find a Pierce-Arrow, a Duesenberg, and a maybe even a Kissel "Gold Bug" Speedster.

The result is the same: a little tingling in your spine because you are there at a moment being sealed in time, to be seen over and over by people throughout the world for years to come.

Every time we watch New York featured on film, we are reminded of the city's universality and endurance. When we walk by one of these places, we claim a little piece of the city's qualities—actually touch them. And when viewing one of those TV shows shot in the city, can we resist straining for a setting we recognize?

New York offers these touchstones to visitors and residents every day, whenever we feel the need or desire to access them. The city is an endless collection of places and events and happenings that reach into our psyche and dazzle our senses. They are all part of what the city represents to us: not just concrete and steel and glass but vibrations from an emotional tuning fork that we feel throughout our very being.

High on the list of sources of these vibrations are the city's museums, devoted to exhibiting various forms of art and also Native Americans, Jews, black people, fashion, jazz, rock and

roll, tattoos and other curiosities, the history of New York, of the United States and the universe, and nearly everything else you can think of. They are the repositories of the symbols of our existence, experiences, ideas, and dreams, collected in relatively small spaces.

Access to some of these can be expensive—in 1965 as today—but the better one knows the city, the more one learns to work around this obstacle. Most museums have some time when admission is free—usually one day a week or at least an afternoon. There are also special reduced rates for children and students. And there is one big but little-known secret: one of the most popular can always be really cheap. The posted admission price at the Museum of Natural History is only "suggested"; they'll accept whatever you offer. Try it. Offer a dollar and the response will likely be a polite "Thank you." (A similar policy exists at the Metropolitan and its adjuncts, the Cloisters and the Met Breuer, but only for residents of the state and students from New York, Connecticut, and New Jersey.)

My favorite, the Museum of Modern Art, does not embrace this egalitarian policy; it is unique to museums affiliated with New York City. MoMA, as it is known, is free for children under sixteen and everyone on Fridays from 4:00 p.m. till 8:00. It does, however, have a tempting offer, one I accepted soon after moving to 77th Street. For something like fifty dollars a year, I became an out-of-town member; I used my family's address in Ohio. This bought me unlimited access to the museum, free catalogues of major exhibits, and

entertainment that included movies and jazz in the sculpture garden, originally every Thursday night during July and August. The little theater in the basement showed films twice each afternoon and on the one evening when the museum was open late.

New York of the mid-1960s—lower octane and less crowded than today—had yet to fully discover these added MoMA attractions, and so the movie theater was rarely filled and there was always plenty of space at jazz in the garden. The few chairs that were available might be taken, but twenty-five cents rented a cushion, and a place to sit was always available around the pond and among the sculptures of Rodin, Renoir, Moore, Calder, and my personal favorite, Lipchitz's *Figure*.

Before New York, live music for me meant theaters and concert halls. Listening in the open air beside some of the world's greatest sculpture redefined the experience, opening it to more than one of my senses. My first summer in the city, I saw the Earl "Fatha" Hines Septet, with Earl on the piano, and the Booker Ervin Quartet; Booker played tenor saxophone.

Attending movies in the afternoon was part of my process of getting down to work. And while there were plenty of choices on the Upper West Side—the Embassy and Beacon showed first-run movies, the New Yorker and the Thalia specialized in Hollywood revivals—MoMA was free. Programs were organized by themes: a week of German Expressionism, one of silent Charlie Chaplin films with a real piano player, and lots of Alfred Hitchcock. I still remember

the scene from *The 39 Steps* where Hitchcock cuts from a screaming woman to the screaming whistle of a train as it steams north from London to Scotland. Dozens of other films have made similar cuts, but I saw it first at MoMA.

Jazz and movies at the Modern, watching crews inflate the giant balloons for the Macy's parade, and immersing yourself in firsthand accounts of past events in the public library are unique New York activities, highly praised by natives and visitors. But one of the secrets of getting to know the city is to savor simple, everyday treasures often taken for granted by both groups.

The return trip on the Staten Island Ferry still offers the best view of Lower Manhattan at night. A walk through the same area during the day reveals an up-close look at some of the city's true architectural wonders, from the grand entrance of the Cities Service Building and the lobby of the United States Assay Office to the terra-cotta birds, gargoyles, and alligators peering down from high on the Liberty Tower. Guards will prohibit you from the buildings themselves, but the lobbies are open to the public.

And in the summer heat, while a subway will get you to Rockaway, Orchard, Brighton, or Coney Island beaches, a little covert exploration will reveal which hotels have rooftop pools that are easy to crash. My favorite (name intentionally withheld) was just south of Columbus Circle, a short walk along 9th Avenue to 54th Street. If this obvious transgression makes you squeamish, remind yourself that it's no more illegal than sneaking into the theater at intermission without

a ticket, a practice so well accepted on Broadway that the artsy crowd has christened it "second acting." Pool crashing is a little more involved, but a quick change in the restroom and the pool is yours for the swimming, a treat on hot August afternoons.

This is the magic of New York, the multiplicity of situations available to everyone. Just be there and step forward. An estimated billion people worldwide watch on television as the ball drops on New Year's Eve in Times Square; if you are willing to arrive around three in the afternoon, you can watch in person, be a part of the excitement as the ball drops. (Back in 1965, my date and I arrived about 10:30 p.m., two of only three hundred thousand people compared to an estimated million in 2018).

If you thrill to the Brooklyn Bridge—the cables above and the river traffic below—you can experience that feeling firsthand by walking across and on the other side enjoy a stroll through Brooklyn Heights. If you crave the best cannoli you've ever tasted, it's Café Ferrara in Little Italy. Oppressed by the madness of Midtown? Stop in at the Ford Foundation Building on 43rd Street and relax in its 230-feet-high atrium, one of man's great tributes to nature and solitude.

These are not activities that guidebooks recommend and travel agencies tout, attractions afforded only by the rich; they are part of everyday living in the club called New York. Engaging at the most modest level initiates membership and a sense of belonging, though some adjustment in

conventional thinking may be required.

The general rule among subway riders is to avert your eyes; look at your book or the floor, any place but your fellow passengers. I propose the opposite; the conditions are ideal. Unlike buses, where most passengers face front, subway riders sit on benches lining both sides of cars and so face each other. This arrangement invites observation, the first step in the exercise that offers a revealing glimpse into what makes a New Yorker, thereby enriching the experience of being in the city.

Sitting recently in a crowded Number Two train as it sped up the West Side, I saw a man across the aisle, his New York Times folded in that linear fashion that permitted him to read an entire column top-to-bottom, known as "the New York wrap." A woman standing to the left of me held her purse tucked under her arm with the straps over her shoulder to thwart thieves, consciously ignoring the well-dressed man who carried on a conversation with himself, not using Bluetooth to communicate with someone else but fully engaged in a one-person dialogue, providing both sides of the exchange. These are typical scenes in the subway, the quintessential people-moving machine in the city, and I was part of it just by being there.

This inclusion contributes to writing. The city offers a setting for stories and also stimulates with its energy. Particularly Manhattan. From Battery Park in the south to the edge of Spuyten Duyvil in the north, the borough is comprised of blocks densely packed with humanity and wide-open

acres of nature, different conditions with their own kinds of attractions.

I believe it is this diversity of opportunities that, at least in part, pulls people from every nation, and, once they arrive, the quality of their energy pushes us to be better at what whatever we do. For those of us who write, it helps us fight the trap to be satisfied with a good draft when we can push for a better one.

At least it did for me. I have written in the country surrounded by fields so silent you think you could hear the corn grow, and by the sea, with the rhythmic pattern of waves hitting against the shore. But for most of my life I wrote best in the city, amidst its sounds and smells and actions, indicators of different people going about their business of living and making it work on that one island, not divided by their differences but enriched and stimulated by them.

Or maybe it was the sound of all those people typing, other writers working on their manuscripts in the middle of the day and the dead of night and in doing so, pushing me to write faster and better.

Many people talk about how competitive New York is. They're right; it is. But the challenge is not only to compete with other peoples' success but to match their commitment to work. And while the first can be intimidating, the second can be inspiring.

TEN

"'Cause I Could Pass the Football"

It is worth noting that I am one-third into this book and have mentioned practically nothing about sports—odd since so much about my being in New York had to do with writing and so much of my writing was about sports. Four published nonfiction books, prolonged stints with ESPN, *BusinessWeek* and the *Wall Street Journal*, all of it working on sports, at least tangentially. But that would come later. It started almost by accident.

I never intended to write about sports when I moved to the city. To be honest, I don't really like sports, as a participant or even a spectator, not in the same way that rabid fans live and die with their hometown favorites, display team colors with near-religious fever and clothe their infants and pets in team merchandise, despise fans of competing teams, even hate the opposition's mascots and symbols. (Remember the University of Alabama fan who

in 2011 poisoned Auburn's historic Toomer's Corner oak trees? Unbelievable!)

That said, there is a quality to some games—especially baseball—that I find satisfying, even therapeutic. On bad days, when work proceeds at a glacial pace—or stops dead—a game that would normally not interest me suddenly takes on value. There is something about baseball, on radio or television, that moves me along emotionally and helps me out of a hole.

It has little to do with who wins or loses and more to do with rhythm, to the windup and delivery by the pitcher, to the batter as he times his swing at the ball, to the shortstop who ranges to his right to field the ball and fire to the first baseman, to the outfielder who gauges his approach to a fly ball so he can catch it and fire in one continuous motion to the cutoff man and stop the runner on second base from advancing to third.

And then there is the pace of games, often described as leisurely, which leaves room for the stories that baseball generates. I love the stories.

Growing up in Cincinnati in the mid- and late-1940s, I attended not a single Reds baseball game and yet was fascinated to listen to Waite Hoyt's radio broadcasts. Not because he so eloquently described what was happening on the field; he wasn't very good at that. Hoyt had a habit of forgetting that we were out there listening. I can hear him now: "Adams leads off first, McCormick at the plate. And there's a line drive over the shortstop's head." Then silence, five, six

seconds of nothing, until: "Adams is on third, McCormick on first." No, play-by-play was not the attraction; his storytelling was. I was mesmerized by each tale, every behind-the-scenes memory.

Hoyt as a young man pitched on those great New York Yankees teams that included Lou Gehrig and Babe Ruth, and he liked to reminisce about them, especially Ruth. Any delay was an excuse, even a foul ball off the catcher's mask. "Wow," he once said after one such incident, "that must've hurt. You can imagine how staying a catcher would have changed the Babe's career; he began as a left-handed catcher, you know." We didn't; at least I didn't.

Those Reds teams of that era were not very good, rarely won as often as they lost, but I tuned in to hear Hoyt spin tales about the Yankees, how he played with them and hung out with them, how the Babe was a great teammate but could not remember the names of the other players, called them Joe or Pete or Happy or anything else that came to mind, but nobody cared because everybody loved the Babe.

We moved in 1951 to Florida, where there were no Reds games on radio. What I got were the Dodgers, the result of team owner Walter O'Malley creating a network that stretched from Brooklyn south to Miami, a popular retirement location for New Yorkers. But these were not Dodgers games called live from the ballpark by those great announcers Red Barber or Vin Scully but games recreated by Nat Allbright sitting in a studio and reading bare-fact telegraph messages augmented by sound effects; Barber and

Scully in those days were heard only in New York. Allbright's games defied credibility—every hit a screamer; every catch spectacular—and worse, lacked stories of carousing with Babe Ruth.

I substituted with sports fiction, like Irwin Shaw's short story "The Eighty-Yard Run," in which Christian Darling scores a touchdown in a college practice then spends the next fifteen years of his life trying to match the exhilaration of that moment. And there were old movies, a staple in that period for television: *College Coach* (1933) was about the ethical sacrifices made for a winning football team, *The Champ* (1931) about the health risks in boxing, and *The Big Fix* (1947) covered gambling in college basketball.

A favorite in our house was *Wonderful Town*, first a Broadway musical and then a TV special, both loosely based on a series of stories in the *New Yorker* about two sisters trying to make it in New York City. The attraction for us was that the sisters came from Ohio. For me it was the character named Wreck, who was in town hoping to sign with New York's professional football team.

In his one song in the show, Wreck made it clear that his path to graduating was eased because of his skill playing football. Not only was he on a full scholarship with food and vacations paid for, famous professors tutored him, all because, as the title of his song says, he could "Pass the Football."

The song was humorous but the situation real and not so funny. That it should surface on Broadway decades before becoming a popular subject in the media is a testament to

how well ingrained it was in the culture that athletes got a free ride so long as they could "pass the football."

Sport is the ideal stage to illustrate the defining realities of life. And while Wreck and Christian Darling were fictional, sport is made up of real people, their lives changed by the twists and turns that occur in competition. Elena Ivashchenko, the four-time European judo champion from Russia, committed suicide after failing to medal at the 2012 London Olympics. Len Bias, selected second in the 1986 NBA draft, died forty-eight hours later, reportedly from a cocaine overdose taken at a celebration party. Monica Seles never returned to her number-one world tennis ranking form (1991 and 1992) after being stabbed in the back during a match in Hamburg in 1993 by a man reported to be an obsessed fan of Steffi Graff, a frequent opponent of Seles.

Players committing suicide after a failed performance or being attacked by a crazed fan make headlines worldwide. Routinely ignored are how everyday winning and losing impact athletes. And while success and failure take place throughout society, in all professions, sport is unique in that its climactic moments are played out not behind closed doors but before thousands of people in stadiums and millions on television.

Everybody knows when a kicker misses a field goal that would have won the game or a batter strikes out with the bases loaded. In a world of subjective judgments, where success is left to someone's opinion of what is good and what

is bad, in sport it goes to the last competitor standing. For all its harsh realities, there is beauty in that, and in its unscripted nature, frequently yielding surprise endings any dramatist would envy.

The ripple effect of these events is often life altering and so more important than final scores. This side of sport attracted me; it still does. But I never got the chance to write about it. While I briefly worked in sports departments in Miami, Bethlehem, and Mount Vernon, game stories filled their pages, winners and losers. *Sports Illustrated* introduced a new, theme-driven attitude toward covering athletics when it began publishing in 1954, but it took time for most news-papers to catch on. Then toward the end of 1975, with the definition of what is and what is not a good sports story changing, I got the opportunity to join the party.

I had been writing for *Audubon* for about four years when one of the editors invited me to attend a meeting with exec-utives from Chanticleer Press, a packaging publisher. These are companies that produce books that are distributed by established publishers under those publishers' imprimaturs. Chanticleer created mostly large-format books, also known as coffee-table books, with finely reproduced photographs—the kind of books generally beyond the technical skills of tradi-tional publishers. Since 1952 they had taken what seemed like esoteric subjects and turned them into beautiful and successful books, among them Mary McCarthy's *Stones of Florence* about the history and quality of life in that city and Peter Matthies-sen's *The Tree Where Man Was Born* about Africa.

They brought me in to explore new ideas that might fill out their list. For more than an hour we mined my recent work and future assignments, looking for some theme that might work. Nothing sparked their interest until the conversation circled around to my interest in sports. I took a deep breath and explained about these dynamic little situations that happen out of the spotlight, not just to stars but to those foot soldiers of sports, to which the Chanticleer woman responded with something like, "Huh!" And then, "I think I like that."

I wish I could tell you that Chanticleer gave me a contract for this great coffee-table book filled with fabulous photographs and supported by my scintillating text, but I can't. The final response was no thanks.

By then Jim Brown was my agent and he liked the idea, leading to my first book contract, signed by Jonathan Segal at Times Books. It followed a chronology, starting with young players filled with confidence and hope, struggling to make a team, surviving as fringe players confronting the new crop of top prospects every season, ending with others as they were released for the last time.

They played different sports and experienced different levels of success but shared a passion for their sports and the life lived while competing. No one exhibited that more than Norman Snead, who had been a star quarterback in the NFL but was a backup for the New York Giants when I met him in 1976, the last of his sixteen seasons that included being traded and released on multiple occasions and required three knee surgeries.

"I love the game and I love the people in it," he told me. "I love all the craziness, the going to bars and drinking beer and telling stories. I love the locker room and the smell of the sweaty uniforms and the guys I'm sharing it with. My wife is concerned about how I'm going to be when I'm fifty. I couldn't care less. I don't care if I'm crippled. This is worth it."

Segal took the book with him when he moved to Simon & Schuster, where it was published in 1979 under the title *One Step from Glory.*

If this sounds like a roundabout way of landing a book contract, it is, but that's often how it works, and for me the pattern usually involved sports. Months after that first book appeared, a magazine editor asked me to develop an idea connected with the upcoming Olympics in Moscow. He had only one caveat: "Do not tie it to a single athlete; they're always getting injured. We know there will be an Olympics."

I pitched a story about the decathlon, focusing for editorial security on the top three athletes—an American, a German, and an Englishman. Weeks after I filed my story, Russia invaded Afghanistan and President Jimmy Carter announced a boycott of the games. There would be no Olympics for America, reducing interest for US publications. My story was killed.

At Jim Brown's suggestion I refocused on the Brit, Daley Thompson; Brown sold the idea as a book in England—not boycotting the Olympics—and there I was back writing about sports.

The Thompson book led to my writing Steve Garvey's autobiography, which helped me get a job writing something called advertorials for *Sports Illustrated*, the bumpy but lucrative marriage of editorial and advertising. These led to a contract to write a book about sports business that led to a column in *Sport* magazine on sports business, which led to my writing for the sports business section of *BusinessWeek* magazine.

All the while I kept proposing articles of general interest and books having nothing to do with sports and writing novels. I sold some of the non-sport articles but none of the books. At some point it became clear that to make a living as a writer, I needed to write about sport in one form or another. I considered it a professional imperative, my own version of publish or perish, but I do not consider myself a sports writer.

Except when sports in their many and varied forms pull aside the curtain of privacy and permit us to peek into the otherwise personal spectacles of peoples' lives. They constitute theater without a script, and I am thankful for the privilege of sitting in the audience, taking notes.

Cautionary Tales

Much as I prized these insightful moments, there is a trap in valuing them too much: we think they represent the real people at the center. Because the nature of our work encourages them to share instances of success and failure and their feelings about these moments, we think we have an understanding of the whole person. This is an arrogant assumption and frequently flawed.

I spent the best part of two years working on the autobiography of Steve Garvey, the baseball player, observing him, traveling and interviewing him and people from his childhood in Tampa, Florida, his early years playing for the Los Angeles Dodgers, and later the San Diego Padres. It was a good experience. He was generous with his time and forthcoming on his feelings about sport and life.

My conclusion was that Garvey was an excellent ball player who worked hard at his craft, was personally earnest and held closely to traditional values. I believed his "Mr. Clean" image, earned for his his well-documented adherence to the unwritten and official rules of baseball and society.

He was eminently likeable and not guarded. I found him to be a bit square—or maybe just very conservative—and he seemed comfortable with that label. I even suggested that our publisher subtitle our book "Straight Arrow," a proposal that was rejected.

And so I was among those most surprised when, within three years of the book's publication, news surfaced that Garvey had become simultaneously involved with three different women and was the object of a paternity suit filed by one.

"Some people have a midlife crisis," he told Rick Riley of Sports Illustrated in a 1989 article detailing Garvey's domestic problems. "I had a midlife disaster." These were lesser revelations compared to contemporary transgressions but actions I would not have predicted, which is why I mention them here: They served as an introduction for me to the fallacy of making assumptions about people. Harder lessons followed.

One involved Steve's teammate on the Padres, pitcher Eric Show. Tangential to the Garvey story, he and I connected on a level separate from baseball. We spent hours talking at the Padres spring training camp in Yuma, Arizona, and later when I covered Garvey during the season. We talked about writing—he inquired whether I had read Ayn Rand, which I hadn't—and about music; he'd played guitar since his youth. I found him warm, smart, friendly, engaging, and focused. Once when our locker-room conversation carried on into the area of the urinals—usually denied access to reporters—he

casually finished peeing and followed me back to the unrestricted area without interrupting the point he was making.

He seemed to be a man at peace with himself and the pressures of being a professional athlete. In 1985 when I watched TV footage of him sitting on the mound in Cincinnati as Riverfront Stadium fans celebrated Pete Rose breaking Ty Cobb's all-time hit record with a single off Show, I thought, *Yea, that's Eric, carving out a place for himself while the world goes nuts.* I remember thinking, smugly, *I know this guy.*

Disbelief best describes my response to his death in 1994, just two years after he retired from baseball. His body was discovered in a drug rehabilitation center in San Diego. I subsequently read Tom Friend's article on ESPN.com that chronicled Show's relationship with an abusive father and his history with drugs. I knew none of this or much else about the real Eric Show.

And I was not alone. From Ira Berkow's piece in the *New York Times* soon after Show's death: "For most baseball fans, Eric Show was a decent pitcher who had once been lucky enough to make it to the World Series. But to the people who were close to him, he was, in the end, someone they did not fully know."

My most serious misreading of the inner person concerns Michael Wayne Current. Mike and I met in 1976 while I worked on my first book, interviewing players at the initial football camp of the expansion Tampa Bay Buccaneers. As with all new teams, this first camp was a gathering of mostly desperate athletes. They once played at a high level but at this

point were considered expendable, left unprotected by their teams in that unceremonious dumping of athletes officially known as the veteran allocation draft. This is how newly formed professional football teams fill their roster: partly through the regular draft of college players, partly by signing free agents, but mostly from other teams making players available from the list they no longer want.

Some players at that Bucs camp had impressive résumés. Larry Ball, a linebacker out of Louisville, had played on the Miami Dolphins undefeated team in 1972. Joe Blahak helped anchor the defensive backfield on Nebraska's undefeated national championship team in 1971. Pat Toomay led the Dallas Cowboys in sacks in 1973. But all were left unprotected by their teams at the end of the 1975 season and were in Tampa the following July, trying to extend their careers while the rest of America celebrated the nation's bicentennial.

Mike Current was among them. He had played left tackle on offense for Ohio State, was co-captain in his senior year, and was drafted in the third round by Denver in 1967. The Broncos quickly traded him to Miami, who after two games traded him back to Denver, where he remained into the 1975 season; a knee injury took him out in the seventh game. He was a starter until then and in 1969 was selected to the Pro Bowl.

We became friends over the month I spent with those first Bucs. I met his wife and young son and had dinner with them back at their house. We kept in touch and saw each other when he came to New York to play the Jets during that

long season of frustration; Tampa Bay became the first NFL to complete a fourteen-game schedule without a victory.

Mike was traded to Miami for the 1977 season, and we continued to see each other when the Dolphins came to town once a year to play the Jets. We had dinner in town the night before the games and met at Shea Stadium early on Sundays, before the stadium was open to the public; press credentials gained me entrance.

I remember one bright, sunny November morning, meeting at midfield. Mike liked the hazelnut cookies from Éclair's and I had brought him a box. We sat on the grass, saying little but marveling at the quiet in that near-empty stadium. I carried the image of that Sunday with me for years, the peace in that huge stadium before the raucous fans and mayhem on the field turned it into a modern-day Colosseum, and this six-foot-five-inch, 276-pound football player leaning protectively over his box of cookies.

He had over our time together shared personal truths that helped me understand my subject, the tenuous existence of a professional athlete. Mike was clear that he didn't like the two-a-day workouts at training camp or all the hitting during the week in season, but he put up with it all just so he could play in games. He came to represent for me all those fringe players fighting for one more season.

We lost contact once he left football when the Dolphins released him after the 1979 season. His wife called me occasionally, just to keep in touch, even though they had split up. She was not part of my official research, but

sometimes the illusion of intimacy from prolonged communication extends beyond the principle subjects, at least for a while. Soon those calls ended. Eventually Mike Current slipped out of my consciousness.

Then early in 2012, while scanning the internet in what has become a frequent exercise to catch up with incomplete storylines of my life and work, I came upon the following headline from the Denver Post: "Former Bronco Mike Current found dead, he faced child-sex charges in Oregon."

I'm not sure I am enough in touch with my emotions to describe how I responded. I think I didn't believe it. *A prank,* I thought. A dumb, cruel prank; the internet invites such shit. I felt compelled to read on.

"The 66-year-old apparently shot himself sometime overnight at the viewing area along the Baskett Slough National Wildlife Refuge," said Sgt. Michael Holsapple of the Polk County Sheriff's Office. There were no signs of foul play or a struggle in the pullout along the road northeast of the small town of Dallas.

"In November, Current, who lived in Silverton from the mid-2000s to 2010, was charged with five counts of first-degree sexual assault and one count of luring a minor, according to the Marion County district attorney's office. The alleged offenses occurred at an unspecified address in Marion County."

I did not need to read more of the article. A quick survey of additional postings online convinced me that, whatever the details, Mike had gotten himself into enough

of a bad situation that he viewed his only way out as taking his life.

My mind flashed back to that Sunday on the fifty-yard-line of the Shea Stadium field, sitting there with my friend and his cookies. I could not escape the reality that I had no idea who he was.

The lesson, I guess, is to never assume we know the people we encounter in public life, as reporters dealing directly with them and particularly as consumers of the media, but even this comes with a warning label: a healthy dose of skepticism is important if not taken to extreme; no one benefits from looking for the worst in the figures we read about or view on television.

Moderation is the key, an approach I define as holding back a little trust. The next time you are tempted to idolize that running back streaking along the sidelines for a touchdown, remember the complex manner in which we now view O. J. Simpson.

The Nexus

While I continued to pursue work by conventional means—submitting stories and ideas cold to editors I did not know and applying for jobs on my own—most of my success came through the recommendation of someone I did know or someone I knew who knew someone else.

The first short story I published—in a literary magazine called *The New Renaissance*—got the attention of the editor because the young man I traveled to South America to find sent it to her, and she liked it. My introduction to *Audubon* started with a book designer at Time, Inc., whom I met at one of Joanna Steichen's parties, who knew a magazine designer who knew an editor at *Audubon*. These were different people encountered in different situations. What they had in common was New York, the center where all of these forces interacted.

This is part of that New York connectivity, people talking to people talking to people, and some of them willing to help another person. Vital as these opportunities are, they represent only an entrée, the proverbial foot in the door. An

editor would be foolish to risk his or her job by publishing inferior writing, especially in national publications, where there is so much competition for every column inch, so much scrutiny with every editorial decision. Once that introduction is made, the work must stand on its own. But this all begins with forces that come together in New York.

A similar mechanism—placing people in close proximity to the many elements of the city and its environs—permits a growing familiarity with a tantalizing array of settings one might otherwise have missed. Over the years I wrote about Fort Tryon Park at the northern tip of Manhattan for *Audubon* and covered news events throughout the boroughs for *Time* magazine and *BusinessWeek*. While researching *One Step from Glory*, I interviewed dozens of players at Yankee and Shea Stadiums, the Meadowlands in New Jersey, Madison Square Garden in Manhattan, and the Nassau Veterans Memorial Coliseum in Uniondale on Long Island.

Every one of these encounters brought me closer to the true character of the city and its people. This is the natural result of being a reporter; we push ourselves into situations we would otherwise miss, and we learn in the process.

On a Thursday morning in May 1970, I received a call from the *Miami Herald*. This was three days after Ohio National Guardsmen shot and killed four students who were protesting the expansion of the Vietnam War into Cambodia and the presence of the Guard on campus at Kent State University. The *Herald* learned that funeral services for one

of the students, twenty-year-old Jeffrey Miller from Long Island, were scheduled for that day and asked me to cover them for the paper.

The site was Riverside Memorial Chapel on Amsterdam Avenue, four blocks from my apartment. My intention was to arrive early, slip inside and report on the service, observe and perhaps interview the parents—ghoulish, I know, but that's what reporters do.

The minute I reached the scene, I realized this was not going to work. The street had already been blocked off by police, as was the entrance to the chapel. Prominent mourners were escorted in, among them New York Senator Charles Goodell and Dr. Benjamin Spock, by then better known as an antiwar activist than for his books on rearing babies. But I was not among the invited and carried no press credentials, leaving me stuck among the reported four thousand spectators outside.

This was decades before Instagram, Snapchat, Twitter, and all those other methods to quickly disseminate news. How had all those people learned of the time and place for the funeral? Within minutes I found the answer was WBAI, the listener-sponsored FM radio station, left leaning and heavily antiwar. Others told me it was the word of mouth network that linked all of New York, where diversity of population seemed to empower them to act on their shared concerns.

On this morning they had come to express their sadness and anger about the death of young Jeffrey and their

opposition to the war. They jammed onto the street outside the funeral hall, respectfully silent. They strained to hear the speeches of Dr. Spock and Senator Goodell broadcast from the service inside; I doubted they could understand their muffled words any better than I. When the service ended and the hearse bearing the casket drove away, there was a spontaneous appearance of index and middle fingers forming V-signs for peace and circulars passed out bearing the chilling message: "In memory of Jeffrey Miller, murdered at Kent State." This was a New York kind of event.

While working in 1983 for the New York bureau of *Time*, I was one of their three reporters covering the centennial celebration of the opening of the Brooklyn Bridge. Equipped with a large, plastic-encased press pass that permitted me to cross police lines that blocked off the bridge, I scooted among the 1.5 million spectators on the Manhattan side and 650,000 on the Brooklyn side who gathered for the 28 minutes of fireworks, ending with a "3,600 detonations in a giddy 2½ minutes, 25 flames-a-second" finale, according to *Time*.

Reporting on the pyrotechnics was not my assignment; *Time* relied on celebrity fireworks enthusiast George Plimpton for that. I was there to talk to people, the famous like former mayor John Lindsey and the not-so-famous. I was rewarded with expressions of passion about the bridge but also more than a few Brooklynites bemoaning its existence, insisting that it had robbed their home of its uniqueness and voicing their wish that Brooklyn would someday secede from New

York and return to the days when it was its own city, as it was prior to 1898. They blamed the bridge for paving the way for what they considered was that ignominious demotion. One woman expressed her local chauvinism by demanding that Los Angeles give back the Dodgers.

Later that same year I was part of a larger group from *Time* working on an early cover story on AIDS, "Hunting for the Hidden Killers." Bureaus around the country sent reporters to conduct firsthand research then turn those files in to the New York office, where writers and editors created the story that appeared in the magazine.

My job was to interview people at the Gay Men's Health Crisis, a nonprofit volunteer organization formed the previous year by six men committed to alerting the general population and homosexuals to the threat of AIDS and supporting those infected. This was early in the AIDS pandemic. The *New York Times* published its first article about AIDS in July 1981, reporting that forty-one homosexuals had been diagnosed with a rare form of cancer; eight died in the United States in less than twenty-four months after being diagnosed. Two years later our *Time* article reported 644 deaths. (A high of 42,144 people died in 1996, the year that the three-drug "cocktail" was developed to combat the disease, after which the death rate began to decrease.)

But in that summer of 1983, the death rate was rising, as was the anxiety, especially among the gay population where most deaths occurred. There was no cure—and still isn't—but even the source was a mystery. While medical researchers

attacked the science, the Gay Men's Health Crisis mounted an offensive against the escalating fear. Working out of an apartment in Chelsea, the group of volunteers operated a twenty-four-hour-a-day hotline to dispense up-to-date information and offer counseling and legal aid. At the time of our reporting, they had just sponsored the first fundraising event, a performance of Ringling Brothers Circus at Madison Square Garden. "There are a lot of frightened people out there and it's our job to offer them comfort and information," one volunteer told me.

Every assignment made it more clear how engaged New Yorkers are with their community. Much of this is obvious. Benches throughout the five boroughs sport plaques bearing the names of donors and often messages attesting to their affection for New York, more than four thousand of them in Central Park. Buildings, theaters, and concert halls are named after benefactors who paid for that honor with the swipe of a pen.

Other indications materialize spontaneously in the course of not-so-normal events. During the transit strikes of 1966 and 1980, cars and even limousines picked up people walking downtown to work in the morning and back uptown in the afternoon and early evening.

And then there is Fort Tryon Park and the Cloisters museum with its collection of European medieval art, famous for its Flemish unicorn tapestries. It is common knowledge that the complex was donated to the city by John D. Rockefeller Jr. in the mid-1930s. In research I also learned that he

guaranteed a pure, natural view for visitors at the park—prized for being the highest natural point in Manhattan—by purchasing several hundred acres of the New Jersey Palisades on the other side of the Hudson.

The week I spent at the Cloisters and Fort Tryon for *Audubon* afforded me more than a picture of how the very rich support their favorite causes. Talking to one of the docents, I learned of the different people drawn to this lovely but seriously out-of-the-way attraction, nearly nine miles north of Times Square: flower lovers for the gardens, art enthusiasts for the unicorns, geologists there to study the glacial striations from the last Ice Age on which the park is built, and historians who came to examine the fort near the site of the Revolutionary War battle of Fort Washington, fought on November 16, 1776; a plaque honors Margaret Corbin, considered the first woman to fight in the war.

We were standing outside the museum on one of the walkways that led to the stone fortification referred to as the ramparts. "Just last week," the docent said, "an elementary school teacher brought his entire class. They stood out here and sang 'The Star Spangled Banner.' You know," she said, and began singing: "*O say, can you see by the dawn's early light.* When they got to the part that went, '*O'er the ramparts we watched,*' they all pointed to the ramparts and they applauded."

Stories everywhere, and the more we tap into them, the more we feel a part of the city, its history, and its pulse.

This is not unique to New York. William Faulkner, Willa Cather, and William Kennedy did pretty well writing about their favorite regions of America; Willie Morris wrote fine books set in a place called Yazoo City. New York just seems to offer more stories and a greater range of stories and more opportunities to sell them, with more publications and more people willing to offer an introduction. As long as a writer has the energy to keep trying—and the resilience to deal with the rejection—there seems always to be another editor willing to at least read a few lines.

This coming together of subject and opportunity, rejection and acceptance, happened most dramatically for me with one of the shortest, simplest stories I've ever written. It is the one I mentioned earlier, about that vending machine in the basement of Lewisohn Hall. While not in any meaningful way a New York tale—not in its characters or the graphic nature of its setting—its track from obscurity to at least marginal prominence is pure New York.

Lewisohn is today as it was in 1967: the home of Columbia University's School of General Studies, where I took writing classes. The machine dispensed not only coffee black, or with milk and maybe sugar, but also tea and hot chocolate. I would stop in before class to purchase a coffee with milk, an experience that inspired the story I called "The Coffee Break." Yes, this is the story that was rejected with a "Not funny—yuck" by that magazine editor in 1968. I have efficiently wiped the name of the publication and editor from my mind but not the circumstances.

In the 1970s *Harper's* magazine published a monthly section called Wraparound, a special feature of relatively short pieces focusing on two or three subjects. It got its name from its design: eight pages of newsprint wrapped around the main glossy body of the magazine, four in front and four behind. Each month the editors sent out letters identifying the subjects and a deadline.

In January 1975 the principal subject was villains. Unable to come up with a fresh idea, I recycled the vending machine story; because it frustrated the human character by denying him his choice of beverage, I thought it qualified as a villain.

Harper's agreed, renamed it "Big White," and ran it. (Read it following this chapter.) A year later Scholastic Books published a little paperback called *Loving, Dying, Living: Faces of America*, and filled it with poems and short stories; one was "Big White." Later that year Reader's Digest published my story under the headline "Duel with the Devil."

Since then it has been reprinted more than twenty times, mostly in textbooks about writing. I like to think it's pure brilliance shining through. More likely the editor of one textbook saw it in another textbook and thought, *Why not my textbook?*

Frankly, I don't care. Seeing it makes me happy, and it reminds me of an important writer's reality: What one editor thinks is "Yuck," others might think has value. This exercise in mental health compensates for a lot of rejection letters. Doesn't wipe them out, mind you, but helps balance the scale.

Big White

This story first appeared in Harper's Magazine *in January 1975.*

A strange calm settled over me as I stood before the large, white vending machine and dropped a quarter into the appropriate slot. I listened as the coin clunked into register. Then I pressed the button marked "Hot Chocolate." From deep inside a paper cup slid down a chute, crackling into place on a small metal rack. Through an unseen tube poured coffee, black as night and smoking hot.

I even smiled as I moved to my customary place at the last table, sat down, and gazed across to the white machine, large and clean and defiant. Not since it had been moved in between the candy machine and the sandwich machine had I known peace. Every morning for two weeks I had selected a beverage, and each time the machine had dispensed something different. When I pushed the button for hot chocolate, black coffee came out. When I pushed the button for tea with sugar, coffee with half-and-half came out. So the cup of coffee before me was no surprise. It was but one final test; my plan had already been laid.

Later in the day, after everyone else had left the building, I returned to the snack bar, a yellow legal pad in my hand and a fistful of change in my pocket. I approached the machine and, taking each button in order, began feeding in quarters. After the first quarter I pressed the button labeled "Black Coffee." Tea with sugar came out and I recorded that on the first line of my pad. I dropped in a second quarter and pressed the button for coffee with sugar. Plain tea came out and I wrote that down.

I pressed all nine of the buttons, noting what came out. Then I placed each cup on the table behind me. When I had gone through them all, I repeated the process and was delighted to find the machine dispensing the same drinks as before.

None was what I had ordered,

but each error was consistent with my list.

I was thrilled. To celebrate, I decided to purchase a fresh cup of chocolate.

Dropping in two dimes and a nickel and consulting my pad, I pressed the "Coffee with Sugar and Half-and-Half" button. The machine clicked in response, and a little cup slid down the chute, bouncing as it hit bottom. But that was all. Nothing else happened. No hot chocolate poured into my cup. No black coffee came down. Nothing.

I was livid. I forced five nickels into the slot and pushed the button for black coffee. A cup dropped into place but nothing more. I put five more nickels in and pushed another button, and another cup dropped down—empty. I dug into my pocket for more change but found only three dimes. I forced them in and got back a stream of hot water and a nickel change. I went berserk.

"White devil!" I screamed as I slammed my fists against the machine's clean enamel finish. "You white devil!"

I beat on the buttons and rammed the coin-return rod down. I wanted the machine to know what pain was. I slapped at the metal sides and kicked its base with such force that I could almost hear the bone in my foot crack, then wheeled in agony on my good foot, and with one frantic swing sent the entire table of coffee-, tea-, and chocolate-filled cups sailing.

That was last night. They have cleaned up the snack bar since then, and I have had my foot X-rayed and wrapped in that brown elastic they use for sprains. I am now sitting with my back to the row of vending machines. I know by the steadiness of my hand as I pour homemade hot chocolate from my thermos that no one can sense what I have been through—except, of course, the great white machine over against the wall.

Even now, behind me, in the space just below the coin slot, a tiny sign blinks off and on: "Make Another Selection," it taunts. "Make Another Selection."

—Skip Rozin

Skip Rozin, a freelance writer, is based in New York City.

151

Change

New York was a great place to be single, straight, and male in the second half of the twentieth century. There were all kinds of women, smart and attractive and interesting, older women and younger women, all shapes and sizes, local, from all over this country and most others. If a man wanted company and could put a subject and a verb together to form an intelligent sentence—in any language—there was plenty of good, smart companionship available.

I am talking about the '60s and the '70s, so there was no fear of AIDS and most women were on the pill, making sex easy and fun. Many were also confidently gregarious; an occasional knock at my apartment door initiated an unexpected evening of social contact. And without expectations, let alone talk of marriage, which was fine for me as I was terrified of marriage, of the commitment and responsibility, emotional and financial. Working as hard as I could, I barely made enough money for one, and this while living in an apartment that by then, with small but regular increases, cost me around $165 a month, depending on the date.

Work not only took up most of my time but proved to be a good source of recreation. Every assignment offered interesting and often exciting travel for research. The best of this coincided with my writing for *Audubon*, affording a perfect match for my taste. While friends spent vacations sunbathing at Club Med or gambling in Las Vegas, I was delighted to tramp onto the Greenland permafrost in search of calving icebergs and rise before dawn to accompany the oystermen of the Chesapeake.

None of this could have happened without an assignment; I needed an excuse to court the exotic and someone to cover expenses. The rewards invariably extend beyond supporting an article. Exploring ghost towns in Michigan's Keweenaw Peninsula, I discovered three steam locomotives stored away decades before under circumstances that eluded my inquiries with regional historians and one old codger who professed to hold all the local secrets. Writing about Wrigley Field, I spent an entire game with the crew inside the manually operated centerfield scoreboard.

The highlight of my Chicago trip was happening upon Bill Veeck in the bleachers. Veeck was famous for owning five different baseball teams, most notably the Cleveland Indians, where he integrated the American League by signing Larry Doby in 1947 and winning the World Series a year later, but his heart belonged to his hometown Cubs. His father was club president from 1919 till 1933 and hired young Bill in a variety of jobs, including popcorn vender. I sat enthralled as he spun tales of his exploits while he smoked one cigarette

after another, depositing the ashes into the hole he had built into his peg right leg—not an artificial leg and foot but an actual peg, like a pirate—replacing the one that was amputated after a World War II accident.

The fact that I was alone for these encounters contributed to their success; alone was the nature of the work. I was there to concentrate on the place and the people, to feel and understand how these elements contributed to and in fact created the story. This was not a social act to be shared with a friend or a mate. Some writers I knew worked that way, but I never had.

If being alone for research was at least a subject for discussion, it was not for the writing, a job that for me could only be done by myself. And considering how much of my time was spent writing, that same condition set the pattern for most of my adult life. I was not unique in this. Among my acquaintances in New York at that time, plenty of single men and women in many professions were leading what they thought of as good lives, some in their forties but others in their fifties and sixties. They were sometimes with companions but not continually, and with no lasting responsibilities other than to themselves.

These people were almost role models to me; their situations seemed that good. We shared a reluctance to form close attachments or embrace accountability to anyone other than ourselves. Mostly alone was just fine.

Big cities support this attitude. Small-town living is more geared to couples; pairing up is almost necessary for

survival. People alone are viewed with suspicion, especially as they grow older. But cities accommodate singles more easily. Look around New York; single people are everywhere. Life there seems designed to form temporary attachments, filled with opportunities to meet other singles, and friends with friends looking for companionship, short-term or long. You are together with someone for a while, and when that relationship falls apart, you find someone else. Or not. That's just the way it is. A shop on Fifth Avenue even ran a publicity campaign for a specially designed ceramic pot and cup advertised as "Tea For One." It seemed like a natural item to sell in Manhattan, where nearly one in every two adults lived alone, a trend that I embraced.

Then came that unexpected September night on the French Rivera. A friend, a lawyer with business dealings all over the world, invited me to join him on his weeklong vacation.

We were cruising along the Cote d'Azur on his client's ninety-six-foot motor yacht and had put in for a few days at St. Tropez, famous for enticing women to go topless on its glistening beaches and hosting international celebrities dating back to Coco Chanel and later Brigitte Bardot. A late dinner on deck was finished; nearly everyone else had gone to their staterooms. I lingered over one last cognac and remained to watch the parade of tourists walking along the docks. Casually dressed and tanned, they were leaving restaurants that ranged from cafes that offered an entire meal for eight dollars to Mouscardins at the top of

the street, where a couple would have trouble getting away for less than $200.

The deck was quiet and, out of the glare of lights from the shore, cast in shadow. I took that time to appreciate where I was, docked in St. Tropez, drinking fine cognac aboard a yacht. This was very nice. There was even talk of extending our stay a day or two.

Suddenly there came an odd feeling, a questioning of my joyful circumstance. In the next instant it came to me: I could take off at a moment's notice because nobody relied on my being back home. Every assignment could take me as far away and last as long as warranted because nobody cared when I returned. Good as this was on one level, it indicated a lack of responsibility to anyone but me, to anything except what I considered important. In the quiet of that night I suddenly saw my life played out as lyrics in a sentimental country song, how living free meant having nothing left to lose. I doubt that the temperature dropped at the moment, but a shudder ran through me.

This was 1981 and I was about to turn forty. Maybe that was the stressor, the stimulus that made me look critically at my situation. Those friends leading good lives were happy, but applying their standards to myself seemed suddenly shortsighted. I wasn't questioning whether it was right for them, but did it work for me? Even in New York, which many consider the capital of self-indulgence, shouldn't there be more? Focusing totally on my own needs and happiness hadn't seemed selfish before, but approaching forty, I found

myself challenging it, even in that luxurious setting. And as I looked down the road toward fifty and sixty, it seemed even less attractive. I warmed the cognac in the large crystal snifter, lifted it to my nose, and inhaled the aroma. Maybe I should rethink my course. And so I did.

Instead of looking at women as potential dates, I began seeking a woman with whom I might share a life. The primary qualities were the same for both groups—physically attractive, intelligent, sane, interesting, and willing to compromise—but they were weighted differently. Attractive ranked high for dating, less so when choosing a wife; sanity was essential in a wife while eccentric was charming in a date. Intelligent and interesting—and they are different—ranked high for both. Willingness to compromise, while valuable in a date, is essential in marriage. (Admittedly, I understand this better now, but even then I could intuit the different values and how I ranked them.)

I didn't need to look far. I had already met Julie Guibord through mutual friends, and we connected from the start. I found her smart and attractive, a runner, tall and thin, with lovely hands, long and gracefully tapered fingers; nice hands were inexplicably important to me. She was a marvelous illustrator, though she dismissed her artistic talent as a facility and her degree from Cooper Union's School of Art as time wasted. She placed greater value on her skill with a camera and earned a master's in fine arts from Yale's school of photography. That determination looked to me like independence, a quality that would serve us both well as I committed

to my own professional path. I felt a strong attraction. Love? Probably, though the course of our latter years together have colored what I see looking back.

We had our differences. I liked wine; she drank no alcohol. She had been a vegetarian since she was a teenager and I embraced eating all manner of meat, fish, and poultry. She was critical of my taste in music, accused it of being stuck in the '60s. But these issues seemed minor, and we tried to accommodate each other. I never urged her to drink with me or to prepare nonvegetarian portions of my meals; she tolerated my records and bought tickets for us to attend a Joan Baez concert at the Beacon Theatre.

The only issue was that Julie wanted children. While being a parent sounded good in theory, it was for me one of those someday things, something other people did—you know, adults. Marriage did not seem so risky, but parenthood was scary. And yet here I was, seeking a fuller life, one focused less on myself. But the woman I wished to marry wanted a child. I was at an impasse, which was how I got to psychotherapy.

Most of my friends had time with a shrink in their history and eagerly recommended it as a positive force in my personal growth. I always resisted, insisting that my growth and I were progressing nicely. This time they augmented their argument with therapy's value resolving dilemmas. I definitely had a dilemma. Eighteen months of twice-a-week sessions revealed that my issue was one of control, control of time and money, and how selfishly I guarded my physical and emotional space

to write. I slept, ate, and worked at specific times and spent money only on what I deemed necessary. A family would put that delicate arrangement in jeopardy.

While therapy was valuable, I'm not sure we ever resolved my deeper issues—why I so feared a loss of control, which I now suspect was tied to my fear of failure. (Of course, the bigger question is if I was so afraid of failure, why did I chose a profession so filled with it, but confronting that would have required much more therapy.) The best we did was to agree that men had been getting married and starting families for a long time and few had died from it. I proposed marriage to Julie; she accepted and we married in May 1983.

I was confident that we would never part, and I was positive that Julie felt the same way. (On our third anniversary, she made me a card that read, "Skip and Julie forever.") Initially it was the same as living together. We resided in Julie's one-bedroom apartment on 75th Street and Columbus Avenue and each morning I went off to work at 336. Even the birth of our first child, Rebecca, in October 1985 didn't change much.

Julie swears the pregnancy was easy, and I believe her. She signed up with the midwifery program at Roosevelt Hospital—no bright lights, drugs, or surgery for her. On the morning she delivered she insisted on walking the sixteen blocks from our apartment, stopping once for labor pains and a second time for a Tofutti cone.

She had gained so little weight and was so fit that when we told the guard in the lobby we wanted the maternity floor,

he looked at her and exclaimed that visiting hours weren't till one o'clock. This was about 10:30 a.m.; Rebecca arrived at 3:45, smiling and reaching for her mother's face. At 8:30 the following morning Julie called and said that if I could pick her up by 10:00, we would not get charged for an extra day—my kind of reasoning.

Rebecca mostly smiled through infancy, with the exceptions of some bouts of colic. More often than not it was Julie who cared for her, to lift her from her crib and walk around our little apartment, bedroom to living room to kitchen and back, bedroom to living room to kitchen and back, until she fell asleep.

When it was my turn I followed Julie's pattern: bedroom to living room to kitchen and back. But I never had her patience; two trips and I was done with the repetition. My fallback cure was to put Rebecca in her Snugli, zip her inside my down jacket, and walk through the wintery streets of the Upper West Side, occasionally stopping in at the International Market on Broadway and 77th, where Rebecca charmed the cashiers with her babble until she tired and fell asleep. My biggest challenge was keeping her asleep while I unfolded her from our walking gear and lay her down in her crib.

She was a take-me-anywhere kid. At one party she happily played on the floor for a time, somehow avoiding the feet of the adults. When she got tired we put her down on our host's bed, surrounded by the guests' coats as a barrier from rolling off. She remained asleep even as we picked her up and carried her home to her own bed.

And she was a great traveler, on a five-hour drive to visit Julie's parents on Cape Cod or all the way to Ohio. I remember one drive west when she was two; we had left New York at sundown and she was asleep before we exited the Lincoln Tunnel. Eleven hours of driving later, much of it through hard rain, we arrived in Ohio shortly after dawn. Rebecca sat up in her car seat, peered out at the morning fog, yawned, and said, "Cape Cod already?"

Those were good years for all of us as a family. We traveled by car to Ohio and the Cape, by plane to Miami to visit my mother. Julie had friends in California, and she and Rebecca flew there. At home we did New York things, some of them silly. We had friends over for our first New Year's Eve; I dressed as the old 1985, complete with a long gray beard, carrying the young New Year, Rebecca, with a sash that read 1986. (See page 194.) I watched Rebecca in the morning while Julie ran to Central Park and around the reservoir, then headed to 336 while the two of them engaged in mother-and-daughter activities.

It was particularly good for Julie and Rebecca. They did everything together. They went to playgrounds in Central Park, to Chinatown for recreation and Julie's soy sauce and tofu, and on cold or rainy days to museums: the Metropolitan (Julie's favorite) and the Museum of Natural History (Rebecca's top choice). Summer was the best, with the wading pond near the boat basin in Riverside Park and Lincoln Center's Out of Doors festival, nearly a month of free music, theater, and dance performances. They were the

perfect pair and totally mobile: Rebecca strapped into the baby seat affixed to Julie's bike for neighborhood trips, public transportation for more distant destinations.

Then in 1987, when Rebecca was two, Julie introduced the subject of a second child. I was—What's the expression?—taken aback, but I dismissed my anxiety. After all, we were just having another kid, probably like Rebecca, fun and easy and giving joy.

All the while, a subplot was about to impact my little utopia. Julie at thirty-three—I was forty-three—had trouble getting pregnant with Rebecca. We finally sought a fertility specialist, who prescribed Clomid, a drug he insisted was safe, a euphemism for having a low risk for causing multiples. Sure enough, after one dose and timing our efforts to Julie's ovulation schedule, she got pregnant. Now three years, one miscarriage, and six months of failing to conceive on our own sent us back to the specialist. Again he recommended Clomid. This time it took two doses—one for each of two consecutive cycles—for the drug's magic to work.

That was March 1988, and everything seemed fine. We again signed up with Roosevelt's midwifery program, looked for a larger apartment, and began the process of introducing the idea to Rebecca of changing her status of one-and-only child. Somewhere around the twelfth week we got a call from Roosevelt that she should schedule a sonogram—strictly routine, we were told, something about high hormone levels.

The procedure was done in an outpatient office of Mount Sinai Hospital, about 100th Street and Fifth Avenue. While

Julie was being examined, I read *Cinderella* to Rebecca. All around us the dearest of hopes were being realized. Women, most of them accompanied by their husbands, filled every chair of the waiting room. One by one they were summoned to be examined and then, moments later, their husbands were called in. Before long the pair would emerge, smiling, hands usually clasped, reassured that everything was progressing normally.

Couples entered the office and left. Rebecca and I sat and watched as the drama played on. We waited as fifteen minutes became thirty minutes, then forty-five. I plodded through *Cinderella* a second time, but my mind was not on the words. Something was going on behind that closed door. I reached inside for some inner strength and found very little. What I did find was a desperate longing to be somewhere else.

Rebecca was growing restless; I was fighting an anxiety attack. My mouth was so dry I could hardly read; my heart pounded. And then, while I am not religious, I issued a silent prayer: *Please God, let Julie be OK . . . and don't let it be twins.*

Finally a nurse came out of the examining room and motioned for us to follow her. The instant I saw Julie lying on that table, saw the expression on her face, I knew something was up. She reached over and calmly took my hand. Her palm was cool, her stare fixed. And then she said, "It's triplets."

I could feel the blood drain from my face, my legs weaken. I have no idea what I said or what else was said to me. I remember a doctor coming into the room to confirm the readings. He moved the sensor along Julie's belly and analyzed the

ghostly impressions on the little screen before us, counting aloud: one, two, three dark sacks. He said there was a fourth shadow but assured us that it was only a blood clot. Medical humor! I did not even blink.

Roots

Outside the afternoon was cool and gray. On the ride home Julie and I exchanged only the most ordinary of pleasantries—not a single "Wow!" or "Son of a gun!" I should have offered words of comfort, embraced her as a sign of support, but I couldn't. I was in shock. My temples throbbed with the pressure of what lay ahead; I can still feel the dizziness that came over me.

Then as the bus traveled downtown, I made a terrible mistake: A few blocks from our apartment I got off. I had to walk, I said. In fact I wanted everything around me to stop; no conversation, nothing. I needed time to figure out how to cope. It was a decision I later learned impacted the rest of my relationship with Julie. I am really sorry, honest. A better person would have put his own fears aside and comforted his wife, but I was on the verge of panic and this was all I could think of to stop it.

I headed for West 77th Street, mostly an automatic response. I sought the safety of my apartment, a place to hide. I walked in, secured two of the three locks, switched

off the radio intended to ward off potential burglars and sat down in the one comfortable chair, positioned before the television. I did not turn it on. I just stared at the blank screen, a panel as dark and devoid of images as my mind. On the two buses from Mount Sinai—the M96 crosstown and the 104 heading downtown—I had but one thought: *What the fuck am I going to do now?* Slowly, sitting in the solemnity of my apartment, calm began to settle over me.

Solace was the impact that 336 had on me, an environment permitting me to block out stress and anything even bordering on negativity, from the day-to-day risk of city life to the chance that anything I wrote might not find an enthusiastic editor. I had created an alternate reality there, one better than what I actually confronted. Delusional or not, within those walls I felt strong enough to effectively deal with any obstacle. Now I hoped to evoke that power to ease the transition of our going from a family of three to six, news transmitted in shadowy images appearing on a sonogram screen.

Ambitious as this sounds, it was a skill I had spent years cultivating. And while I had perfected this mental exercise in Apartment Four, I had begun the process in Lancaster, Ohio, far away and many years before.

Lancaster was the site of the paper mill that formed one half of Loroco Industries, the family business. Our father used government loans to purchase it at the beginning of World War II, resurrecting it from its Depression-era shutdown in order to supply paper for the company's converting

plant in Reading, outside Cincinnati, making parts for field stoves and artillery shells during the war, packaging material in peacetime.

From then on our father drove three hours every Monday morning from Cincinnati to Lancaster to oversee operation at the mill, returning on Friday afternoon. This marked the end of our family as a normal, stable unit; I was about three. It was also the beginning of my growing closeness with my mother, for bedtime stories and occasionally to Howard Johnson's for after-dinner ice cream and with my older brother, teaching skills normally left to a father: how to ride a bicycle, early reading lessons, and assembling model boats and planes.

Soon after purchasing the mill came the farm, about a half-mile behind and so long abandoned that it required nearly two years to upgrade: new wiring and plumbing, modern heating, a complete new bathroom and kitchen, and renovation of the two bedrooms, dining, and living rooms.

Once modernized, the farm held great appeal for me. At first, when I was about six, it was the chickens producing fresh eggs, horses I learned to ride, a pair of dwarf deer that soon bred into a small herd, curiosities to amuse our father's business associates and the family during holidays. When we moved to Miami, and with our father commuting between Florida and Ohio, Lancaster time grew to accommodate month-long summertime visits.

Everything about the farm sparked conversation. The interior of the powder room downstairs was festooned with multicolored lights that flashed on and off in a preset

sequence. An aquarium with live goldfish ran the length of the bar, guarded by a caged parrot proficient in duplicating any voice she overheard.

Then there was our father's penchant for lifting serving spoons from his favorite Manhattan hotel, the Waldorf Astoria. For years I told visiting friends that the ornate design on the handles was the family crest of a long-dead relative. I assumed my ruse was safe until Rebecca traveled to New York as an adult and sent the following letter on Waldorf writing paper: "Just wanted to write you a quick note on The Family Stationery to say hello!"

But the real appeal of the farm was that time spent there represented family to me, more than any other place. I'm not suggesting things were substantially different, but they were different enough to create pleasant and lasting memories. In Cincinnati and Miami, our parents vacationed by themselves—White Sulfur Springs and French Lick from Ohio, Cuba and the Bahamas from Florida—while in Lancaster we were more often together. The farm became a place where life in general was better. When I went through hard times, struggling during my freshman year in college or breaking up with my first serious girlfriend, I regrouped at the farm.

Years later, after I returned from Europe and moved to New York, the farm continued to present a better side of life, providing a welcomed respite from my subsistence-level existence. While on 77th Street I built my cuisine around ground beef, our father's charge account at Bay Food Market

in Lancaster afforded me fresh chicken and especially rib eye steaks expertly cut onsite by butcher Charles "Chum" Kraft. It was not a style I could afford but one I was happy to assume twice a year. The farm became my go-to place when my early struggles in New York got me down.

Gradually I began to inject some of this appeal to New York. There were physical aspects: the farm had dining room speakers connected to the stereo in the living room and I installed speakers in both rooms of Apartment Four; the farm's master bath had a set of heat and sun lamps, and I positioned one of each near the ceiling of my otherwise ordinary bath.

More important was the sense of security I felt in both places. The two possessed the power to accentuate the most positive aspect of any situation. During those early years when my writing knew mostly rejection, a week at the farm recharged my emotional batteries and made me ready to confront the next project with renewed energy, and my little one-bedroom apartment could produce a similar effect.

Arthur died in 1974 (only then could I think of him by name). About that time my Ohio Shangri-La collided with reality. It began innocently. On one of those trips west some of the older mill employees invited me out for a drink.

This was nice, these men revisiting their memories of my father; they never could call him Arthur. They recounted the hurricane-force winds that felled the mill's three smokestacks in 1952, shutting down the operation until my father leased a locomotive from the Baltimore and Ohio Railroad to generate steam for the paper machine. They talked about the United

Mine Workers strike of 1961, which lasted through a cold winter. "I walked the picket line," said one of them, "wearing an old coat from your father."

After the second round of beer, the reminiscing moved to the farm. One of the men mentioned parties; "wild parties," contributed another. Over the next hour I heard stories about how, when the rest of the family was in Cincinnati or Florida, select people—including the police chief and important customers—were invited to catered parties, with "lots of booze and not just beer," as one man put it. And then came the topper: "And women, some local but others from as far away as Columbus," said another with wonder, though the distance was only thirty miles.

What I got that evening was sourced from local legend, from men who had no firsthand information. But I believed them. They wanted to honor the man they called "the boss." They liked him, respected him, and wanted me to know that he was quite a guy, living the high life.

Fact-checking came through my brother Lee, who had started working at Loroco's Reading plant while in high school and, eight years my senior, had a firmer grasp on family dynamics. Yes, he told me, he'd heard the stories, and then he went a step further. There was, he said, one woman with whom our father carried on an extended relationship. I pushed for details but got little, except there was an event, after the family had moved to Miami, when the woman called our mother, Freda, and demanded that she give up Arthur so that they could be together.

Years later, before Alzheimer's disease totally robbed our mother of her memory, I asked her about the woman. "Oh, yes," she told me without hesitation. "She called me once, told me she and your father had a daughter and demanded that I give him up. I told her I knew that was a lie because my husband was sterile and both our sons were adopted." I had no idea if she had actually issued that fabricated retort or concocted it later to soothe her wounded pride; I hoped she had said it.

Either way, I was left with a half-told tale, of an event that did or did not occur when I was a teenager and ill-equipped to draw important conclusions about adult behavior, especially involving my parents. What I did have was an uncomfortable feeling about the farm, a place that was dear to me.

Over time I learned more fragments of information. There was a woman, and a daughter who was given up for adoption. I never knew the circumstances of the woman's becoming pregnant, how my father responded, or who decided on the adoption. I didn't want to know. The story made me uncomfortable. I felt for the woman and her daughter and for our mother.

Apparently I took this worse than those directly involved. Between Arthur's death and when Freda lost her mind, she and I spoke of many things, including their marriage. When we got around to the affair, she dismissed its importance, as if it was a product of the times and my father's personality. "He was not perfect," she said, "but neither was I." I was unable to get her to go further. I looked for a smile, or a twinkle in

an eye, but her expression revealed nothing.

As for my sister, the relationship became an important part of her personal history. She tracked down her mother, connected with her, and gleaned as much information as she could about the affair, a word she did not use. She referred to the farm as "their love nest," shared during "those best of years" by her mother and our father. Then one January evening she called me at 77th Street to tell me that her mother had died. "She's drinking champagne with Arthur," she said, her voice choked with emotion. "He was waiting for her, and now they're together."

This romanticized vision was something my sister proudly shared with her family. She sent me her grown daughter's account of her grandmother and the grandmother's relationship with our father: "She was very beautiful and had many suitors, but her love was only for Arthur. They would travel to New York and Chicago, stay in the best hotels and drink fine wine."

They expressed no anger and dismissed my attempt at a family apology. They seemed to be saying to me, "Get over it; we're OK. Nobody got hurt. A child got born who embraces her life, so what's your problem?" Good question; I don't know. But from then on the farm was never the same. I made the drive to Lancaster less and less often. My brother noticed and, sighting the cost of maintaining the house and property, suggested that he sell it. I did not object.

Before the house was sold I took one long, slow walk-through. I salvaged some old books and records and the brass

bell that mysteriously disappeared when that steam locomotive was returned to the B&O. I guess these items escaped the taint I came to associate with those years. That was it; I was done with the farm. All that emotional investment, the sense of home and security embodied for so long in the farm, got transferred to the apartment on West 77th Street. The process had actually already begun.

This was only right. The farm was five hundred miles away, and while I considered it a permanent fixture, it was actually in constant jeopardy after Arthur died. And it was, after all, his.

Meanwhile, the apartment was mine, the place where important events occurred for me. I was in the apartment when I learned that my father had contracted cancer and two years later when word came he was dying. When my first book was published in 1979, the party was there. The night before Julie and I were married, my friends and I met there for a celebratory drink before going out for my bachelor dinner. The night in 1985 after Rebecca was born, I went there to reflect on how my life would change upon becoming a father at forty-four.

And now, three years later, that shift was complete. The farm was gone, first trashed in my mind and then actually sold; the apartment became my sanctuary. So upon learning that our second child would be triplets, that the nature of our lives was about to forever change, the apartment is where I went to try and figure out how to cope.

A Brave and Scary New World

My time at the apartment—less than an hour—did not begin all that well. My panic ran deep.

What was I going to do about those babies? How could we feed them? What about all the diapers? Once out of diapers, what about clothes? My mind raced ahead; I tried to stop it but failed. Three more children would need three cribs and then beds and three high chairs. And shoes—think of the shoes! My vision of the years ahead sped by faster and faster, overwhelming me with the responsibility of caring for four children in New York, of putting them through school, and eventually college. Oh, God, what about college!

This last thought stopped me cold. Why was I worried about college, years away? I had no idea where we were going to live. Julie and I had just pooled our resources and with the assistance of my family bought an apartment on West End and 69th Street. True, it was Lincoln Towers, one of those huge complexes of appallingly similar co-ops. My dream

apartment was in a classy, pre-war building (New York short-hand for built after 1900 and before World War II) with high ceilings, thick plaster walls, and hardwood floors. Lincoln Towers consisted of eight high-rise buildings—some as tall as thirty floors—crowded together between 66th and 70th Street, 3,800 apartments that differed from one another only in their size, from one-room studios to three bedrooms.

If you could get past their cookie-cutter designs and all those people jammed into five blocks, they afforded us two bedrooms and two bathrooms, enough space for four of us, as much of a family as I felt sure we would ever be. Our apartment was on the twelfth floor with an enticing view of the Hudson River. While a compromise, it was an apartment that I felt a family of four could live in forever or at least till our kids graduated from college and made their own way in the world. No longer. That afternoon in March our two-bedroom apartment—and the fantasy of its perpetuity—became obsolete. We were not to be a family of four but of six. What indeed was I going to do?

I fought to gain a measure of calm. This was not the end of the world, I told myself. It's another change—a really big change but just a change. I took a deep breath and let my eyes drift along the surface of those walls that had provided my security for so long. I was twenty-four when I moved in, forty-six by that afternoon, and had experienced many ups and downs along the way. I had survived by exerting a little control, control over my work and my schedule, control over my state of mind. Let the past be my guide and design the

future accordingly was my philosophy. Surely I could exert a little more control and make my plan continue to work.

That quickly, I was back in the present. The most urgent piece of control at that moment was to get myself back to Lincoln Towers, if for no other reason than to assure my wife and daughter that I had not skipped town.

There were obvious and essential details to deal with immediately. First, we needed a doctor. Julie had signed up with the same midwifery program that we used for Rebecca, but triplets disqualified us. We sought an obstetrician specializing in high-risk pregnancies; the recommended choice was Thomas D. Kerenyi, with offices on Park Avenue and admitting privileges at Mount Sinai, one of the city's best hospitals.

Apparently the word was out on Kerenyi. Even at four in the afternoon on a Thursday, his office was jammed, filled with women in various stages of pregnancy. Some were in their twenties, but most were older. We had left Rebecca with friends, a decision I debated as we waited our turn. Better for her not to sit through another doctor's visit, but she would have provided distraction for us. We could have used one. Sitting there for nearly an hour, I filled my mind with guesses as to why all these women needed a doctor with special abilities. What dire concerns grew within them?

Finally the nurse called us in. Kerenyi began by asking the normal questions: Julie's age, when she had her first period, the conditions of her first pregnancy, her first labor, and finally about Rebecca. All the while he took what appeared to be casual notes. After hearing the answers that described

the history of her remarkably normal first pregnancy and delivery, he refitted the cap on his Mount Blanc fountain pen and looked up.

"So," he said, "why do you need me?" Julie paused and then smiled at our new doctor.

"You don't know, do you?" she said. "We're the triplets."

"Ah," he said, nodding his head and removing the cap from his pen. "I knew you were out there. I just didn't know which ones."

We got down to serious business. Now Kerenyi diligently took notes throughout the remainder of our visit. He seemed surprised when Julie said she had taken Clomid. A minimal dose, taken only twice over a short time, was rarely responsible for multiple births, he said, but at twelve weeks into the pregnancy and considering triplets were the reason for the appointment, the drug's reputation was no longer relevant.

He went on to address Julie's questions about how much weight he hoped she would gain and how long he hoped she might carry, about how much activity she could handle and what method of delivery Kerenyi would use.

It was about then, when Julie had run out of questions and there was a pause in their exchange, that he again put down his pen and took on a more serious expression. "You know," he said, "you do have an option here." Julie and I looked at each other. What could he mean? Kerenyi went on to explain the procedure called "selective reduction," whereby one or more fetuses in a multiple pregnancy are aborted. Julie immediately went stone cold. I do not recall her uttering a

word; she just shook her head, once to the right and once to the left. "OK," said the doctor, "let's have a look," and he led the way into the examining room for another sonogram.

As I stood before the monitor in that darkened room, staring at the pulsating images on that screen, I considered what had just happened. I had originally envisioned Julie carrying one baby, but seeing the physical confirmation of our future children at that moment, I could not possibly imagine one or more of them being eliminated. Whatever my personal preference had once been, whatever my fears, these three babies were ours, and they were on their way.

At the desk, while Julie made our next appointment for a month away, I took Kerenyi aside and asked if there was anything he wanted to say to me in private, any advice delivered directly from obstetrician to prospective father of triplets. He took my hand and gently but firmly squeezed it, ensuring that he had my attention. "Yes," he said, "start saving money."

That was May 5. As the birth of the triplets drew closer, I became strangely influenced by the people around me. Whatever their response to the situation—joy or dread—I adopted it as my own. And being New York, there was no shortage of both responses.

At a dinner party my announcement elicited an immediate and complete cessation of conversation. One guest dropped a shrimp from its toothpick; another gagged on his chardonnay. Later our hostess accused me of casting a pall over the entire evening. Our neighbor in Lincoln Towers,

a mother of two, bubbled with enthusiasm. "It's a miracle," she said. "Think of all that love."

And then there was the letter from a purported friend who sent us a harrowing account about the birth of triplets suffering horrifying defects. I have no idea why she felt compelled to send this, but I can tell you that it was not welcomed. It only increased our fear, reminding us of the nightmares that could await us and forever change our lives.

Julie and I discussed none of this. Our attention was absorbed by more tangible issues, decisions that surfaced not as conversations or debates but as bickering. We argued about how we would change an apartment comfortably designed for four people to one accommodating six. We argued about where we would send Rebecca to nursery school, for how many hours a day and how many days a week. Once we found ourselves arguing about the ice cream that I had brought back from the A&P at midnight. She had wanted coffee; I bought chocolate chip.

Most of these expressions of temper came from me; when Julie's nerves got stretched taut, she became sullen. Regardless, it was often unpleasant. Naturally, Rebecca was affected.

When we first told her that triplets were coming she was wildly enthusiastic. She wanted to know what the babies were doing at that very moment. Were they playing? Were they happy? When they came out, what would they be wearing? Her only demand was that out of the group we guarantee her one sister, and that we could call her Rachel, after her favorite doll.

None of this was a surprise. Rebecca loved a party, and she totally accepted triplets as one more festive event. She told everyone she met, holding up three fingers to avoid any confusion, and included the unborns as if they had already joined the family. Early one morning, she crawled into our bed and patted Julie's round, hard belly. "How are those babies doing in there?" she asked with glee.

But as we showed signs of stress, so did Rebecca. After two particularly bad days she flashed some temper of her own and burst into tears. "I don't want those babies to come," she sobbed. I tried to console her. I took her in my arms, rocked her, and confessed: "Sometimes, I don't either." It did not help. What Rebecca wanted and needed was her mother's assurance that their good life together was not going to change. This was just not true.

The next five months were filled with tiny explosions, moments of real fear for what was coming. There were the rushed calls to Dr. Kerenyi because of bleeding or some other internal sign that convinced us the babies were in trouble. And it seemed that more and more magazines, more television talk shows contained some horror tale that demonstrated that any woman carrying more than twins was courting disaster. Everywhere we saw warnings, some more upsetting than others.

One afternoon, waiting to see Kerenyi, we sat beside a young pregnant woman; she appeared to be in her late twenties. With her were her normal-looking son of about five and a second son, maybe two, who sat in his stroller for the hour

while we all waited. His big blue eyes never focused; his head swung continually from side to side. The mother paid him little attention, as did the older brother. Neither played with him or tried to calm him when he became agitated.

No one else in the waiting room was able to ignore the child in the stroller. The place was filled with expectant mothers, mostly over thirty-five, and I swear I could read their thoughts: *If this can happen to her, so young and with one perfectly healthy boy, what chance do I at my age have of delivering a normal child?*

Dramas played out daily. Because it was New York, they often contained extra flair. Our debate about altering the apartment was joined by a friend who wrote for *Metropolitan Home*, a magazine covering, in its own words, "high end modern design and interiors." She sent over one of its architecture specialists who drew plans for a little room just for Rebecca positioned in the corner of the living room. He recommended a builder who put the whole thing together and even went to the site of a house being remodeled and purchased an antique window.

Rebecca was thrilled. Though she gave up her room to Julie and me, as we gave up the master bedroom to the triplets, she had a brand new room, smack in the middle of the living room, complete with a window, a portal of inclusion to everything happening outside, qualities no other bedroom had.

Then there was the Yulla Lipchitz saga. The widow of Jacques, who had died in 1973, had remained in contact,

mostly because of my ongoing friendship with her son. At this point, fall of 1988, Yulla was friendly with a self-proclaimed psychic who performed readings for viewers who called in to his cable television show; most of his income came from privately scheduled readings.

She called one afternoon to tell me that he had a vision about Julie. The triplets were mostly developing nicely, she assured me, but one was in some distress, and it was her suggestion that Julie spend the remainder of the pregnancy resting. Then she made an extraordinary offer, to pay for a housekeeper to come in and free Julie from normal chores. I never told Julie of the warning or Yulla's offer; we had enough scares to ward off. (More on this later.)

Kerenyi at our first meeting said he would be pleased if Julie carried the triplets thirty-four weeks. That would bring them to within six weeks of full term and give them an excellent chance of developing normally. As Julie approached that mark, Kerenyi wrote a prescription for Ritodrine, a drug that slows the onset of labor. "Don't start taking it until I tell you," he said, "but get the pills and keep them handy." He also informed us that from the sonograms he could tell they were two boys and a girl; Rebecca was delighted.

Then came that Friday night late in October when the contractions began and would not stop. Julie had felt them before, ever more actively in the last weeks, but abandoning whatever task she was about and sitting down—or at the most lying down—always resulted in their subsiding. That

night they kept coming, no matter what she tried. Kerenyi started her on the Ritodrine, one pill every four hours.

The pills worked, at least for a while. But by Sunday the contractions were back. To keep Julie from going into labor, Kerenyi increased the dosage to one pill every three hours. Eventually she would be taking two pills every two hours.

Late one night the following week, I woke up and found myself alone in bed. Lying there, I could hear my wife in the kitchen, then in the living room. I did not want there to be something wrong; I desperately did not want those babies to start coming in the middle of the night. I got up and joined her in the living room. She was stretched out on the couch, her hands shaking, her heart pounding. Ritodrine does that too.

We saw Kerenyi the next morning, a Monday. No waiting this time; the nurse rushed us right in. Everything was fine, Kerenyi said, but he shared with us that during the previous sonogram it was confirmed that one of the babies, a boy, was being pushed up against the left side of Julie's rib cage. While the other two continued to grow, his development was hindered by his position. My mind flashed back to that telephone conversation with Yulla Lipchitz and the warning from her psychic.

Kerenyi complimented Julie on getting through thirty-five weeks and said that she had done enough. (And she had, even adding fish to her usually vegetarian diet for the protein it provided.) She offered him another week, palpitations and all, but he declined. "Let's do it now,"

he said, "before there is an emergency." He scheduled the Caesarean for Wednesday morning.

The next forty-eight hours had a surreal quality. Few of the projects that we planned in preparation for our family's doubling in size had been completed. At first I tried to catch up, but as the time sped by I found myself getting further and further behind and concentrated on the basics: clean the apartment, shop for groceries, fill my prescription for Xanax.

It was a smart move. For me those hours were spent underwater, walking through a sea so dense that my movements and thoughts occurred in slow motion. At moments public and private—crushed in the subway and waiting for sleep in the middle of the night—I heard the same haunting refrain: This is real—they are coming.

At 10:15 on the first Wednesday morning in November, nurses wheeled Julie into one of the delivery rooms at Mount Sinai. Someone dressed in operating garb—a nurse, I think, but maybe a doctor—suggested that I should not be there while they administered the epidural anesthesia; another shrugged and tossed me a mask, gown, and cap.

The room looked small. I had anticipated a size commensurate with the magnitude of the event, maybe one of those operating theaters with a terraced observation area featured in old black-and-white movies. This was just a room, but packed with equipment. First to catch my attention was the enormous instrument tray, more suitable for a GMC garage than an operating room; four feet long, three feet wide, and

filled with terrible-looking pieces of apparatus. Sure, they were stainless steel and glisteningly clean, but so big—not just scalpels and forceps but gadgetry with the unmistakable suggestion of torture.

Then I saw the three transparent boxes, each covered by a sheet. I knew these babies were five weeks premature and the boxes were transporters with heat and oxygen equipment, all very necessary, but covered up they looked like—I'm sorry—little coffins.

The sight let loose the fear I had fought to push below the surface, fear that something terrible would happen to one or more of the babies; fear that something terrible would happen to Julie and I would not only lose my wife but be left alone as the father of three more babies. The lights, the equipment, it all made the seriousness of this event undeniable, along with the realization that anything could happen. Whatever it was, it was going to happen now.

Doctors were everywhere. An anesthesiologist injected some numbing agent into Julie that seemed to take forever to work. We all stood there for ten minutes, twenty minutes, until Kerenyi announced that he was ready. A pin gently pricking Julie's side indicated she was not; we waited some more.

While we waited, three-doctor teams of pediatricians —one team for each baby, a total of nine—came up and introduced themselves. The head pediatrician explained that because space in the delivery room was limited, they would work in shifts, taking the babies away as each was born to

check it over and clean it. Not to worry, he said, they would bring them right back—more medical humor.

As I listened, out of the corner of my eye I saw people gathering at the entrance of the delivery room; twenty-five of them, maybe thirty, all in those light-blue operating outfits, their faces masked. At first I thought they were part of the surgical team, waiting to perform some essential task. But they were just standing there at what appeared to be a set distance, as if there were an actual line drawn four feet beyond the delivery table, and I realized they were spectators. I stood back by Julie, a sheet walling off our view of the surgery. Then one of the masked doctors explained to us that as a scheduled, nonemergency delivery of triplets—apparently unusual—staff members knew what was happening and wanted to watch.

Twice more they tested Julie's awareness of the pin; twice more she responded to the pain. Kerenyi was impatient. Finally they tilted the table back, dropping Julie's head a few degrees below level to help the drug drain to the unaffected area. Suddenly the mood got serious; everybody moved to his or her assigned place. The next pinprick told them that Julie was ready. Behind the draped sheet that blocked her view, they were beginning.

Someone kindly provided a stool for me, back behind the sheet with my wife, both of us wracked with anxiety. I had seen lots of blood as a police reporter and considered standing up to see beyond the sheet but thought better of it. By then my breathing was quick and shallow, my mouth too dry to easily swallow. Sweat poured down my back and sides, down

along my legs, and into my shoes. I girded myself; fainting would contribute nothing positive.

The room was still. Only Kerenyi and his assistant, Dr. Victor Grazi, spoke. I could hear little of what passed between them; the pounding of my heart was too loud. Then, after about twenty-five minutes, the great assemblage let out a gasp of anticipation. Kerenyi leaned forward. As he straightened up, the delivery room became Yankee Stadium. "Here comes the first one," said someone from the back. "It's a girl. Doesn't she look big for a triplet?"

Applause exploded throughout the room. Actual applause! Kerenyi handed our baby girl to the waiting pediatricians. They whisked her away as Kerenyi disappeared behind the sheet. A few minutes passed and then: "Here comes a boy— he looks great." Now they were cheering, their arms waving in the air.

More pediatricians moved in to take the second baby, their actions quick and efficient but not hurried as Kerenyi returned to work. After another minute or two: "And look at this one—another boy. He's a big fellow." More cheers, louder than before. Kerenyi lifted up the third baby as if showing a trophy to the crowd then handed him to the last of the pediatric teams. Everybody applauded.

The entire room seemed to be spinning around Julie and me. My ears flooded with the sound of applause, reverberating applause from the spectators, from every doctor and nurse not caring for one baby or another. I was applauding, too, inside. Or maybe I was crying. I only know I experienced

a flash of relief. Three babies got born and nobody failed to survive, not even me.

Within minutes the pediatricians had checked over our babies—designated by Mount Sinai as Triplet A, Triplet B, and Triplet C—cleaned them and returned them to the warming tray beside Julie. And then the doctors were gone, leaving three little red babies, all healthy. To us they were Alexandra at four pounds, eight ounces; Matthew at four pounds, one ounce; and Jacob at five pounds, two ounces.

I stood there and looked at them, and as I did I felt something I did not immediately understand. This was more than relief. Yes, they had arrived and they were healthy. And while there was a palpable rush of exhilaration, what I felt at the moment was more profound. Suddenly all those practical responsibilities that had plagued me for six months—providing food and clothes and space—faded into the background, overshadowed by a new reality.

That control I had fought for most of my adult life, control of time and mood and work, came under question. This wasn't totally new. When Rebecca was born and I was introduced to parenthood, I felt it slipping away but fought to regain it.

But on the morning of November 2, 1988, sometime between eleven and eleven fifteen when the triplets were born, I gave up the fight. Seeing them and imagining my part in their future, I realized that control was an illusion, probably always was. So in that flash of creation, I surrendered any claim to that fantasy.

Living room of Apartment Four, 336 West 77th Street, with writing loft reflected in mirror, 1970. Photo by Skip Rozin.

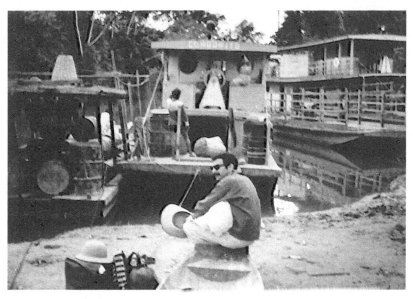

Waiting for the riverboat to load, Porto San Francisco, Bolivia, 1970.
Photo by Tom Lyons.

Researching travel article in Yellowstone National Park for the New York
Times, *1978.* Photographer unknown.

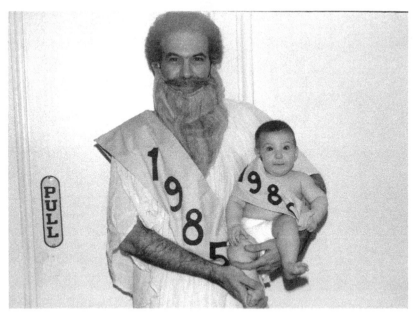

Father Time with ten-week-old Rebecca as Baby New Year,
New Year's Eve, 1985. Photo by Julie Guibord.

Rebecca (at about a year) and father, face to face, 1986.
Photo by Julie Guibord.

Rebecca (eleven months) and Julie in Lake Logan, Ohio, 1986.
Photo by Skip Rozin.

Bewildered father with, left to right, Jacob, Alexandra, and Matthew, about three weeks old, 1988. Photo by Julie Guibord.

Triplet stroller fully loaded with, front to back, Alex, Matt, and Jake, about six months old, 1989. Photo by Julie Guibord.

196

Cuddling with, left to right, Jake, Alex, and Matt, about seven years old on High Street in Orleans, 1995. Photo by Beverly Hall.

In Bled, Slovenia, before a 2,500-mile, seven-country trek to deliver racing shells to Northern Iraq, on assignment for the Wall Street Journal, *2012.* Photo by Bruce Smith.

On the roof of the Miami Herald, *1962.* Photo by Lewis McLain.

Matt, Alex, Jake, and Rebecca (clockwise), posed for a birthday present for their father at seventy-five, 2016. Matt in San Diego. Photo by unnamed pedestrian. *Alex in Pocatello, Idaho.* Photo by Jarrod Zweigart. *Jake in Paris.* Photo by Céline Meyer. *Rebecca in Philadelphia.* Photo by Lacy Clark.

Identity

In my early days in New York, when I wrote regularly and sold nothing, I comforted myself by connecting with that honorable tradition of the struggling writer fighting depression to produce a good page or a paragraph—on bad days, a decent sentence. One weapon in this battle was to create a parallel universe, one in which I was a success. Every article was published. Critics praised my novels; whole chapters were reprinted in the *New York Review of Books*. And in the Oak Room of the Hotel Algonquin, an attractive woman touches my arm. "Excuse me," she says, "aren't you Skip Rozin, the writer?"

I know this is frivolous, not the thinking of a serious writer. Perhaps, but it was necessary at a time when I knew no success. Did I really fantasize being approached by fans? No. One attraction of writing was—and still is—that it's done in seclusion. I prize that aspect of the profession, but it takes a strong ego to produce copy good enough to be published, and in those days of constant rejection, my fantasizing acceptance—and maybe a whiff of celebrity—was how I strengthened my sagging ego.

Eventually, as I passed through my thirties and started to publish—first articles, a few short stories, and then nonfiction books—the work itself was enough to sustain my personal version of a writing life. Every aspect, from the initial research at the city's massive library system in those pre-internet days to travel and reporting, to writing, editing, and publication, increased my sense of being a professional.

Even my social life became tied to writing. Early on there were informal gatherings at Dick Humphreys's apartment near Columbia, meeting with other current and former students from his writing classes, some editors, and eventually Jim Brown. I wasn't publishing, but those parties had the feel of literary circles, filled with talk of writing, the good and the bad. And because of who was in attendance—serious people doing serious work—the level of conversation was high and so enriching. Those gatherings were not a substitute for publishing but offered a taste of that revered goal.

Later came Jim Brown's parties; he never missed the opportunity to introduce his writers to anyone who might advance their career. They were evenings filled with writers and editors, leading to invitations to other parties filled with writers and editors but also broadening those attending to include artists and actors and musicians, most of them generating interesting conversation. To a Midwesterner, this was dream New York.

James Oliver Brown was an anachronism. He would be more so if he were alive today but was even when we met in 1967. He was a conservative dresser, rarely attired in anything

other than one of his many dark blue three-piece suits from Brooks Brothers. The first time I was invited to his apartment was for Saturday afternoon tea, served promptly at four o'clock in a sterling silver tea set—even the strainer was silver, to catch the loose tea (he never used tea bags)—and accompanied by little triangular cucumber sandwiches. After five o'clock he broke out the whiskey.

Born in western Pennsylvania, he morphed into the quintessential Easterner, proper if peripatetic. He attended the Naval Academy but resigned his commission upon graduating and earned his law degree from Harvard, setting up his practice on Wall Street in 1936. He served in the army from 1940 to 1944 and then worked as the New York editor for the publishing firm of Little, Brown and Company till 1948. He left to become a literary agent, work he continued until he retired in 1985.

Proper was at the center of Jim Brown's persona—proper attire, proper use of the English language and, most important, proper behavior. He prized what he considered good breeding as indicated by good manners, which he defined as the standards of conduct that show an individual to be cultured, polite, and refined.

Part of this picture, in Brown's view, was a public acknowledgement of his status and that of his family. It was important that he was listed in the *Social Register*—a copy was always placed conspicuously on the desk in his living room—and that reference to him and his family frequently appeared in the *New York Times*. The *Times* complied. It

covered his engagement to the debutant Honour Dickerman and the several formal parties leading up to their marriage in 1938: "Henry Ashforths are Dinner Hosts; Miss Honour Dickerman and Her Fiance, James Brown, Are Entertained" read one headline in March.

Their marriage ceremony earned a two-column photograph of the bride and an article that included such details as the presiding official, a full description of the bride's gown, a list of the maids and ushers, and biographical information of the bride and groom. There was, of course, no mention of the couple's divorce, but in the years to come there was active coverage of the debut and marriage of their two daughters, ending with the news of Brown's death from cancer in 1992 at the age of eighty-two.

He died on September 1, but the article did not appear until September 7. *The gap would have troubled him*, I thought as I perused each day's paper in search of his obituary. For his beloved *Times* to ignore the newsworthiness of his passing, perhaps even leaving it to the obscurity of the paid death notice column, would have angered and saddened him, an indignation from which he was saved by one of his former clients, I was told. Reportedly the *Times* was persuaded to rethink its lapse by the well-respected Louis Auchincloss, whose own obituary ran promptly the day after he died in 2009, praised his novels exploring the experiences and psychology of American polite society and old money, and was nearly ten times the length of Brown's.

If pride diminished Jim Brown, generosity and support for his writers elevated him. He did more than represent my work and invite me to parties; he was an advocate, as he was for all his clients. Though when we met I had written only two dozen short stories and sold none, he believed in my ability and encouraged me to keep working despite the rejection. That this was happening in New York amplified the impact in my mind and increased opportunities. Conversation over drinks often extended to dinner, where more subjects were explored and, over time, a friendship developed, providing even more opportunities.

Brown was a member of some of New York's most prestigious clubs—among them the Union Club and the Century Association—and he frequently invited clients, for their pleasure and whatever professional good it might afford them. The Union Club was the city's oldest social club, founded in 1836 with the stated goal of supporting the federal government of the United States, in jeopardy in those years leading up to the Civil War. The Century Association, established eleven years later in 1847, was less political and made up, in the club's own words, of "authors, artists, and amateurs of letters and fine arts."

Because they considered themselves social clubs, conducting business was frowned upon if not officially forbidden. Members were discouraged from bringing in work papers from their briefcases, and briefcases were not allowed in the dining room, at least according to Jim Brown. But there were plenty of discussions about work-related matters, such

as which magazine was looking for what kind of article and maybe even whom to approach.

I was pleased to accept whenever Jim extended an invitation for lunch and occasionally for dinner. The ambiance, the architecture, and furnishings transported members and their guests to a time before casual Friday, personal stereos, and cell phones assaulted the essence and spirit of decorum. There was a sense of associating with the inner circle of New York. Unlike watching them on television or reading their books and articles, you dined a table away or enjoyed a drink while sitting in the next club chair.

When I was working with Steve Garvey on his autobiography, he liked to go for dinner after games at Shea Stadium to the Midtown restaurant owned by retired baseball player Rusty Staub on Third Avenue and 73rd Street. Steve enjoyed the food but he also appreciated that Rusty maintained a special section for celebrities, mostly athletes, an elevated space at the rear of the restaurant discretely roped off from the public. These clubs were entire roped-off buildings where the elite could associate without being hounded by common folk. To slide in under that rope, if only for a few hours, was a kick.

It was also clear that I did not belong. These were the kind of gentlemen's establishments we identify with nineteenth-century London, clubs like White's, Brooks's and Boodle's. The one club of Jim Brown's where I did feel comfortable was The Coffee House. He proposed me for membership and I joined in 1971.

Smaller, newer (founded in 1915), and less pretentious than the others, it shared many of their qualities: men-only clubs located in Midtown and devoted to eating, drinking, and conversation. The food and drink were passable, but the conversation was, well, smart. One day after meeting with an editor, I stopped in between lunch and dinner, mostly for a break from the Midtown insanity. The place was practically empty, except for one other member seated in a winged club chair reading the *Wall Street Journal*. I took a chair across from him and picked up the *Times*. Several minutes of silence followed and then: "I have to refrain from my normal habit of tearing out pages containing long articles to read later," he said.

I laughed. "I do the same thing; the good ones I file for future reference."

He put down his paper and looked at me solemnly. "Ah," he said in a knowing tone, "you file. That way lies only madness."

On another occasion I was there for lunch. Unlike the Union and Century clubs, which serve members and their guests lunch at individual tables, The Coffee House has one long table, intended to promote conversation among all in attendance. That afternoon I was seated beside a member I did not know; the instant he spoke I recognized Alexander Scourby, the actor famous for his deep, resonant voice. A member I did know introduced us, in direct violation of the club's custom of no introductions. ("At The Coffee House, everybody is supposed to know everybody else," according

to the regularly printed pamphlet of the club's members and notes. "No introductions are necessary. Indeed it is a custom of the Club for strangers to treat members—and vice versa—as if they had long been friends.")

After engaging in this transgression, Scourby said, "Skip? SKIP! I can only assume that is a sobriquet for something and the name that comes to mind is Scipio Africanus." I had no idea who that was and my expression must have revealed my ignorance. "You know," said Scourby, "the Roman general who defeated Hannibal in the Second Punic War. From now on you shall be Scipio." For a lunch or two I was, and then it was forgotten.

The Coffee House became a frequent stop for me whenever I was in Midtown, providing an opportunity to interact with some of the city's most interesting people. Among them were Roger Angell of the *New Yorker*, Russell Baker and Seymour Topping of the *Times*, and Norman Cousins, Willard Espy, and Arthur Schlesinger Jr. It was a private club, so the atmosphere was congenial; the nature of membership made the conversation lively.

In those days it was all male, which somehow eased the atmosphere. (All three clubs were men-only through the '70s but have accepted women as members since.) Women were always welcomed as guests at The Coffee House after four o'clock for tea, drinks, and dinner. While their addition as members in 1980 was certainly positive, there was something liberating about being in the company of only men: discriminatory and politically incorrect but also more relaxed. Men

behave differently around women, are more competitive, more easily distracted, and more concerned with appearance. Not that there is no posturing in an all-male group, just less.

Although I possessed few of the credentials of most other members, belonging boosted my self-esteem, as did living in New York. When the walls in my apartment closed in and doubt made producing a decent sentence impossible, there was relief to be found in the city's bars that had offered comfort to writers for generations. More often than I like to admit, I took myself down to the White Horse and looked for inspiration from the ghosts of Dylan Thomas and James Baldwin, to the Lion's Head for Norman Mailer, to the Cedar Tavern for Allen Ginsberg and Frank O'Hara.

This balancing act became more vital once I entered the realm of adult responsibility with the birth of Rebecca in 1985. I tried to be a good husband and a good father, but work was never far from my mind. I went every day to 336, sometimes returning there late at night, fighting to squeeze out a few pages leading to an assignment that I could approach with excitement and pride. Nothing made a difference. The best I could do was land some editorial work that helped pay our mounting bills but did little a feed my artistic soul.

Then came the morning the triplets arrived. That afternoon, in the Mount Sinai nursery or waiting for an elevator, I kept meeting hospital personnel who were present at the delivery. I did not recognize them; everyone in that room had been masked. But they knew me. "How are those triplets doing?" I heard over and over. Or: "Hey, Mr. Triplet,

wasn't that something?" Each time I smiled politely then dismissed what appeared to be an extreme level of interest. *These were medical people whose specialty was delivering babies,* I told myself. Triplets were a major event to them. But it did not end there.

Soon after the babies were home, friends started stopping by, some to offer congratulations, others out of curiosity. Several greeted us with the same lines: "We didn't even tell the doorman your name," they laughed. "We just said we're here to see the triplets. He sent us right up."

We quickly became a child-centric household. Julie's mother arrived every Monday morning and stayed with us until Friday afternoon, serving as our much appreciated nanny. Neighborhood outings involved the triplet stroller, one formidable conveyance. For trips requiring a subway or bus, Julie or I used a Snugli in front for one baby and a backpack carrier for the second, and the other of us took the third in another backpack; Rebecca walked. During the week I took Rebecca to school each morning; Julie and the triplets picked her up in the afternoon while I worked.

Or tried to work but with little success. I reassessed potential articles I had intended to write for years but never got around to, scanned magazines and newspapers for new ideas triggered by current events and found nothing I had any confidence could produce a worthwhile article. Slowly I began to lose hold on my cherished sense of being a working writer.

Not completely. I broke through to write about Rebecca and the triplets, less because I felt driven to do so and more

because I found that I could. No assignment, not even a clear idea where to submit—just because I could, and thankful for that. When I finished I called around to anyone who knew someone who might be interested. In that New York way of friends of friends willing to help, my contact at *Metropolitan Home* knew an editor at *New York* magazine who had a friend at *Parents* magazine. I ended up selling a four-part series and followed that up with a long piece for the *Washington Post* travel section about taking the family for a Cape Cod vacation to visit Julie's parents, the only invitation that came our way after the triplets arrived.

I would like to say that this unleashed a torrent of productive work, but the opposite happened. I found myself less willing to struggle with my writers' demons. Either by intellectual fatigue or guilt inspired by my expanded family, I tried getting home a little earlier, if not to actually help then to present a physical presence. A similar combination of forces led me to give up visiting the Lion's Head and the White Horse about the same time I resigned my membership at The Coffee House.

Inexplicably, these changes were reflected in a highly diverse portion of the Upper West Side community. In our apartment building, buying diaper rash ointment at the pharmacy, even standing in the bread line at Fairway, over and over I heard complete strangers call out to me: "Excuse me," they said, "aren't you the father of those triplets?"

Sweet Chaos

How do I describe living in New York City with four children, one three-year-old and three infants? "Chaotic" works.

The first months were not so bad. Newborn babies mostly lie there. We had one crib left over from Rebecca; friends firmly committed to no additional children contributed two more. Soon we discovered that the boys' wheezing was asthma, apparently not unusual in babies born with less than thirty-seven weeks of gestation. We purchased a nebulizer, in those days a relatively hefty apparatus, mostly a compressor to administer medication that helped the boys breathe. This joined the breast pump that Julie used to express enough milk, two of the essentials needed to keep our newly configured family growing and healthy.

Much of that first year was filled with events known to every new parent, except times three. Most memorable was the stomach illness that spread through the triplets like a biblical plague: four days of projectile vomiting and diarrhea. At first we tried keeping up by repeatedly replacing diapers and putting their soiled clothes in a big garbage bag and

making trips every few hours to the laundry in the basement, but then we gave up and left them naked, mopping up what they ejected from either end and then cleaning that end. But in so many ways it was the routine that was most amazing, how quickly we got accustomed to feeding the three of them simultaneously, keeping track of them as they increased their mobility, and the ritual of bathing, an event that Rebecca insisted being part of.

These antics constituted our private theater of the absurd, a new show opening every day. The incongruity had started early, on the day we telephoned the grandmothers and informed them that triplets were coming. Julie's mother, Mona, casually announced that she would take early retirement from her job at a senior citizens' center on Staten Island to become our volunteer nanny; my mother abruptly ended the call before I got the news fully out, calling back to explain that she hung up because she was "so upset."

All this before they were born, and then came their dramatic debut at Mount Sinai, amidst applause and cheering. Understandable—that was a hospital and their arrival was a minor medical miracle. Surely the city would not be so impressed. This was New York, where famous movie stars and seven-foot-tall athletes mix among the populous and draw not a second look. Apparently triplets are another matter.

To understand why, you need to envision a Midtown sidewalk on a typical day. New York is jammed full with people, streets and sidewalks alike, especially the center of the city—from 14th Street to 96th Street and two blocks off

the Hudson and East Rivers—between 8:00 a.m. and 10:00 p.m. These people are not only traversing between home and work but shopping, heading to and from restaurants, museums, and movies, and sitting at one of the thousands of tables that restaurants insist upon positioning in front of their establishments for a little alfresco dining as if it were Paris. Navigating any stretch for even a single person approaches the level of physical confrontation.

Now imagine you are not walking alone but are pushing a triplet stroller. These come with three seats abreast, configured with two seats in front and one behind or one in front and two behind. Ours was different, the three-in-line tandem design, the only possible option for New York but still a challenge, a monster vehicle with carriage-style wire wheels and three seats aligned one behind the other, each with its own canopy. (See page 196.) The logistics—keeping that loaded three-seat train with three-year-old Rebecca either leading or trailing on course without hitting anything or anyone—commanded the full attention of the adult providing locomotion and much of the city's as well. Nobody failed to react, even if it was only with a quick flick of the head. Most froze in their tracks and stared. They smiled. They pointed. They whispered. They laughed aloud.

One Sunday morning in Riverside Park, a basketball game stopped dead while ten sweaty men watched us pass. A woman riding her bicycle looked once as she pedaled by then jerked her head back for confirmation and stared so intently that she collided with a large garbage receptacle.

And there were comments, positive and otherwise. Julie reported expressions of sympathy and some snarky, unkind references to overpopulation. I mostly received admiration, especially from men. Another Sunday—Sunday was my day with them—as I pushed the stroller by Tavern on the Green and into Central Park, four young black men raised their fists in unison as if choreographed. One of them shook his head and shouted, "You sure didn't shoot no blanks."

Rebecca took most of this in stride, especially in the beginning. We had done our best to prepare her. We talked to her about the wonder of growing up the big sister of three adoring siblings; we bought her a "sister to be" T-shirt with a bumblebee on it. Julie took her to visit another little girl recently confronted with newborn triplets. We allowed her to pick out her own dresser for her new room and to choose the color of paint for the walls. Our efforts were largely successful. The triplet visit was a hit, and she loved the new room . . . with light purple walls.

Even the week that Julie gave birth went well. I took Rebecca to visit her in the hospital each afternoon. At night, although she missed her mother, she accepted the situation with an ease that was no doubt aided by the presence of her grandmother; without Mona, I can't imagine our making it through unscathed.

When all three babies were finally home—they kept Matthew through the week until the doctors judged him strong enough—Rebecca showed more pride than jealousy. She went through our extensive collection of gifted

hand-me-downs and sorted baby clothes, making two piles of ordinary items for the boys and one pile of especially nice contributions for "the sister." She was always there to pick up a fallen bottle or change a baby's frown into a smile. Nights were more complicated, but she coped nicely. She often joined us in our bed sometime before dawn. Once, when Julie and I slept through two screamers, she shook me until I awoke. "Daddy," she said firmly but cheerfully, "your babies are crying."

But after several weeks her enthusiasm began to flag; maybe it was when she realized the triplets were here to stay or when she saw how much time they were taking. One afternoon she held a sale of their clothing, playing both clerk and customer; tiny pairs of pants went for a nickel, shirts for a penny. Could we possibly interpret her actions any way other than she'd like to sell the triplets as well? On occasions, extreme tiredness and frustration led to more aggressive behavior. She snatched toys from the babies, even shoved them. It was not unusual for her to tumble dangerously close to a precariously seated infant.

She also showed them enormous amounts of love. She comforted them when they cried, helped feed them, and always wanted them along on outings. Once, when she began sniffling from yet another cold brought home from nursery school, she rubbed her nose hard as if to chase away the symptoms. "I don't want a cold," she said. "I want to be able to kiss the babies." On a rare occasion bathing alone, she complained aloud, "I don't have any company in here."

Even at three going on four, she was a dynamic individual, ricocheting from one emotional extreme to another. There was regression: She tried to squeeze into the babies' outfits, climbed into their cribs, crawled like them, and imitated their cries. In a demand to be treated as an adult, she defied the house rule of plastic cups for all children and insisted on taking her juice in a glass. (This lasted until that unfortunate evening when she dropped a tumbler and cried as it shattered on the floor. "I know," she yelled. "I'll never get glass again.")

Whatever her mood, happy or sad, content or frustrated, Rebecca made her feelings clear. And even at her young age she usually managed to put those feelings into words. If she decided we were too busy caring for cranky babies, she did not hesitate to state her rights. "Somebody better hold me," was a frequently issued demand.

She was not the only one trying to figure out this new family paradigm. Julie professed instant connection and unconditional love. I took a little longer to fathom my place and define my relationship with our new family members. As I spent most of my days at 336, this occurred mainly at night, gradually over those first six months, nine months, maybe longer. Join me in the course of one of those late nights.

It is 4:30 in the morning and Jacob has a cold.

Alexandra and Matthew sleep peacefully in their cribs. Their breathing is barely audible in the darkened nursery, what originally was the master bedroom—our bedroom—before

the triplets arrived and we rearranged the apartment. The faintest trace of light reaches from a single bulb out in the hall to the rocking chair where I hold Jacob.

He leans across my chest, his head flopped against my shoulder, and coughs; at least the loud spasms have ended. Jake still suffers from asthma; Matthew, too, but he is quiet tonight. The condition does little more than prolong his colds and worsen their symptoms; his coughs become gasps as he struggles for air through a sea of mucus. It was that wrenching sound that woke me and led me to take him from his crib, hold him upright, and rock him. And it works; the fluid drains. The worst of his symptoms have subsided, but the coughing, the slow hacking, goes on.

He may be asleep but I dare not return him to his crib—not yet. If I try and fail and he wakes up, we will have to start all over. But the longer I wait and the more I rock, the greater the chance of disturbing the others. This must be avoided. And this damn old chair creaks with every movement. No matter how I shift my weight or alter the rhythm of my rocking, it creaks, a sound seemingly amplified in the quiet of the night. And so I continue to rock as gently as I can, keeping the pattern as smooth as I can, holding my breath at each creak.

This is not what I do best in our family, but I'm adjusting. I am good at earning the money to pay the bills and buy the groceries. I take Rebecca to school. I clean up after dinner and do the driving on trips. I change broken light fixtures and put triplet strollers together. My father used to call these

kinds of things the really important work; he said they made the world safe for democracy.

Julie does the other stuff. She feeds the babies and bathes the babies and cleans up after them. She amuses them with education-promoting blocks and games and teaches them to back down from the couch instead of going off headfirst.

And she takes the very early and the very late shifts in the nursery, partly because she is more responsible than I and partly because she is so maternal—but also their crying wakes her up and not me. She could nudge me, of course; I could never sleep through a good nudge. But she would never do that; it's not her way. This is a mixed blessing. I get more rest, but now and then I am the object of subtle rage.

She had already been up two times during this long night and had just fallen back to asleep when Jake began again to cough. Still, I barely made it into the nursery before she showed up at the door. I assured her that I could handle things. Too tired to argue, she shrugged and returned to bed.

Jake is the biggest of the triplets and in his first year, the slowest to develop physically. While Alexandra crawled at six months and Matt at eight, Jake was in his eleventh month before he devised his own style of locomotion, a kind of seated lurch accomplished by leaning forward on his hands, his right leg tucked under his left, and using all parts to propel himself forward.

It was awkward but effective. Those months before he perfected this style were frustrating for him, especially watching his brother and sister speed by him and occasionally directly over him. But his anguish was forgotten once he gained mobility, and he reveled in the freedom. Now, at thirteen months, he laughs his way from one end of the apartment to the other.

This kind of temperament, his ability to appreciate the moment despite what preceded it, makes Jake easy to love. Actually, they are a loveable group, and in no way identical. Alex, brash and the quickest of the three, the first to walk and crawl, established herself as an early ring leader, the one who would push a chair over to the dresser, climb onto the seat so she could take the treasures hidden out of reach, and throw them down to the boys, at that point still floor-bound. Matt, the smallest at birth and so physically frail that Mount Sinai kept him that week, continues to be sensitive, upset by changes and the one most likely to wander off to seek his own space. Jake is smart though needy. But his eagerness to respond when those needs are addressed—and his joy in that instant—make me want to scoop him up in my arms. (Everyone, actually. During that first year when Julie's mother was in residence every weekday, she would enter a room of crying babies, lift up Jake, and upon leaving the nursery say, "I've got mine.")

As I rock him now, back and forth, back and forth, holding his solid little body close, he clings to me,

burrowing his head into the crook of my neck. He is thanking me for bringing him comfort, for helping.

He is asleep, I am sure. The pattern of his breathing changes when he sleeps, becomes slower, deeper. And his body loses that resistance of the child awake. The coughing has stopped. He lies against me, every muscle relaxed, all tension gone. This is the time to ease him down, but I cannot. Holding him feels too good. I no longer rock for him but for me. It is one of those times when the obligation of being a parent and the reward converge.

I remember this from when Rebecca was an infant, especially during those late nights walking around the neighborhood or rocking in this very chair. I loved those nights. Being a father was so new, so different from what came before, forty years of thinking mostly of myself. When Rebecca came along it changed, and I first sensed the impact of that change on those long nights. They showed me how much I cared for her and helped form the relationship that we now share.

Somehow I lost sight of that process. Somewhere in the panic I felt when the triplets were still gray impressions on a sonogram screen, in the months filled with worry about who would survive and who would not and in the tumult of their arrival, I forgot that other time and what it meant to me. But on nights like this, holding them in the dark and the quiet, giving them comfort and feeling that comfort in return, I remember.

Suddenly I hear a faint rustle, the sound of footed pajamas moving against a sheet. It is Alexandra. I draw Jake closer and stop rocking. In the eerie half-light of the nursery, I see the quilt move. It rises up, holds there for an instant, then falls. Again it rises. If I can just get Jake back into his crib before she is fully awake, maybe I can get her back to sleep.

Too late. She is standing, a tiny phantom behind the crib bars. I know what comes next: She cries out, a quiet little whimper of a cry. Once, then a second time, now louder. She is delivering a message: *Why am I stuck in here while you are holding him?* That quickly, Jake is up, and now he is crying. Soon the coughing will resume.

Matt's crib is in the far corner. I can see nothing of him, but I do hear him throwing off his quilt, using the bars of his crib to climb to his feet. A moment passes. I envision him thinking, pondering, then he starts to cry.

All three are crying.

And here comes Julie.

I wanted to avoid this. I wanted to handle everything, just this once. I wanted to give her one morning of sleep.

She pats me on the head, one of those "Nice try, kid" pats. She picks up Matt, offers some comforting words to Alex, and heads toward the kitchen to get three bottles.

"Think we can get them back to sleep?" I ask.

She stops halfway out of the nursery and turns back to me. "It's five thirty. They're up!"

"What can I do?"

"Unless you're up for the day, go back to bed."

I wait for Julie to return from the kitchen. Then, placing Jake down in his little reclining seat, I take a bottle from Julie and hand it to him. I kiss him on his forehead and leave for bed.

So it goes, for that morning and for many others, for me and for Rebecca, learning to connect with Alex, Jake, and Matt. And in my spare time, I make the world safe for democracy.

Family and Life Reconfigured

As you might imagine, going from having no children at forty-four to four children in three years induced many changes. Actually, almost everything changed.

It began with my quantitative concept of family or, more precisely, my need to stabilize the size of our family, to staunch its propensity to grow. Julie had been eager for a second child, probably even before Rebecca was born; I came to embrace the idea. Now both of us were convinced that four was enough and we sought a permanent method of birth control for one of us. The conversation was brief. Considering what Julie had gone through to produce the triplets, and the fact that my option—a vasectomy—was less invasive that hers—tubal ligation—I had little rebuttal for her contention that it was my turn. And I was good with that, at least until the night before the scheduled surgery.

This was early 1990, a little over a year after the triplets were born. A new outpatient procedure called the "no-scalpel

vasectomy" was reputed to be easier than the old method, cause less pain, require a reduced recovery period, involve only a local anesthetic, and take about fifteen minutes. It had been developed in China in 1974 and introduced to the United States in 1986 by Dr. Marc Goldstein, the very doctor who would perform my procedure in his office at New York Hospital/Cornell Medical Center. So there you have it, slam-bang by the nation's leading expert. Should be no problem.

But here I was, lying in bed at three o'clock on the morning of the surgery, Rebecca and the triplets and Julie asleep and me wide awake. Over and over Goldstein's words, meant to be reassuring, played in my head: a tiny puncture is made in the middle of the scrotum, one vas duct that carries sperm is pulled out, cauterized, clipped, and replaced, then the other duct, all in about as much time as it takes to hard boil an egg.

Lying there, key words flashed through my mind: puncture, cauterized, and worst of all, CLIPPED. I envisioned pain, disfigurement, even death. If none of these, I risked alteration to my masculinity. While I was certain I wanted no more children, this operation could have wider implications. I was being changed in a fundamental manner, my sperm bottled up, the essence of my manhood thwarted from its natural course. Not making more babies was a good thing, but what unintended consequences might result? Goldstein insisted his procedure was medically safe and simple, but was it also personality altering? My imagination took over from there. I was able to dismiss upsetting images of me as horribly

deformed with a withered scrotum and shrunken penis, but worried about libido, already inconsistent as I approached middle age. Then I fell asleep.

The next day came and went in a fog. I do remember being sore after the surgery, as predicted, and I had planned accordingly. Instead of spending the night at Lincoln Towers with my loving but exuberant family, I chose to carry out the doctor's prescription—twenty-four hours of bed rest and an ice pack held fast to my crotch—back on West 77th Street, my safe refuge. I rented three movies from the VCR store on Columbus Avenue, bought a pastrami-and-coleslaw-on-pumpernickel sandwich from Fine & Schapiro on 72nd Street, and laid in plenty of red wine.

I dropped off easily and slept soundly through the night. Wine and pastrami, you say, the perfect sleep-inducing formula. They must have helped; I certainly needed help. My memory of those two days—of that entire period—was of a time devoid of inner peace. Added to my normal anxiety about work was everything to do with the subject of parenthood.

From when Julie and I decided to marry—and by extension to become parents—my becoming the sole provider for a family of three had gnawed at me; it was why I went into therapy. Up till then, I had managed to patch together a living without taking a fulltime job since I left the Mount Vernon *Daily Argus* in 1967. One way or another, through freelance editorial tasks from typing to indexing and finally when I began to sell articles and then books, there was enough work

and enough money.

Things soon got murky. After finishing the Garvey book—turning in the final manuscript and welcoming Rebecca into the world both happened in the fall of 1985—I returned to trolling for magazine assignments. I had envelopes filled with ideas waiting to be fleshed out and turned into proposals, and I attacked them with vigor. But few of them gelled into viable pitches, rarely even reached a point where I felt enthusiastic enough to approach an editor. I kept at it but with little success. I also wrote book proposals; none landed a contract.

The situation was not good and I knew it, but I felt a need to remain calm, to push down my anxiety. This was a phase, I told myself, a temporary dark valley; I'd been through them before. Muscle on, I said, and I did. Day after day I haunted 336 then headed back to my family having accomplished nothing for the eight or nine hours invested.

At no time during this period did I entertain the possibility that fatherhood had crippled me as a writer, that the pressure of supporting our newly created unit had real impact. How could I? This was my new life and I was committed to it. Sending back the kid was not an option.

My only choice as I saw it was to ignore that anything serious was happening and keep banging my head against my typewriter, my same old approach to hard times. Can't get a paragraph to read the way I want or find the right word, work harder. Not surprisingly, this caveman approach

yielded nothing of value.

Eventually, as my financial resources continued to shrink, I sent out a contact-wide SOS: will work for money—writing, editing, typing, indexing, anything vaguely connected to my thirty years' experience as an itinerant reporter and editorial handyman.

One month went by, then a second. Nothing. I was on the verge of panic when I got help from a most unexpected source. A woman I once dated had recently been hired by the American Kennel Club as their vice president in charge of communications. She remembered my varied résumé and called to ask if I wanted to create a newspaper about hunting dogs.

My first reaction was massive relief; a job with money coming in. And while I knew little about dogs and less about hunting, wasn't this like any other new subject, strip mining or lighthouses? Of course it was, and that was how I proceeded: research and write and in my position as editor, assign articles. My little staff and I ended up putting out a newspaper that was interesting and helpful to dog owners. We covered the AKC's new proficiency tests for hunting dogs, ran articles about nutrition and training but also issues like caring for your retriever while hunting in winter, important for sportsmen who might otherwise leave a wet dog in the open cargo bed of a pickup.

This was good enough to create in me a sense of security that eased me through the coming of triplets. I took none of this lightly. Maybe editing a dog newspaper didn't match my

fantasy of journalism, but it was editorial work that kept us in the city I loved. And, I reminded myself, this was what adults with adult responsibilities did—adjust.

Then quite unexpectedly the AKC killed my newspaper; I never knew why. After the last issue was published at the end of 1989, I was told it was over. I stayed on to edit their annual report but in 1990 my five years of steady work ended. With it vanished that sense of security.

Unemployment was short lived. Weeks later I received a call from the AKC's former graphic designer, the man who laid out my dog newspaper. He had resigned from the organization in 1989 to set up his own business. One of his first clients was *Sports Illustrated*, designing advertorials. Like hunting dogs, they were something else I knew nothing about, but I was desperate to learn.

Advertorials, as their name suggests, are a blend of advertising and editorial; literally advertising made to look like news or feature articles. Some are one page, more often several, forming little sections within a magazine or newspaper. Often the only perceptible difference to the reader is that advertorials carry a label, usually in very small type: "Special advertising section." I wrote my first one for *SI* in 1991.

The big advantage for the advertisers was that the text was related to their products—or, in the language of Time, Inc., "a special advertising feature puts the advertiser's message in a tailored editorial environment of his own choosing, as opposed to run-of-book positioning." The advantage for

me was that there was plenty of work, for *SI* and through the *SI* connection for *Fortune* and occasionally for *Time*. And the pay was better than regular journalism, a factor of increasing importance. I liked writing advertorials and am to this day thankful to those people who continued to hire me to write them.

On so many levels, life seemed good, with all basic needs met. The triplets were born without incident, were generally healthy, and while there were three of them, they were just toddlers with simple needs. Rebecca was coping nicely with her new siblings, her relationships with them improving steadily. And I had enough work to cover our expenses.

I was almost giddy with confidence. Against what appeared to be mounting odds, we were ensconced as New Yorkers. Potential obstacles appeared and then vanished. Yes, we had four children instead of two, but had taken steps to avoid further surprises. We had settled in an apartment big enough for the six of us albeit a little cramped, not uncommon in New York. My job at the American Kennel Club vanished, but it got replaced by *Sports Illustrated*. These were not my dream jobs, but neither the *New Yorker* nor the *New York Times* was calling, and I was still writing.

That it was happening in New York was important. One of my neighbors at 336 used to rail against out-of-towners who said, "How can you live there, without trees?" Her response was always the same: "How can you live out there without museums?" We did not have to make that choice;

no New Yorker does. Our kids were growing up with trees and museums, along with all those sights, sounds, and experiences that make New York unique.

In those days I felt confident that we had it all and that it would go on forever. You can probably guess that I was wrong.

Reality Interrupts

My education began abruptly. One afternoon, after Julie had picked up Rebecca from school and was pushing our train of a stroller back toward Lincoln Towers, a taxicab making a right turn against the light onto Amsterdam Avenue hit the stroller. Not hard—nobody was hurt—but hard enough to buckle the frame and leave Rebecca, Alex, Jake, and Matt terrified and screaming and Julie shaken.

It was over quickly. Julie did her best to calm the children then pushed them in the damaged stroller slowly back to Lincoln Towers, an arduous and stressful trip. The building's handyman repaired the stroller, and we were soon back on our old schedule. But not really. That day exploded the myth that we were doing great.

The assumption was bravado, intended to impress, well, me, I guess. What a joke! If I had considered our situation more realistically I would have seen that we had been riding an incredible streak of good luck, and that good luck in life, as in gambling, is temporary. But I didn't; I couldn't. We had our hands full taking things one day at a time.

Every trip outside required planning rivaling a military engagement. Not that we had many places to go, not socially. While friends had welcomed us to their homes when Rebecca was our only child, the addition of Alex, Jake, and Matt was apparently too daunting. Invitations stopped, and after that first wave of curiosity, few friends were brave enough to visit.

And these were the early times, when we were still bathing in the glow of surviving pregnancy with triplets and three healthy births, producing three very cute babies. Any long-range projection about dealing with early adolescence and then those teenage years was just too intimidating. So we didn't think about it, or at least I didn't.

Then came the accident. No one was physically injured, but any of them could have been, or all. If the cab had been going just a little faster, the driver a little slower to the brake . . . you can fill in the rest. For years Julie refused to discuss the incident in the presence of the children, fearful of making them relive the trauma, scarring them emotionally. The time it took to return the stroller to functional shape afforded us a peek into our soon-to-be future. Julie tried navigating the sidewalks of the Upper West Side with the kids tethered to her by leashes. The expression "herding cats" came to mind, and it seemed unlikely that the procedure would improve with practice.

That quickly, it became clear that we had to leave New York. At least that's how I recall it: a rapid progression. First came the accident and with it my recognizing the fragility of our existence in the city, then the decision to leave. I suspect

that Julie was ahead of me; she was the one coping with the triplets-in-the-city circus every day. But she was not a complainer and, sadly, I did not realize—or did not want to realize—how hectic and even precarious our situation was. Did I ask how her day went when I returned to Lincoln Towers each evening? Probably, but was this more than a pro forma gesture? Probably not. I was scrambling to line up as much work as possible. Either way, partly through 1990 we both openly accepted that it was time to go.

Typing these words makes it all seem so simple: "time to go." It was not simple and I damn well knew it. All my talk about wanting a more balanced life, with a wife and family, was true, felt to my depths, but all the while I held on to the hope that I could accomplish this with a minimum of disruption.

I sought to keep my feet in two worlds. I had built a life that I liked in a place I loved and wished to hang on to. Change but don't change everything; leave the city but not entirely. Ideally, I would take the elements of my writer's world—contacts and experience and work habits—package them up and move to a place safe from the garbage, noise, and reckless cab drivers, a location more conducive to rearing four young children. My family and I would live in this model setting and I, when necessary, would return to the one place synonymous with the best that I had known over the previous twenty-five years, my apartment, amidst all that concrete and traffic, and, not incidentally, firm up my work connections.

The timing seemed right. By then I had formed a foun-
dation of work, some of it pretty far afield from my original
definition: fiction and journalism. I had begun writing for
TOPPS, a baseball magazine published by the TOPPS base-
ball card and bubblegum people—this also via my old AKC
designer—provided copy for a newsletter for Citibank about
extending cash management to an oil production project in
Kazakhstan, and wrote non-fashion articles for *Vogue*. One
SI advertorial had me working with Ernst & Young, the
accounting firm that represented several major sports teams
and leagues. They were convinced that a book about the
business of sports published under the byline of two of their
top accountant executives would increase their professional
profile. I became their designated writer.

Leaving the city forced me to embrace the computer and,
soon after, the internet, two things I had fought against while
the technology era boomed around me. Clearly they were the
future, but I suspect I would have clung to my typewriter
for years, even while it was hurtling toward obsolescence.
This was a time when the theory was being advanced that
computers and the internet permitted work like mine to be
done easily from anywhere. I bet on this being true.

The real question for us was where would "anywhere" be?

This was a quandary. Julie, I think, dreamed for years of
California; my covering the oystermen of the Chesapeake
left me with a fondness for Maryland's eastern shore. Both
got lost in debate, leaving us with the Northeast, an option
I confess to influencing.

Leaving the region meant surrendering the apartment and my connection to the city, to those familiar blocks that formed my route when trying to get to work, to Riverside Park and the Hudson; I loved to lean against the railing and watch pleasure crafts out for a spin and barges propelled by powerful towboats. Even shopping was a New York experience. Zabar's and Fairway offered not only a unique selection of products but their own brand of customers, hardy souls willing to brave hordes of bustling shoppers and long checkout lines in order to compete for the store's combination of the exotic and mundane. Abandon all that? Not easily.

Still, we had to do something. Rearing four children in New York was not a viable option. After much conversation, Cape Cod loomed as a natural choice. Julie's parents had maintained a vacation house there for nearly twenty years and were planning to retire there in late 1990, he from his position as a high school counselor and she from the senior citizen's center. They would sell their Queen Anne Revival house on Staten Island and move full-time to Wellfleet, past Orleans and Eastham and before the very distant Truro and Provincetown.

My connection was more tangential. Each October from 1968 through the '70s, I had spent two weeks at a friend's summer cottage on Nantucket, that island thirty miles south of the Cape. Usually alone, I wrote and walked the beaches then closed the cottage for the winter. I developed a fondness for Nantucket and fantasized about moving there, but the extreme expense of island property and its isolation—a good

storm renders it inaccessible by boat or plane—made the Cape a more reasonable alternative.

It all seemed very logical. Julie's parents would provide us with a social base and we would gradually form friendships as most adults do when moving to a new town, through the parents of our children's friends. We would buy a house with a separate office, and I would drive into the city as needed. That house ended up being in East Orleans, a town with more full-time residents than Wellfleet and less remote than those towns considered part of the Outer Cape.

I felt a surge of momentum as these plans coalesced, a fast-moving current that had first materialized only five years before when Julie and I married and was now carrying me along with a force provided by our little army of a family. This feeling was generally positive, except for those times when it was not, when it sputtered and I found myself steeped in doubt. Never were they more pronounced than the night before the move.

With everything prepped at Lincoln Towers, I worked late at 77th Street, deciding what would be left as my New York office and packing what would create the Cape Cod version. Somewhere after midnight I became disturbingly sentimental, unexpectedly concerned with what I was leaving. Not me personally—I would still have 336 as my portal to the city. Instead I fixated on the changes for our children. This was, of course, the reason for making the move, and it was certainly a positive one.

Still, it was not being made without cost, and I wasn't even thinking about all those famous big city advantages but the little New York things that we often take for granted, like that level of awareness that comes from living in a true metropolis. Once that door in my thought process opened, much more rushed through, most of it concerning Rebecca, our most advanced child at that point.

Even at five years old she was already showing signs of sophistication common among New York kids. She developed an obsession with smoked salmon, which she had sampled once at a brunch when she was about three. Suddenly, it became a proxy for what was really good. One Saturday afternoon, I had picked her up after a school friend's birthday party at an uptown McDonalds where hamburgers, French fries, and Cokes were served. We rolled down Columbus Avenue on Julie's bike, chatting at each red light. I asked how the party was, leaning back to talk to her in her bike seat. "Fun," she said.

"What did you eat?"

"Smoked salmon," she said, "my favorite."

One other day, we stopped at Fairway on the way to school so I could finish the shopping early. As a treat for her patience, I offered her something from the baked goods section. She considered each category and said, "Oh, I see they have scones. I think I'd like a scone. Cranberry, please."

Would a five-year-old growing up west of the Hudson incorporate smoked salmon into her fantasy meal or recognize a scone? I doubted it. And will the triplets growing up on

Cape Cod prosper from the same kind of exposure? Again, doubtful. Maybe none of this was essential for intellectual growth but it was for a certain quality of life.

I became conflicted about moving. It was necessary, but I was less confident. And in that moment I felt a kinship with so many other New Yorkers who had packed up and relocated to nearby Connecticut, to Westchester County or New Jersey, or to far-off Phoenix or Los Angeles.

This book is primarily about living in New York, and what of that experience we take with us when we leave. But it is also about what we leave behind. And while at some level I recognized this, on the night before we left, it was not how leaving would impact me that filled my thoughts but the impact on my children.

Cape Life/City Life

Cape Cod seemed to be the tonic I needed.

The basics of our house—five years old, seven-tenths of a mile from the Atlantic Ocean and with a separate apartment over the garage for my office—were important, but it was that first sight that hooked me. As we drove up the long, curved driveway, hundreds of tiny goldfinches suddenly took flight from an acre of uncut grass and wild flowers. It was stunning.

We continued to be drawn by the Cape's beauty, from the dazzlingly bright days of sunshine to those hauntingly overcast to when the thick fog rolled in and swallowed even a view of our one neighbor. And wildlife, not just the feathered creatures that drive birders crazy as they seek a glimpse of a snowy owl, king eider, or painted bunting among the more than three hundred species known to frequent the Cape but sporadic sightings of foxes, coyotes, and deer, hawks soaring overhead in search of prey and, especially in the fall, flocks of huge wild turkeys that seem to materialize out of nowhere, take over yards and roads for weeks, then vanish.

But the greatest value of moving to the Cape was the sense of community that it presented to our children. We felt it early. Rebecca started right in at Orleans Elementary School as if she were a native. Within a year the triplets began preschool at the Federated Church, whose letterhead stated that it had "gathered as a congregational society since 1646"; obviously not Jewish but well meaning and not preachy, at least not at their level. For what religious support we required there was Am Hayam, an ad hoc group that met in any available space for Jewish holidays—actually more social than spiritual for us but an important link to the Upper West Side.

It was classic small-town America. Rebecca took tap and ballet lessons and quickly became active with the Orleans Academy of Performing Arts, a relationship that lasted throughout her time on the Cape. During our second summer, she danced on stage when *Sesame Street*'s Bob McGrath brought his family concert to the "Picnic in the Park" at the Hyannis Village Green. Later she performed with a local ballet company, acted in school plays and at the Academy, and tapped with Elaine Chase, famous for teaching and performing dance on the Cape for forty years. In high school she worked on a summertime attraction for kids, the Pirate Adventure, alternating between playing Riptide Rebecca, shooting the water cannon at pirates in Town Cove, and Pirate Pete, in the water being shot at.

Alex, Jake, and Matt were not far behind. All three studied ballet and soon began performing in the annual production of *The Nutcracker*. In 2000, with the release of

the film *Billy Elliot* about an eleven-year-old boy in northern England fighting the negative stereotype of the male ballet dancer, Jake and Matt were quoted and pictured in an edition of *CapeWeek*. The article explored the joy of dance and also boys' suffering being teased. "I think it's stupid," Jake told the reporter. "I really don't care because I like ballet." Matt cut right to the point most important to him: "I can do as many pushups as my friends. I'm the strongest."

Before that all four children became accustomed to appearing in print, so different from New York, where one must do something remarkably good or bad to it make into the pages of any newspaper. A year after we relocated, Rebecca's picture appeared in the *Cape Codder* selecting stickers she'd earned as part of the statewide summer reading program, "Reach for it. Read." The following year, there she was again, along with other cast members for the Academy's production of *The Best Christmas Pageant Ever.*

A photograph of five-year-old Jake, crash-landing off his sled at the bottom of Baker's Pond Road, made it to the front page of the *Cape Codder* in March 1994. The same month I took the triplets with me to town hall to pay our tax bill. They quizzed the Orleans treasurer about why the building was called "town hall." She responded by calling the *Cape Codder*, resulting in a reporter and photographer being dispatched to our house. "We know what town means, but what does the hall mean?" they were quoted in the paper, under the headline, "Triplets Wonder About Orleans Town Hall Origins."

The three took their minor celebrity for granted. Though they did not look much alike, especially to themselves or us, they knew they were a unit and were surprised when someone didn't recognize them as part of one. On a summer afternoon upon leaving a children's program at Orleans's Snow Library, we were stopped by an elderly woman just entering the building. "Oh, what adorable children," she said in that grandmotherly way. She asked Alex her age—"I'm six," was her response—and then Jake, who gave her the same answer. When she turned to Matt and repeated her question, she got this retort: "Lady," he said, "we're all six years old."

They were proud of being triplets, despite their mother's resistance to their being lumped together. Julie never dressed them alike, lobbied Nauset Elementary to place them in separate classes, and if anyone referred to them as triplets, she was quick to point out that they were Alex, Jake, and Matt.

These well-meaning attempts were countered by the subjects she was trying to protect. Sitting three abreast in the rear seat of our minivan—a necessity for our family of six—they regularly locked their arms together and swayed back and forth while singing, "We are the triplets! We are the triplets!" Much later, when they got their first cell phones, Jake listed contacts Alex and Matt as Trip 1 and Trip 2.

They were our version of Norman Rockwell models, with scenes that included outings with the Brownies and Cub Scouts, attending parades during the day on July Fourth and fireworks at night, and pulling their albino pet ferret, Joey, on a red wagon for the annual "Most Unusual Pet" competition.

Most Rockwellian was their lemonade stand, strategically located at the beginning of High Street where it intersected with Beach Road, the only way to reach Nauset Beach. During July and August, cars waited in line for a space in the beach parking lot for up to an hour . . . in the sun and the heat, stuck there along with all those other cars. What better place for a lemonade stand! They started off selling plain lemonade and ice, added pink lemonade then brownies, and finally jewelry made by Alex and Matt from beads that we bought in New York. They could hardly keep up with the demand.

This is not to suggest that life among our children was perfect. While outbursts were few, Rebecca continued to mourn the loss of her exclusive status with her mother and the triplets continued to compete, almost as if they were fighting for space in the womb. Soon after entering public school (kindergarten or maybe first grade—I'm not sure), Jake came home with a stomach virus. It was one of those fast-moving ailments; a night of throwing up and he recovered, but not before he passed it on to Matt. As Julie and I sat with Matt in the bathroom around midnight while he disgorged his dinner, there came a call from the boys' bedroom. "Is Matt's vomit as disgusting as mine?" demanded Jake.

The real competition was with Rebecca, forever their big sister and a star on stage in middle school and then high school. Their awareness that she was first and secured the bulk of the attention lessened some when they were all in college and making their own ways, but reminders of her early

edge continued. Years later, I shared a Father's Day present that Rebecca had made for me, a CD of songs I had sung to her in quieter times before the triplets were born, favorites of mine from my early collection of 45s, among them "The Girl That I Marry," "Pittsburgh, Pennsylvania," and "Ghost Riders in the Sky." I thought they would find them interesting but instead the reaction was silence until Jake spoke up, addressing his siblings. "I don't recall his ever singing to us, do you?" Alex and Matt shook their heads in agreement.

Cape life also showed imperfections. Perhaps most important, it was socially narrow: white middle-class Americans, except for the brief summer when young Asians and Europeans were shipped in to work in service jobs for the tourist trade. We balanced this with 272-mile drives to New York.

Most ritualistic were the annual trips during the week between Christmas and New Year's. It was one of the few family traditions, begun about our third or fourth year. The routine was always the same. We left about seven in the evening, all four children wearing their pajamas and with their own pillows and quilts. The triplets were asleep by the time we crossed the Sagamore Bridge linking Cape Cod to the mainland. Rebecca usually joined them within twenty minutes when we hit I-195, the beginning of the interstate highways that led to Manhattan.

It was the perfect time to travel with kids, dark and quiet with little traffic and few distractions. The guaranteed exception was the Rhode Island Adult Correctional Institute in

Cranston, just south of Providence. From the southbound lane of I-95, we could see the lighted guard towers off to the right; the children insisted that we wake them as we drove by. They got a thrill from reading the sign along the highway warning drivers not to stop for hitchhikers; it was their version of a ghost story. I thought it would have caused nightmares, but it worked like a lullaby.

Without construction or weather delays, the trip took about five hours, including one toilet and gas stop. Other than that, they slept, sometimes waking up in the bright lights of the Cross Bronx Expressway but often not until we reached West 77th Street, double-parking right in front of 336.

Unloading, too, followed a routine: Julie stayed in the van while I herded the four kids—each with his and her quilt and pillow and without a word—out of the van, into the building, and up to Apartment Four. I headed back down to unload the bags while Julie sat guard in the car, then she went upstairs to get the kids to bed while I sought a parking space.

This usually happened around midnight, and accomplishing it as quietly as possible was essential. Because we were good New Yorkers who didn't want to disturb our neighbors? More like we were bad New Yorkers perpetuating the fiction that I was the single tenant of Apartment Four, still rent controlled and only legally mine if I lived there full-time. The children were drafted into this conspiracy. If stopped by anyone in the building during our visit, their line was that they were the nieces and nephews of Skip Rozin, just in for the holidays; Julie, their mother, was his sister.

I know, unethical, even illegal, which added to the excitement of those visits for the kids. I can see them now, urging each other to be quiet as they lugged their quilts and pillows out of the van and into the building. And while we were all together in the apartment, their climbing into one loft or another to play, they would fight to control their laughter in response to my reminding them to hush. It was a great game.

The best part of the game was New York itself, especially after Cape Cod. Could there be a more dramatic contrast? Like any other tourists, we hit the museums. The Museum of Natural History was a favorite stop. The triplets loved the Hall of Gems even more than the dinosaurs or the ninety-four-foot-long blue whale. They seemed annoyed that it was a fiberglass replica—big but a poor substitute for the real whales that periodically washed up on their Cape beaches or might be spotted offshore mid-April to mid-October. From there it was a brisk walk across Central Park to the Metropolitan; their new interest in theater drove them to the museum's costume collection. A little good planning could also allow us to take the van north to the Cloisters, returning by one thirty to salvage a good parking spot.

And there were the New York attractions less valued by the average tourist but treasured by our children. Every trip included the bead store on 37th Street in the Garment District to restock their supplies for jewelry to be sold at their lemonade stand, Chinatown for exotic candies and

to glimpse the fresh-killed animals hanging or jarred for sale—with a combination of fascination and disgust but nothing they would see on the Cape—and several stops at Fairway to shop for dinner, snacks, and scones. By then not just Rebecca but everyone liked scones, though they differed as to flavor, an even split between chocolate chip and cranberry.

Perhaps their favorite thing was the subway. It particularly appealed to the triplets, who at six still fit under the forty-four-inch free admission limit—a luxury they pushed till the age of eight. The real thrill was the ride, always in the first car, their view of the track ahead illuminated by the car's headlight as the train sped through the tunnels of underground New York.

How, you might ask, did you fit six people in that apartment for a week, especially when Julie and I took the bedroom for ourselves? Parental rights, I declared. Easily. By then I had given up my writing platform, installed a conventional mattress above and moved my desk below. The couch slept one, and blow-up mattresses accommodated another two. Each child had a preference, and Julie and I decided to leave that decision up to them. The plan, however, failed in practice. We ended up rotating each night of our visit, as everyone always wanted the loft.

Arrangements got more complicated when the kids started bringing one or more friends to New York. Then came that one post-Christmas/pre-New Year's trip when Rebecca invited her current boyfriend, a girlfriend, and her mother, a

total of nine; we needed two cars. In the apartment we had five nights of wall-to-wall people. Yes, bathroom use was a challenge.

My own trips to the city were simpler. I drove in for work, and in those early years that arrangement went well. My preparation for moving to the Cape, setting up as many jobs as possible beginning about 1990, kept me busy. Advertorials for *Sports Illustrated* and later *Fortune*, and the business-of-sports book written with Ernst & Young's accounting experts, formed a solid foundation and kept me driving in once a month. My regimen was always the same: leave High Street at 8:00 a.m., arrive at 336 about 1:00, then double-park till it was safe to move my car to the open side of the street and sit there and read the *Times* till 2:00, basically the same as I'd been doing since I moved to the city in 1965 but with a longer transfer time—six hours instead of forty-five minutes.

Driving in regularly did not satisfy all of my work needs; even living in the city hadn't guaranteed that. The normal passage of time takes a toll. Editors lose jobs or change jobs, even die, and there was a lot of all that during the twenty-six years that I lived and worked full-time in New York.

Keeping work connections in that dynamic environment is hard for freelancers. Writers on staff have set positions, but freelancers need to reprove their worth every time a new editor is hired. I wrote for the travel section of the *New York Times* over ten years under four different editors. Then somewhere around 1985 they changed editors again and I got lost in the transition.

Remaining connected is easier when you can physically pop into the office albeit on the lamest excuse but really to remind them you are alive and available. This kind of gentle prompting is harder to accomplish once you leave the city and are making contact over the phone.

Maintaining friendships was less of an issue. Since I saw my friends on no regular pattern as a resident, hooking up once a month was not difficult. It simply required a little more planning than before—less spontaneous, but we all adjusted. We met for dinner at Coppola's on 79th Street off Amsterdam or headed uptown to Jay's for a late drink and jazz; just through that black door on Broadway, upstairs to squeeze in at the bar, and it could have been Small's Paradise in Harlem circa 1965.

Those first years out of the city were the best of times. And if I forgot, someone was there to remind me. "Let me get this right," said a woman making conversation while we waited in line at Fairway. "You live on Cape Cod and keep an apartment in the city?" I nodded and she laughed. Then, with a dose of envy: "That's about perfect."

I knew that, but hearing it from a stranger made the truth of it all the more clear. We did have this great life on the Cape, filled with safety and nature and domesticity, and when I needed—or just wanted—a break from all that tranquility, I would drive five hours and park right in front of 336, which always felt like home to me.

So Rare

What made this idyllic situation possible was my landlord, believe it or not.

New York is famous for bad landlords. For evidence, go online to your favorite search engine and type in New York City's worst landlords. Listing after listing will appear, along with specific and graphic horror stories complete with names and addresses of the most egregious offenders. Complaints include the presence of mice, roaches, and other vermin, exposed wiring, leaking pipes, trash in the hallways, and of course, no heat or hot water.

My landlord was guilty of none of these. In fact, my relationship with him was so cordial that I am refraining from using his name here—though he has since died and by my rules for this book qualifies for full identification— for fear that landlord vigilantes will take vengeance on his descendants.

Things did not begin so friendly, mostly because back then he wasn't my landlord; his father was, and he was more in the classic mold. Not cruel, just tough, like so many

first-generation European Americans working hard to make a place for themselves and their families.

He purchased the building from Florence Lescot in 1970. By then she and I had become relatively friendly. I think she liked the idea that I was a writer, perhaps a connection to her previous life as an artist or maybe a patron of the arts, someone who hosted wonderful soirées where talented poets and sculptors made marvelous conversation and drank wine till dawn. This is the impression I got from the few times I was invited into her apartment, dark and furnished with antiques and filled with primitive art that she proudly told me had been created by her father, who by then had died.

Florence was, however, terrible at business. She owned another brownstone about five blocks away that was nicer than 336 and into which she poured all kinds of money in restoration. She took me over there to show off the craftsmanship that was lovingly and patiently devoted to returning an old, ornate wooden bannister to its original condition—far too lovingly and patiently for an owner whose other building was continually in need of the most basic repairs.

I suspect it was her investment in renovation that cost her both buildings, selling 336 to the father of, well, my friend; I feel comfortable calling him my friend. The father owned six or eight buildings in our neighborhood and employed a staff of plumbers, electricians, painters, and other men to keep his buildings in operational shape. All were Italian, for while he prospered in the New World, his ties to the Old

World were strong, as evidenced by the poster-sized picture of Benito Mussolini over his desk.

The son was more Americanized, having been brought to the States by his parents in 1947 when he was eleven. Not that he completely embraced the ways of his adopted country. I never saw him speak disrespectfully to his father—though he was taller and stronger and, at least in my mind, had plenty of provocation—and was most deferential to his mother, more Old World characteristics than those exhibited by the rebellious youth of post-war America.

Dealing with his father had to be difficult. The old man made sure that his son learned every aspect of the business, and I don't mean accounting. Plumbing, electronics, carpentry, tile work, tearing down and putting up walls—his son had to know it all, less for him to complete the work himself and more for him to know that the men he hired were doing it correctly.

If he and I had common ground besides Apartment Four, it was nature. In those days I was writing for *Audubon* and he was an avid hunter. We swapped tales about his trips into the wilds of Alaska and my trips to Labrador, Greenland, and Michigan's Upper Peninsula.

But those conversations took place out of sight of his father. To the old man, I was the enemy stealing his money. While the city's office of rent control did grant a 7.5 percent increase for every application made, his father still considered me a thief and not without some justification. By 1974 the

apartment that could easily rent for $400 a month earned only $84.93 from me; by 1978 it was up to $113.66.

None of the father's ire filtered down to his son. Not only did he socialize with me, he helped me make the most out of my apartment, all while his father dreamed of my moving so he could charge a market-value rent. When a friend of mine who was renovating her East Side apartment offered me the old stove—an upgrade over mine—it was the son who used the family truck to accompany me and pick it up, deliver it to 336, and exchange it for my stove. When he judged the old radiator in my main room to be too small to heat the space, he advised the purchase of a top-of-the-line Sunrad. And while I paid for the radiator, he drove me to the Bronx to purchase it and then installed it, all of this under the cloak of—if not secrecy then certainly circumspection.

Our need for caution ended in 1983 when his father died. From then on we met openly, in his office or my apartment and talked about a variety of subjects but mostly his hunting trips and the game he did or didn't bag and my trips on assignment. The more exotic my destination, the more details he pulled out of me and the more time we spent together.

I did not tell him when Julie and I married or when Rebecca or the triplets were born. I never considered telling him. My goal over those five years was to keep the appearance of my life as unchanged as possible, even as it was radically changing. The apartment was my ally

in this deception; nothing to the casual observer changed in Apartment Four. I was there most every day just as I had always been, with the odd trip now and then for an assignment. And if I did not go in on Sunday, who was to know? This was New York; the coming and going of its residents were private business.

Then in 1991 when we moved to the Cape, I acknowledged a seismic shift. I was not around every day, not for weeks at a time. Wasn't someone in the building bound to notice? By then the pace of turnover had increased dramatically; only two other apartments had the same occupants for as long as five years, with no holdovers from when I moved in twenty-five years earlier. But the landlord—my friend—how would he feel about being deceived?

I wrestled with this for a year or more. I felt pushed to confess to the landlord and let him make whatever decision he wanted about the apartment. If he wanted to increase my rent, I would pay. If he wanted to throw me out, that would be painful but I would adjust. It was his right; 336 was further from my primary residence than it had ever been and therefore not legally mine.

Finally I took my quandary to an old friend, someone I relied on for ethical dilemmas. He listened as I described my predicament and then asked if I thought the landlord knew I no longer lived there full time. I told him he had to; his office was only a block away, and the plumber he'd brought from Italy to work on all his buildings lived just three floors above me.

He took only a minute to consider, then offered the following: "If he knows and he is doing nothing about it, then it's probably something he wants to do, a kindness. (He called it a mitzvah.) If you confess to him then he's going to feel obligated to throw you out. You would be forcing your unspoken conspiracy into the light; he would be violating the landlord's code to permit it to continue. I suggest you say nothing. Let it continue as your private understanding."

And that was what we did. My landlord died of amyotrophic lateral sclerosis or ALS, often referred to as Lou Gehrig's disease, in 2006. By then his two sons had taken over operation of his buildings. While there was no direct conversation between them and me about our unusual arrangement, there seemed to be at least tacit agreement that it could continue, one of the more unusual landlord-tenant relationships in New York, and yet typically New York.

Tick-Tick-Tock

Good as those early times were on Cape Cod, indications gradually surfaced that life there was going to be short of perfect, at least for me. It began with the connections I did not make.

We had people over for dinner and who invited us to their houses, friends we made at the kids' parties and school functions. Our four children were not only their own gang and a magnet for others but drew us into situations we could have never generated on our own, such as school activities and parties given by parents of their friends. And Julie managed pretty well. She joined a group of women—mostly other mothers of kids—who met once a month to discuss, well, whatever they discussed—how difficult their husbands were, I suggested to Julie, but she dismissed this as paranoia. We also saw her parents at their house in Wellfleet.

Somehow all this socialization did not extend to me, which was a surprise. I thought I was doing enough to plug myself into our new environment.

Soon after moving I met Kay Bader, the director of Snow Library in Orleans. The former New Yorker had worked at the Time-Life library, the very research center I used while reporting for *Time*. Within months of our discovering our mutual history, she shared her view that the library's board of trustees was badly in need of new blood and urged me to apply for the seat that just been vacated.

This led to my serving four three-year terms on the board and to my forming a relationship with the library and its staff that continues to this day, not officially anymore but as a frequent patron. I've checked out books in print and audio format, music CDs, and movies and stopped in for help with research problems. But it became clear that asking librarians to chase down obscure material and imploring the reference department to help with information did not a social life make, much as I tried.

Meanwhile, what I relied on in New York just did not work in Orleans. I understood that these two places were about as different as my life in each of them, but my needs were so minimal I thought I could make it work.

Over my years in the city, I developed a specific pattern to generate personal contacts. Encountering people at bars I frequented, at classes at Columbia, at The Coffee House and the various places where I worked, I acquired a group of acquaintances with whom I communicated on subjects serious and frivolous. What we discussed was less important than the quality of the exchanges, active and supported

by sound information and logic—if not always absolutely flawless then at least plausible.

These exchanges occurred in situations in which meeting people was not the primary goal, eliminating the pressure that often accompanies forced social interaction. Even in places that accommodate that end (bars and The Coffee House), fraternizing was less the goal than simply interacting, a service vastly more important for me than selecting the right place to eat and drink.

But private eating clubs and public drinking establishments are not the only venues that invite mixing. The city has made a special effort to create spaces for people to exercise their need to sit and rest, to read, to enjoy being alone, or, when the spirit moves, to engage in some form of interaction—if not deep in intellectual content, at least an antidote to isolation. In the midst of the noise generated by hordes of people, cars, trucks, and buses, New York provides dozens of areas of relief not reserved for the rich and privileged but dedicated to the average pedestrian proceeding from Point A to Point B. This is not an accident but the result of a conscious effort.

Most obvious are the major parks: mother of all, Central Park; little sisters, Riverside and Inwood Hill Parks; and their smaller cousins, Tompkins Square, Morningside, and the rest. Great cities long ago recognized the importance of carving out areas of nature to balance all that cement, destinations for recreation and respite, to row a boat, pitch a horseshoe, hit a baseball, or stand on a soapbox and

address the woes of society. What New York also does— and I propose does better than any other city—is provide little surprises to be happened upon. They have come into being under different circumstances and are supported by private, city, state, and federal funding. And while they exist throughout the city, the majority are in Manhattan, the most crowded borough and therefore the one whose residents are most in need of relief.

Creating these sanctuaries hit full stride soon after I arrived. It had begun when the 1961 Zoning Resolution granted developers the right to overpopulate certain districts in exchange for creating spaces for the public. Officially "Privately Owned Public Spaces" or "POPS," they come in many forms. One of the most unusual is a passageway often referred to as "6½ Avenue." Pedestrians can walk mid-block between 6th and 7th Avenues, from 51st Street to 57th. Instead of being jostled and bumped on sidewalks, the well-informed urbanite can enjoy peace and potted shrubbery, benches, chairs, and tables.

Many skyscrapers contain POPS in the form of enclosed, lighted plazas, some with toilets and food kiosks. A favorite stop for Rebecca and me, after the zoo and playground at the south end of Central Park, was the plaza at the base of the AT&T building, where she could relax at one of the tables and eat the lunch Julie had packed, then we would head upstairs to the InfoQuest Center, an interactive science museum—this before the building was bought by Sony and AT&T moved downtown.

More common are the vest-pocket parks, introduced in 1965 in a previously vacant lot on 128th Street between Lenox and Fifth Avenues. Now there are more than five hundred throughout the city. Several of the most popular feature moving water. An early favorite, with a twenty-foot-high waterfall, was Paley Park, opened in 1967 off 53rd Street between Fifth and Madison Avenues. Others with an aqua theme are Greenacre Park at 51st Street between Second and Third Avenues, with its twenty-five-foot-high terraced waterfall and snack bar, and McGraw-Hill Park at Sixth Avenue, which offers access between 48th and 49th Streets by passing through a Plexiglas tunnel protecting walkers from the pounding water.

Each of the pocket parks has its own personality. Perhaps the quirkiest is the smallest, Septuagesimo Uno (Latin for seventy-first) on West 71st Street. It occupies only .04 acres and is so unassuming that a sign requests visitors to bring water to nourish its plants and flowers.

In contrast is the High Line, a narrow, elevated, linear park running along the West Side from 14th Street to 34th, a course originally linking the rail yards of Midtown Manhattan. Taxpayers and nonprofit support groups pay $4.5 million annually in maintenance, an effort that does not go unappreciated. The 6.7-acre park has proven to be so popular that any warm day causes a traffic jam of walkers along its 1.45-mile route. And while there are plants, exhibits, and art, the visitors themselves are the main attraction. Benches, chaises, and a full set of bleachers provide ample seating to facilitate people watching.

A respite from the city's noise and bustle may be their primary goal, but they also offer an opportunity for casual comments passed between strangers sharing a moment of nature in this most cosmopolitan of settings. The juxtaposition of their civility within a city where life is so hectic reminds visitors that they are part of a unique experience.

One sunny spring afternoon I was walking through Lincoln Center, a park unto itself, complete with a fountain, reflecting pool, bandshell, and a lawn that invites being walked on. I stopped by the pool that is home to Henry Moore's *Reclining Figure*. The giant sculpture—sixteen feet high and thirty feet long—was so arresting that I failed to notice the Lincoln Center staff setting up long tables beside Alice Tully Hall until a woman seated three chairs away asked what was happening. I watched as the crew struggled in the afternoon breeze to lay the cloths on the long tables; I shrugged in ignorance and issued an admittedly lame, "Some kind of function."

She gave me one of those New York looks reserved for visiting ignoramuses and offered a flat and pointed, "Thank you." She wasn't angry or condescending, just being a New Yorker.

Moments later, after Lincoln Center personnel requested that we sit elsewhere—they were setting up for a reception for incoming students for Juilliard, New York's premier music school housed there—we found ourselves again sitting near each other, this time by the Revson Fountain in the middle of Lincoln Center Plaza. No longer strangers,

we were engaged in a quasi-conversation. "They interrupted my lunch," said my new friend with a kind of half smile that I interpreted as mock annoyance, followed by, "Still, not a bad seat in the house."

It may not sound like much, but this kind of exchange fed my meager need for contact; similar events were just not happening on the Cape. The ingredients were there, open spaces and smart people, but the chemistry didn't work. I accept much of the responsibility for this; I suffer from a bad case of social awkwardness. Somehow it caused me less trouble in New York.

The older film writer and his younger girlfriend who lived upstairs at 336 were smart and interesting and easygoing, the perfect combination for me when running on empty or just stuck. They would respond to my three-push signal on the door buzzer and welcome me up for a cup of coffee and a visit. A brief visit—thirty to forty minutes—and I was ready to return to work. I sensed they were occasionally displeased with my abrupt departure, that those breaks for me were a prelude for them to drinks and perhaps dinner. Sometimes I did stay; more often I made my apologies and returned downstairs.

At some point it became uncomfortable, and we all moved on to more satisfactory arrangements. Theirs was to entertain more affable people. Mine was to see friends often enough and for long enough to reinforce our relationship and fill my need for more human contact with phone calls, sometimes under a pretext but often in genuine pursuit of some nugget

of information. What I really sought was a few minutes' exchange of harmless but intelligent ideas or observations, relief from the isolation of writing . . . isolation I enjoyed but did not wish to be absolute.

This is one of the values of being in New York: options. And while the city is famous for the options it provides for restaurants and movies, plays and music and museums, it is the many choices in personal contacts that elevates it as a great place to live, at least for me—not just contacts for work but for quality communication, be it for conversation at dinner, that quick debate over the latest headline in the *Daily News*, or most entertaining, puzzling out the proper use of the subjective.

There didn't seem to be the same opportunities on the Cape for wonderful little exchanges, either one on one or in small groups. My answer was to rely more heavily on the telephone, calling friends in New York and around the country to debate issues in the news, discuss whatever we were reading, or just to swap stories about friends and family. Then something strange happened. About this time the nature of the technology of communication got turned on its head.

Ever since Alexander Graham Bell registered his patent in 1876 for the telephone, his invention was on its way to becoming the primary instrument for communication over a distance between people. The process was simple: pick up the handset, dial the number you are trying to reach; when the other party answers, begin to talk, first one and then the other. It was not as rewarding as in-person contact, being able

to read facial expression and hand gestures, but it was live and interactive. In the words of experimental psychologist Lloyd Morrisett, "The technology of the telephone favors active participation rather than the passive reception of information and entertainment."

Then came computers and by extension, email. Initially I liked it—quick messages sent as they popped into my head, flung into cyberspace early in the morning or late at night, and responded to whenever the recipient could make the time. It was easy and convenient, a handy adjunct to the telephone.

Far too quickly email began to take over most person-to-person communication over any distance. It seemed that people liked not answering their phones and preferred email responses written at their own leisure, with leisure being the operative word. You send an email and it sits there for hours or days or more. I found the delay disappointing then frustrating. And when the response finally came it was often lame. Inflection, which tells so much about what a person means to say, was replaced by poor if any punctuation or capitalization—both indicators of timing and emphasis—and an appalling form of shorthand, as in "how r u" for "How are you?" (No civilized person would fall into such sloppy habits while writing a letter.)

Worse for me was the lack of immediacy. It is not a conversation when days separate the reciprocal give and take but rather an exchange of monologues. And delays invite

confusion. When your listener misinterprets something you've said over the phone, it is easy to correct the error. "Actually, what I meant was . . ." and you are back on track. Mistakes in email are harder to correct. When days have passed, too often that correction becomes a rebuke.

The emergence of email had an especially negative impact on my work. Proposals for articles went unanswered for days and weeks and longer or were totally ignored. I actually looked back fondly to those years when rejection letters promptly defiled my mailbox. Turndowns were depressing but at least I wasn't being ignored, the ultimate denial of existence. I concluded that the physical presence of a pitch written on paper demanded attention while an apparition magically appearing on a screen was easily ignored, but this didn't help.

My sense of isolation deepened. I missed New York and its many and varied resources for feeding my limited but vital need for a social life. Try as I did, I was unable to create a substitute on Cape Cod. I know they were there—the Cape was filled with interesting people who met in congenial surroundings and, presumably, engaged in stimulating conversation—but I could not find them.

All this made New York even more distant. I longed for what it offered, satisfactorily connecting through the natural selection afforded by interesting and like-minded people who happen upon one another not by looking for companionship but by serendipitously discovering a shared passion resulting in railing against difficult editors over lunch at The Coffee

House, or at *Audubon* assessing the environmental damage
wreaked on the Everglades by draining its water in favor of
agriculture, sacrificing a unique wetland ecosystem to grow
sugarcane, lettuce, and peppers.

I retreated into my work, which was not all bad—more
time to write. But even that silver lining contained a measure
of lead. While the assignments I landed from my long-
distance trolling served my need to pay bills, I was waylaid
by a most unexpected source.

The book about the business of sports required more
than a year to research and write. Toward the end, at a
neighborhood gathering of parents, the host asked about
my current project. I mentioned the book and for a reason
I'm not sure I understand—maybe one of those full disclosure
moments—I added that it was being published under the
names of two Ernst & Young partners, not mine. There
seemed to be acceptance, or a lack of comprehension, until
a woman held up her index finger, the universal signal that
she had a question. "You mean you're a ghostwriter?" she
said as if puzzled. I said yes. She snorted, gave me a look as
if I'd dropped my pants at Shabbat services, turned her back
without another word, and walked away.

At first I was wounded, then pissed. I wanted to catch
up with her and, and . . . I didn't know what, but something!
Instead I did nothing, just stood there while the party conver-
sation moved on, a fog of noise with no distinguishable parts
that I recall.

While I had never seen this woman before, I knew her

kind: people with their own strict sense of what it is to be a Writer, with a capital W. Writing fiction or nonfiction for them was an acceptable pursuit but not all other forms of writing qualified. I understood their point. I, too, preferred writing my own books to someone else's; I just couldn't afford to be that selective, and neither could much of the writing community.

I have friends who have authored books and who write for newspapers and magazines but many more who slave over public relations copy, press releases, and annual reports, or speeches for politicians and celebrities. The work of professional writers is exhibited everywhere. Calvin Trillin dramatized this point in his short story, "Roland Magruder, Freelance Writer," published in the *New Yorker* in 1965. His hero was the writer of traffic signs so well respected that people stopped him at cocktail parties and praised his artistry. "Was that your 'THIS IS WATERMILL—SLOW DOWN AND ENJOY IT' I saw on Highway 27, Roland? asked one fan. "I thought your 'NO PARKING ANYTIME' said it all," gushed another.

It is no accident that his story is set in New York; the city provides a favorable environment for all manner of writers. Stars are treated with deference, and the rest of us are respected for the craftsman-like effort we bring to our jobs and for the needs we fill. While "Yield" and "No Parking" are extreme examples, everything that is read needs to be written—not just books and articles but advertising copy and instructions to operate that new computer.

Even the jokes that come trippingly off the tongues of comedians and guests on late-night television, those supposedly spontaneous lines uttered at the Oscars, are most often written by somebody else. Writing all of it well requires skill. If you don't agree, try following an instruction manual translated directly from Korean or sitting through a performance of *Saturday Night Live* in which every joke falls flat.

Angry as I was at that woman at the party, I understood her hard rules. While I had honed my craft in New York's writer-friendly cocoon, where good writing is respected no matter the genre, I knew the difference between writing signs and writing news, and I valued them differently. I was a ghostwriter out of necessity instead of choice and was happy for the work.

And it was not the only choice I made with reservations. Advertorials, too, were a mixed blessing. Thankful as I was for every one that I wrote, I never included them in my résumé. Some journalists considered them tainted, and with a degree of justification. There are advertorials, and advertorials.

At *SI* advertisers had no control over the content in advertorials. They were as journalistically sound as articles in the magazine, though they were not generated by the editorial staff but by a separate division. Many magazines and newspapers produce advertorials that openly support their sponsors' services and products. And because they are designed to look like regular editorial, pro-sponsor advertorials can be confused with an article presenting independently researched

facts. This blurring of what is news and what is advertising is a serious problem among most journalists.

The separating of news and advertising is sacrosanct. Crossing that line threatens the essence of good journalism, the accurate and independent reporting of facts. Those defending this position envision a wall between business and editorial, often comparing it to the wall between church and state, this in reference to the First Amendment of the US Constitution that provides that "Congress shall make no law respecting an establishment of religion, or prohibiting the free exercise thereof."

My editors at *BusinessWeek* saw all advertorials as advertising, regardless of the rules governing their production. To avoid even the appearance that my reporting crossed that news/advertising line, I wrote no articles on a subject I had covered in an advertorial. I agreed with their position, although it cost me good stories, especially about the business of the Olympics, a subject I covered in many *SI* advertorials.

This was the mid-1990s, early in my relationship with *BusinessWeek* and early in the debate about advertorials, when they were a concern mostly among professional news people. As more newspapers and magazines became desperate for revenue in the digital age, that wall between editorial and advertising came under more vigorous assault, contributing to the erosion of the respect for the field of journalism.

Did I see this coming? No, but I did see my work in advertorials cutting me out of more good assignments, leaving me fewer opportunities to be a reporter. And because of

my conversations with my editors at *BusinessWeek*, I had a clearer picture of how serious journalists viewed the writing of advertorials, and I shared some of their concerns. Not enough to stop writing them—just enough to worry about it.

So when that woman trashed my working as a ghost-writer, she hit a nerve, one that had already existed just below the surface. Once laid bare, it spawned questions: What is a writer and what isn't a writer, and what am I?

All this conspired to wear away at my perfect Cape Cod adjustment. That new set of friends I felt sure I would find, that work I had lined up before leaving the city, none of it played out as I had hoped. As for the technology intended to keep me connected no matter how far away I moved, it didn't work well either. Computers may have made the process of communicating easier, but the poor quality of that communication diminished its value. The result on all fronts was a greater sense of isolation.

Piece by piece, my plan to make a successful transition grew shakier. Here we were, all six fully committed to starting a new life in a new place, and here I was, reassessing the decisions I had made to get us there. I became obsessed, my days and nights filled with questions I could not answer. *What have I done and how am I going to fix it?*

So plagued was I with my own personal crisis that I failed to pay attention to anyone else's issues. And then came that morning when Julie told me she wanted a divorce.

Tick-tick-tick. Tock.

Blow Up

I should have noticed something was wrong, but I didn't. I see you out there now, shaking your head. Big shock, huh!

The short version of why is that it never occurred to me that Julie wasn't happy. She seemed to have everything she wanted: four healthy children, an adoring husband, and a house hard by the Atlantic Ocean, just fifteen miles from her parents.

The subtext is more complicated and has to do with the nature of our situation, and probably, of ourselves. Yes, we were this apparently perfect family living in a perfect setting, but how well did all that really work? If the devil is truly in the details, then the details of our marriage showed serious flaws. Most serious was the uneven sharing of family responsibilities.

Those early years since moving to the Cape made clear the reality that even when I was home, I wasn't home that much—more in my office over the garage than in the house being a father and a husband. Had I been more aware I would have seen the resentment this caused in the marriage. But

Julie didn't complain; it's not her nature. And if I knew or even suspected, I didn't deal with it, which is my nature; I'm not good at reading subtle signs, especially when they reflect bad news. Besides, my focus was on work.

I always spent a lot of time working, probably more than Julie fully realized. But that was the way I had lived when I was single, after we married, and even after we became parents, first with Rebecca and then with Alexandra, Jacob, and Matthew. I thought I was making a major adjustment with parenthood, balancing my time as a father, a husband, and a writer, but I really didn't, not enough, and certainly not when you factor in four young children. How much short of enough became clear only on that day.

Relying solely on my memory, I cannot tell you what day it was or relay any of the conversation, just the sense of shock and, perhaps strangely, embarrassment. Fortunately for this book, I am not left to the frailty of my memory. I did what I usually do during hard times: I went to my typewriter, or by then my computer, less to document what was happening and more to articulate it in an effort to explain to myself where my life was going or maybe just to vent. Even now, reading my description of that day, it is clear how surprised and upset I was. I quote it to you now, as I wrote it late on the evening of May 29, 1994:

"It was probably about 11 o'clock this morning when Julie said the words: 'I don't want to be married to you anymore.' It was so strange. We were alone in the kitchen, standing at the sink. At first I didn't understand, and then quickly I

did. It was no joke; I could see that in her face. I asked her what made her come to this decision, and she gave me one of her nonanswers. Julie claimed she didn't know; she just didn't want to go on being married. She said she had been thinking it for a year or more, but she's now decided. It was so strange because it was so cold, so final. It was done."

If I needed confirmation or some explanation of why, it came weeks later in the office of a psychotherapist in Provincetown. I had started seeing her once a week to help contend with my marriage failing, and she suggested we invite Julie in for a session.

Julie agreed but made it clear upon entering the office—even before she sat down—that she would contribute what she could to the conversation but nothing would change her mind; she was finished. The therapist asked why she was so sure. Without hesitating, Julie returned to that day of the sonogram and my getting off the bus as it headed toward our apartment. And while she did not say it in these words, I took her meaning as, "He left me alone then and he's been leaving me alone ever since."

I remember no more of the session in the office or the drive back to Orleans; there was no mention of either in my notes. I think that I asked if we could talk more about this—that is something I would say—and the answer was a firm "No." The rest of the drive is a blank.

Reading back over my notes covering that period, I see I was surprised by the amount of stress that permeated our lives and how early it surfaced. My conversation with myself

began in December 1990 while we were still living in New York. I felt moved enough by what was happening then to take notes. My informal journal continued sporadically for nearly five years.

Alex, Jake, and Matt had just passed their second birthday and were developing nicely, especially for triplets. Julie's mother, who had signed on as a nanny when they were born, held firm to her weekday commitment the first year, tapered off slightly during the second, and then returned to her own life. This is understandable, but she was missed, never more than when the children began coming down with relatively typical toddler illnesses. The following is from December 24th:

"The sickness has been extreme. First a series of colds, then that bout with stomach virus, then more colds, Jacob's ear infection; now this current stuff, whatever it is. (It ended up being asthma.) These last two weeks have been horrible, hardly a day going by without at least one child and usually more being sick with something."

The bulk of the caregiving fell to Julie. Most of my time during the day was spent at 336, confronting our mounting pile of bills, trying to drum up work from a variety of sources. The AKC had killed my hunting dog newspaper in 1989 but assigned me the writing of their annual report in 1990, a short-lived but lucrative job. After that I courted advertorials for *Sports Illustrated* and *Fortune* and wrote that series of articles for *Parents* magazine. I thought we were getting by, but reading my notes I see

the stress. The result was lots of screaming: my screaming at Julie and her screaming back.

Life at first was better on the Cape. We had moved in June, in time to enjoy the summer. Yes, it was hectic with all that free time for the kids, but it was Cape Cod, with ocean beaches on the south side and bay beaches to the north and planned recreation programs from the town for Rebecca. Fresh from the city, I had lots of work.

But with the coming of autumn and our drifting back into normal activities—Rebecca in elementary school and the triplets in nursery school—old tensions surfaced: bathing and preparing them for bed, getting them up on time, eating or not eating meals. Many of them resulted in a confrontation and many confrontations resulting in, yes, more screaming, more of it reflected in my journal than I had recalled. Worst of all, and most surprising, was the toll it was taking, if not obviously on the triplets—who were two and a half when we moved—then certainly on Rebecca. One reference caught my attention; even now, all these years later, it still makes me cringe and more than a little ashamed. She was just seven.

"Yesterday after I threw a fit over some issue I'm sure was minor, Rebecca came into the bathroom while I washed my face in an effort to regain some calm. She didn't say anything at first, just stood there. Clearly, something was on her mind. 'Dad, why do you yell like that?' I tried to dismiss it. 'You know me, I'm a yeller. It rarely is as serious as much as it sounds.' 'Well, it worries me. I think it's me, that I did

something wrong and I'm in trouble.' 'It's rarely you,' I told her. 'I'm glad you told me; I can be more careful.'"

Reading these notes now, I see how much trouble the marriage was in, how badly I was handling it, and how my response affected Rebecca and probably the rest of the family. This was long before that dramatic pronouncement in the kitchen, yet for all of these years that was the moment my mind seizes on as pivotal in the desolation of the marriage. And clear as Julie's words were—"I don't want to be married to you anymore"—I did not identify them as definitive. We were married! We had four young children! We had left New York and given up our apartment. We had a house with a mortgage, two cars, and a cat! How much more married could two people be? And if it wasn't perfect, couldn't it be fixed?

There were no answers and no further conversations. As days turned into weeks my mind embraced something that can only be described as a sliding reality. It began in a hyper-denial mode, as in, *This is not happening.* That morphed into a strange kind of acceptance, strange in like, *Well, maybe this isn't so bad. Surely I can cope.* I say this now with clarity provided by hindsight; I recognize my cavalier attitude because I had experienced it before.

In 1972, when my father was diagnosed with cancer, I called his doctor in Miami to get direct medical information about his condition. The prognosis was not good, he said. The lesion, about the size of a half-dollar, was in the roof of his mouth, a difficult place to treat. The doctor went through the stages of treatment he would attempt, starting with radiation,

and very clinically assessed the chances for success, which he thought were slim. By the end of the conversation, about twenty minutes long, it was clear my father had little chance of surviving.

I remember sitting in my apartment; it was midmorning. I had taken notes, as any reporter would. The conversation ended but the receiver was still in my hand. The doctor had hung up but I still held the phone as if waiting for something else to happen. I don't recall what—maybe for the doctor to correct his report: *Oh, ROZIN with a Z*, I fantasized. *I'm sorry; wrong diagnosis. A few treatments and he'll be fine.*

This did not happen. After a few seconds, that rapid busy tone of a telephone connection uncompleted brought me back to reality. I hung up but continued to sit there, rehashing what the doctor had really said. What followed was a conversation with myself.

OK, your father is going to die, probably sometime in the next two years (he died almost exactly two years later, in January 1974.) *What does this mean to me? Not much*, I reasoned. *I'm thirty-one years old and see him one to two times a year; maybe we talk once a month.*

When I was growing up in Florida and he spent most of his time in Ohio, we corresponded through the mail, mostly my sending him letters, and cards on his birthday. I don't actually recall this but later found several examples saved in his desk at the farm, elevating them to an importance I did not realize at the time. The only mail I recall from him came after I moved to New York and he sent occasional boxes of

canned salmon and tuna, his effort—at least in his mind—to keep me from starving. This insight, too, came later.

My conclusion, sitting there in the quiet apartment, was that we did not have much of a relationship and I could carry on very nicely without him, that in fact I wasn't going to miss him at all. Yes, I could deal with this.

I revised this confident assessment as each stage of his treatment failed and his condition worsened. I flew down to Miami for each emergency, the trips ever more frequent and closer together. In the time that immediately followed his death and especially in the years since, I abandoned my independent stand. I struggled to come to grips with his loss. Despite his affair and the pain it caused my mother, he was my father and I was naïve to think I could take his death lightly.

Little of this acquired wisdom about the importance of personal connections was available to me when Julie announced her decision to end our marriage. Once again I fell back on my old pattern of bravado. Just as I had with my father's illness, I needed to put myself in a place where I felt safe.

I again grasped what appeared to be a logical approach: if I can't change this, there is nothing left for me but to find a way to cope. *I can do this*, I insisted to myself. And I set out to make it happen.

Lifeline

My chief ally in forging a new path was work. Nothing else demands my attention so completely as being forced to focus on a project. Yes, it was this obsessive behavior that contributed to my marriage failing, but I was desperate and work was all I knew.

This new attempt at coping began with *BusinessWeek*. In 1994 I landed an assignment through a friend who mistakenly assumed that my experience writing about sports made me knowledgeable about anabolic steroids. It did not, but I rushed to catch up, eighteen hours a day of reading and then interviewing so I could write a twelve-hundred-word article that the magazine entitled "Steroids and Sports; What Price Glory?" That spawned an article twice as long in 1995 about the drug's abuse in the general population, "Steroids: A Spreading Peril."

BusinessWeek was typical of my experience as a freelance reporter in the modern age of journalism. In the 1970s I still presented myself to the offices of publications to hand deliver manuscripts typed on paper then sat beside the editor to go

over changes. By the '90s that process had ended. Manuscripts were written, filed, and edited electronically without a physical handshake exchanged. *BusinessWeek*'s research departments chased down reference requests and sent them to reporters by the same magical system.

A little impersonal but efficient. Those two articles on steroids were my introduction to this fast new world. They also led to on and off freelance work for the magazine over eleven years, with an interruption in the middle for me to work fulltime for ESPN.

My time in television was interesting and strange but no stranger than how I got the job.

Remember the woman whose lunch meeting led to my working for *Time*'s New York bureau? By now she had married somebody else, moved out of the city, but remained friendly—casually friendly, as in two phone calls a year. She also had a son who was a producer for ESPN.

Early in 1997, when I was splitting my time between reporting for *BusinessWeek* and writing *SI* advertorials, I got a call from the son. He explained that ESPN was beginning a nearly three-year project leading up to the millennium and covering the twentieth century in sports.

It was big: thirty-five people in house, mostly outsiders but also some ESPN regulars, plus hundreds of freelance editorial consultants, cameramen, producers, and editors working together for thirty months to produce sixty to seventy hours of primetime programming. ESPN, based in Bristol, Connecticut, was setting up a satellite office downstate in

Westport, located on I-95, closer to New York and its airports than Bristol, which is in the middle of the state and near very little. Programs would air from September 7, 1998, through February 2000 on ESPN and its parent company ABC; later they would be sold in the form of home videos. The series was called *SportsCentury*.

Formats would vary. There would be one thousand "classic moments" covering the most famous sports events of the century, among them the final game for Notre Dame's Four Horsemen, a 27–10 victory over Stanford in the 1925 Rose Bowl to complete an undefeated season; Villanova's upset of defending national champion Georgetown to win the 1985 NCAA basketball tournament; Secretariat's winning the Belmont Stakes by thirty-one lengths to secure the Triple Crown in 1973, the first horse to accomplish that feat since Citation in 1948.

A "Blue Ribbon Panel"—that's what it was called—of forty-eight sports writers, historians, a few athletes, and members of the media, some from ESPN, would vote on the fifty greatest athletes of the century, limited to those who either came from North America or competed there primarily. A thirty-minute program would profile each one, starting with number fifty and working toward the one judged the best.

There were separate documentaries on the most influential individuals in sports, the greatest dynasties, the best coaches, and the greatest games. Decades would be covered through the events that occurred within them, starting with a

two-hour special on 1900–1949 then separate shows for each of the five decades to follow. (Of course, plenty important events happened in sports between 1900 and 1949 but without enough film to fill five shows; this is a serious consideration when producing television.)

The variety and scope of programming were broad and ambitious, as were the goals of the project.

"We're taking you back to these events and giving them definition, context, and perspective," said Mark Shapiro, who was only twenty-six when he was made executive producer of *SportsCentury* in 1997. "This project is about storytelling, telling the story of sports events in the time that they occurred, showing how society impacts upon them, and how they affect the society around them.

"It's not the fault of today's kids who think Ken Griffey Jr. is the best baseball player of all time. We are going to introduce that kid to Babe Ruth and Ty Cobb and let him make a decision that is historically better informed. Myths will be supported and destroyed, and others will be left unresolved because we can't find out everything. Some things we just don't know, and we'll say that."

I was invited to join the team as a researcher and fact-checker, a fitting assignment for someone with no experience in television but not the job I had in mind. This was an opportunity to learn how television production worked and find out if writing for it was something I would enjoy and be good at. The question was how to get involved with the heart of production and not just the periphery.

To broach the subject I volunteered to create profiles of those athletes sure to be included in the fifty greatest athletes list, the can't-misses like Hank Aaron, Jack Nicklaus, and Joe Montana. The producers creating these thirty-minute shows would conduct their own research in the field, interviewing those figures still alive or historians pontificating on the dead ones—the real work. But I would provide a solid starting point, a single-spaced page covering the essentials of the athlete's story with emphasis on particularly intriguing points, such as the little-known talents beyond track, football, and baseball of Jim Thorpe: he shot golf in the '70s; bowled in the 200s; was an excellent boxer, wrestler, and marksman; and in 1912 won an intercollegiate ballroom dancing championship.

ESPN bought my suggestion and signed me up as an editorial jack-of-all-trades. The job soon centered on editing, writing, and producing. I ended up working on two major documentaries, *Most Influential People in Sports* (among them George Halas, Marvin Miller, and Babe Didrikson) and *Dynasties* (most notably the New York Yankees, the Montreal Canadians, and UCLA, John Wooden's teams that dominated college basketball in the 1960s and early 1970s).

Working for television was new and yet in one way familiar. The team model employed at *Time* to cover many subjects and quickly publish the results was followed at *SportsCentury*. Researchers combed through documents for basic information while reporters worked with sound and camera operators to conduct interviews and shoot support footage called "B roll" for atmosphere then sent all of

this back to the studio where producers put it together for shows.

The confusing job in this process, at least to me, was writing. For traditional publications—newspapers and magazines—writers conduct research in the field to uncover the intricacies of a story in search of some new truth or an enhanced insight into an established truth. They draw conclusions based on a thorough analysis of that research and then, using facts and quotes and also a deep understanding of how they work together, create an accurate version of that story.

For television the writer takes those facts and quotes that have been recorded to tell the story. Even when breaking news in a documentary, television requires images to put on the screen. If a salient point is uncovered in research, a conclusion reached but there is no one to address it on camera, there is a problem. Some facts not supported by visuals can be covered by "voice-over" narration, but too much of this is frowned upon.

This reliance on visual elements is frustrating, turning television into a medium handicapped when it comes to subtle issues. Nuance, essential in good writing, is lost in most nonfiction television and left to those acknowledged masters of historical documentaries.

But it was fun. I worked with talented young people. They were patient with me, who was probably twenty to thirty years older than anyone else working at that level. There were a few older men—as in my age—among the senior staff, but they mostly worked in another part of the complex, not

only setting policy and controlling personnel but with final say on everything that appeared in the series. After editors and producers put shows together, they sent them to senior writer Pat Smith to be reviewed and polished, all under the supervision of Mark Shapiro.

I felt like a member of a team, so different from working alone at my desk at 336 or my office over the garage on the Cape. I wrote and edited scripts, viewed hours of interview tapes in search of good quotes, and traveled to meet with local freelance camera and sound crews to conduct interviews: Myrtle Beach for Lou Saban, who coached O. J. Simpson when he played for the Buffalo Bills and before "the Juice" became the star of his own American tragedy; Madisonville, Kentucky, for Frank Ramsey and his time with the Celtics; Montreal for Brian Mulroney, who was prime minister on that dark day for Canadian hockey when Wayne Gretzky was traded from Edmonton to Los Angeles.

Initially, much of the writing was done from home, with scripts going back and forth to Westport by email; for travel I could as easily fly out of Boston or Providence as New York. I spent three to four days a week in Connecticut, three-and-a-half-hours' drive from the Cape.

Probably the most fun was working with those kids. I say kids; they were all adults—at least twenty-five years old—and with years in television. If they were not skilled they never would have been hired on for such a high-profile project. But even if they were thirty—and few of them were that

old—that meant they were born after John F. Kennedy and Dr. King were assassinated and had no personal memory of the gas lines of the '70s and burning bras or draft cards and had probably never made out at a drive-in movie.

They were intelligent but still had no cognitive connection with those pieces of history, and this was a series that relied heavily on contextual elements, sounds and photographs and pieces of film that put the viewer in the mood to perceive the events of those times. Along with the older members of the senior staff, I became a link to essential years, especially from 1950 through 1980, vital when it came to selecting B roll to bring that visual note of authenticity to sports events of that era. I supplied ideas and some physical props. For the show on the 1950s, I brought in my Billie Holiday *Lady in Satin* LP in its pristine album jacket; for the '60s, *West Side Story* and *Sgt. Pepper's Lonely Hearts Club Band*.

Late one night, three of my young colleagues were debating between photographs of two Chevrolets, one a 1955 and the other a 1956. They needed 1955; maybe it was the Classic Moment covering Sandy Amorós's outfield catch to preserve the Dodgers' only World Series win in Brooklyn or NHL president Clarence Campbell being pelted with eggs and shoes during a game in Montreal after he suspended Canadians' star Maurice Richard for the season for striking a linesman. It was an easy choice for me—the '55 Chevy is more boxy—but they were amazed. "What were you," one of them asked, "some kind of car savant?"

"No," I said, "just a normal boy growing up in the '50s."

The real education was helping write scripts for two of the long documentaries and splicing them together with quotes and supporting images in the edit, hour after hour, sometimes double shifts, assisted by lots of coffee, primarily with the aid of one of ESPN's best veteran producers, Mark Durand, but occasionally on my own.

It was a crash course in making television documentaries and I enjoyed it, but the more involved I became, the more time I spent in Westport; those last twelve months I was there five days a week. And the more involved I became, the more responsibility I had, the more my weakness showed in the time required to turn out segments and the consistency of my work—some of it pretty good and some of it less so. I had a hard time grasping the technology of editing and even more with the need to rely on visuals to support important points, mostly with the challenge of covering complex concepts and subtle issues with only the available interviews, filling in gaps with a few lines of voiceover.

I never really got the hang of it and after three years of steady work and good money, when the series wrapped, my stint in television was essentially over. They did call me in 2002 to work on a documentary about Brown University disbanding its gymnastics team and the girls who fought to get it back, fought all the way to the Supreme Court. A good story, again good work for good pay, but that marked the end of my television career.

The simple truth is that we were not a good match, television and I. I like toiling over my copy, shaping and reshaping it until my text seems just right. Reporters learn to adjust their writing speed to deadlines, and I got pretty good at that during my years on newspapers and magazines, but my preference was to take my time, write and rewrite, parsing sentences and debating over each word.

I am not suggesting that I turned out golden prose, but the joy of writing, the fun of it, was working toward the best copy that I could produce. Words are important in television but not as important as images.

And writers for print seem to have more say about the final version than in television, where there is always somebody higher up to make a decision about how much time in the edit is too much—actually costs too much—and therefore when a show is ready to air. Ultimately, that higher up decides what goes in and what gets left out. I have had articles cut for space or rejected because of editorial conflicts but never had something injected into one of my stories that I did not want or taken out when I insisted it be left in.

Was this often a conflict? No, but often enough that it caused some serious debates; nearly none were resolved in my favor. I believe that had I been a brilliant producer they would have been more accepting of the points I was pressing; I wasn't and therefore had little leverage.

But it was great while it lasted, good fun with talented people, and for all my bitching, we turned out some really good shows, informative and entertaining.

(Our ninety-minute dynasties documentary was recognized as one of the best television and film productions of 1999 at the New York Festivals.)

In my view, most of those sixty to seventy hours were journalistically sound. I agreed with most of what appeared on air, with one major exception.

The central feature of the eighteen months of programming was the countdown of the fifty greatest athletes. It received the bulk of the network's promotion and was covered most avidly in the press: thirty-minute shows beginning in January 1999 with Number 50 (Chris Evert). They aired once a week on ESPN until the final night, December 26, culminating with an hour-long special on ABC featuring the top two. Both networks built the tension over that last month of the century as the list counted down: Number 5—Wayne Gretzky, ice hockey; Number 4—Jim Brown, football; Number 3—Muhammad Ali, boxing.

And then there were two. Obviously they were Michael Jordan and Babe Ruth—nobody else was left. It was a big secret; not even the staffs that produced the shows knew who would appear first in that hour and who would be last, judged the Greatest Athlete of the Century. But I was certain. Jordan was a great basketball player who had led the Chicago Bulls to six NBA championships and changed the nature of sports marketing; Babe Ruth was a great pitcher and the greatest power hitter of the first half of the twentieth century, the man who literally popularized the home run, brought baseball out of the shadows caused

by the 1919 "Black Sox" cheating scandal, and became an international celebrity before that concept was understood. It had to be Ruth.

But the winner was Michael Jordan. What a sham! What a travesty! It was to me the essence of shortsightedness, caving in to popular culture and the concept of the latest best athlete being judged the best ever, a victory of marketing over culture. It was a total denial of what the *SportsCentury* series was supposed to be: a celebration of athletes in the historical context of their time.

Did I share my views at the Westport office of ESPN? Yes, but more quietly than I am here, probably little more than a "Really, are you kidding?" But this was after the shows aired.

Redemption, I was sure, was right around the corner; the national media would rebel. I scanned the press coverage of that final night of programming in hopes of finding support for my position. Maybe a "Hey, ESPN, get real!" Something.

Nothing. Oh well!

TWENTY-FIVE

Complexity

BusinessWeek and ESPN gave me what I needed: challenging work to help me block out the reality of a failing marriage. It was nonetheless failing and while Julie seemed dead set on ejecting me from her life, there were still four children to consider.

Rebecca was eight when Julie made her pronouncement, the triplets five. That was far too young to lose their father and for me to abdicate an active role in their growing up. Julie was a good mother, very involved with their school and activities. I felt I was more involved with them personally, more one on one, or maybe one on one on one on one on one. The kids needed both kinds of parenting, and so both parents.

By reading this far you must have noticed that my motives are never totally altruistic. This was no exception. The more I deliberated over the future, the more I realized that I needed our children, needed to be their father, engaged, on scene. As reluctant as I may have been to enter parenthood, by the time we became a family of six, I was fully committed to

that entity. And if it could not survive in that form, I was dedicated to salvaging as much as possible.

I suspect I sensed all along the power of this connection; I simply had not codified it, never laid it out in such a way that I could understand it and give it proper credit. I didn't need to; it came with being part of a family, and until that moment in the kitchen, I was.

The nature of this feeling has a lot to do with the perspective that parenthood affords us, its value. That value can be elusive from a distance, is often missed by those who experience adulthood without sharing their concern for anyone beyond themselves, especially children. Convincing these happy individuals that they are missing an important part of life is often impossible; they are enjoying themselves far too much. Or they are too much in denial, having filled their days with other things. I understand; I was a member of that club for a long time.

Recently I had an exchange with an old friend, a New Yorker with a very busy life. Twice married and divorced without children, this person had money from a successful career and now retired, read the *Times* in the morning, practiced piano one hour a day, had lunch with friends, cared for an elderly and ailing pet, addressed issues with an apartment in Europe that was rented when not being used by my friend, planted, nourished, harvested, and cooked produce from a terrace garden, attended the theater three nights a week, made time for a book club, and also met with a married lover four afternoons a week.

Did this sound good? At one point it sounded great. It seemed utopian when I was turning forty and was enjoying time on a yacht docked at St. Tropez before being ambushed by the disturbing thought that maybe that was not the right model for me, which led to my getting married and becoming the father of Rebecca, Alexandra, Jacob, and Matthew.

Sadly, I never did gain the full appreciation of a good marriage. I assume a large part of the responsibility for this, perhaps due to some fatal flaw in my personality. Regardless of the cause or causes, Julie was unhappy and demanded a divorce; no further conversation was permitted. But children are shockingly forgiving, and in the space they afforded me I was able to remain connected and so could watch them grow and become their own people while developing traits physical and emotional taken from both their parents and in that way granted validation, at least for me. I needed that process to continue, needed to be around to make sure that it did.

The glue to all this, the force that created these feelings and held them together, was my loving them, perhaps the only feeling of true love I have ever known. It started early, for Rebecca in the Snugli during those winter walks in our Upper West Side neighborhood and for the triplets in those first years of frenzy in Lincoln Towers. This is one of nature's tricks, creating the young so adorable and loveable and dependent that we bond with them, first as infants and then as they grow, making them forever part of us. Divorce, and the separation it usually dictates, strains this bond.

I can hear all you members of Divorced Fathers Anonymous shouting in protest, insisting that you can be just as loving and involved parents from a distance, but I disagree, especially when the children are so young. Even if I bought a house two doors away, Julie would still rear our children, day in and day out, for breakfast, lunch, and dinner. I could not actively share in their growing up, not from down the street and especially not from 250 miles away, and certainly not on some artificially created schedule: my weekend/your weekend, my holiday/your holiday.

Impossible to deal with? Hardly. This was happening in the 1990s, when more than a third of marriages ended in divorce. Millions of couples with children split up and managed. I knew some, but few of them did it easily or particularly well—rarely the adults and even less so the kids.

Too many things are lost, too many little events that come from the everyday experience of living together and reinforce a sense of family: for us, riding the incoming current on a floatboard at Skaket Beach, parking a mile away and then walking to mobbed Rock Harbor for the Fourth of July fireworks, and of course our trips to New York. Some of our best times were single moments: the night all six of us returned from dinner at a friend's to find a mother coyote and four pups playing at the foot of our driveway; the 1994 Leonid meteor shower, when I woke Rebecca and the triplets in the middle of the night to lie on the cold grass of the side yard and watch the celestial show rocketing high overhead.

No event required more planning than the acquiring of a new dog, necessitated after Kelly, our miniature pincher with occasional bouts of aggression, became infected with Lyme disease and died.

This left us with no animals, a rare state of affairs. Jenny the cat finally fled, presumably fed up with being harassed by Kelly. Joey the albino ferret was found dead in his cage at about the age of eight, old for a ferret. Petless, we called the Animal Rescue League of Brewster and learned that a Weimaraner/pitbull was about to deliver a litter. Individual dogs or cats were common; a full litter of puppies was a big deal and interest was high. That first week after they were born saw the shelter deluged with people eager to adopt. Julie and the triplets were among them, there to assess the newborns; Rebecca was away at college.

Rescue league adoption rules dictated first come first served on a set date after the pups were fully weaned. We were committed to being first. I arrived at 4:45 before the shelter closed and made it clear to the staff that we would spend the night there in our van to ensure our preferred status. About 7:00 p.m. Julie dropped off the kids, who would remain there till midnight; friends rotated in and out with pizza and soda. Julie took over at midnight, sleeping in the van while I took the kids home and put them to bed. I relieved her at 5:00 a.m. so she could return home, get the kids ready for school, and get to work; by then she was working for the Visiting Nurse Association, her degree earned after we moved to the Cape.

Late that night the parking lot began to show activity. At midnight there were about six cars, by dawn twice that many, and when the shelter opened at 10:00 a.m., the lot was full. It was all very civilized and orderly except for the man who drove in at 9:45, double-parked, stood by the door, and demanded that he was first. The staff had been through this before. They knew that the people in the van had been there all night and earned literally the pick of the litter. Luna was our prize, a family victory.

These sound simple, even trivial, but they were important to me because growing up I had so little of them. And while friends' families showed their affection openly—embracing and even kissing among males and females—ours was a more reserved household. Our father set the tone. Lee and I addressed him as sir; hellos and goodbyes were occasions for handshakes.

Instinctively, I must have known something was missing, something I needed. I remember at the age of six or seven crawling into my parents' bed after they had gotten up for the day, just to feel the warmth that they had left behind. There was never any abuse. Neither my brother nor I was ever struck or harshly disciplined, but our parents' love was assumed rather than expressed.

One of the most important lessons I learned in therapy came from my New York doctor, who helped ease my way into marriage and parenthood. For those growing up in a household where affection was not openly expressed, he said, having your own family affords the opportunity to make it

right, to fill that void. Being a father did this for me, nearly every day, and I was a better person for it, happier, a truth that became clearer to me after I was confronted with divorce than before.

Somewhere about this same time I embarked upon a flight of fancy: I considered seeking custody and letting Julie negotiate the in-between space. I know, for a semi-engaged father this was absurd, but I wasn't thinking straight. I sought a local lawyer, who quickly pointed out that no judge would take children as young as ours from their mother. It was Julie, he said, who would set up a new family with our children and without me, adding as if it were an afterthought that it would be a family I would pay for, literally, every month.

I fell into a deep hole. At some point in those weeks of being confronted with only bad choices, I decided that I would do nothing. Did this mean I thought I could get Julie to change her mind? Probably not. But maybe I could stall, slow the process. *If only I could buy a little time*, I thought. To what end? I did not know. Maybe the problem wouldn't go away, but at least I could reinforce the good part of what we had built, and maybe in years to come our children might look back on their childhood with, if not happiness, at least less pain and anger. I could think of nothing else.

And so I tried, on my own, without asking Julie's consent or discussing my plan with anyone, friend or therapist. To help my prospects I attempted to eliminate what I assumed was my most objectionable behavior in hopes that my being more present would magically make our time together not so

objectionable to her. I tried becoming more visible, spending more time in and around the house, even sitting with the family during dinner, if not actually eating; I still couldn't eat as early as they liked, around six.

For a while this seemed to work. I even asked Julie if she thought things were better; she accepted that they were. Slowly, talk of a divorce slipped away. This is not to suggest that a honeymoon period ensued. Julie was cordial but not warm. There was no embracing, kissing, or any other expression of affection. She slept on her side of the bed and I on mine.

For affection I turned to the children, who were more than happy to oblige. Sometimes I went into one of their rooms early in the morning to be with them, just for a little human contact. Mostly I'd lie there and watch them sleep. The boys seemed to rise before anyone else, and then we would hang out and talk. Greeting and leaving always warranted hugs and kisses. It wasn't much but it got me through.

It was the strangest of experiences but a price I was willing to pay to hold at least the structure of a marriage together. And while I cannot speak for Julie, I can only assume there was something of value in this bizarre arrangement for her. There continued to be civil interaction and thoughtful conversation about the children and whatever issues they had, as if we were still a well-functioning family.

Perhaps most gracious was her help with my mother. Freda had been living in an assisted housing facility in Florida when she began showing signs of Alzheimer's disease. My

brother and I agreed that moving her to Cape Cod was the best alternative, close to family. Julie accompanied me to fly her north and helped get her settled, first in a nursing home in Orleans, and when her condition worsened, to an Alzheimer's facility nearby. It proved to be a good choice. We visited regularly until my mother no longer recognized any of us and I began going alone, but with decreasing frequency.

Then came that Sunday morning in 2000 when the call came that my mother had died. Freda was ninety-two and had totally lost her mind, but the news was still a blow. Julie could tell something had happened by my expression. When I told her that my mother had died, she took me in her arms, held me tight, and said she was sorry.

I was touched by what appeared to be a genuine attempt to give comfort, one example of the many compromises we both made over a period that stretched out for nearly nine years, gestures made to a family structure that existed in form but not substance.

Does this sound like a good, well-balanced, healthy life? Not really. I was stalling, holding on to what I had at home and otherwise retreating—hiding, really—in work, but it seemed OK; or at least, it was the best I could manage. I may not have had a happy marriage but I did have four loving children and lots of work.

And the work was good. As imperfect as writing for television may have been, it was new, exciting, and lucrative. That entire period, in fact, was filled with some of my favorite work, for *BusinessWeek* and then for the *Wall Street Journal*.

There were complex pieces that took weeks to research and write, others banged out within three hours between receiving the assignment and filing. And because these were national publications with high standards, the pressure to turn in top-quality work was equally high. It's the kind of situation most of us aspire to in our professions, and I loved it.

However, that professional satisfaction, and my whole-hearted pursuit of it, did nothing positive for my plan to prolong my marriage. To be honest, I can't tell you that it really had any impact; there was so little conversation of a personal nature between us. Still, the situation could rarely have been far from the surface. And if Julie's main complaint was my being absent, that period exacerbated the problem. I was gone a lot, and even when I was home, I wasn't very much home.

At some point Julie decided she'd had enough. In May 2004 she picked a quiet time when we were alone to express her feelings. Once again, it came in the form of a brief announcement.

"I think I've been patient," I recall her saying. "I want a divorce. Now!"

Balance

Julie's demand did not come as a surprise. Psychic powers aren't required to perceive the change in another person's demeanor, to recognize that something is different and that the something is important and probably not positive. Behavior becomes more resolute, the simplest of phrases snapped off with firmness, even an edge. The overall impression was that her tolerance had reached its limit, and it gave me a chance to prepare, to formulate an appropriate response.

I told her I was sorry, that I thought things were better but understood if they were not better enough. She had given me time and I was thankful. Dare I ask for just a little more? Rebecca was already in college; in a little over two years the triplets would be as well. I wanted to wait till then.

Reluctantly she agreed. I'm not sure why, except that conflict was not in Julie's nature—inflexibility, perhaps, but not to the point of confrontation.

That quickly, the future of our marriage was set. For us there were no issues about possessions, no negotiating about who would take what. We would not divide the furniture,

leaving rooms picked over—this chair for me and that lamp for you. Our goal was to accomplish the split with as little disruption as possible. All I wanted were a few pans and knives from the kitchen and the contents of my office. I would take my car and Julie would keep hers. The van would remain to accommodate family needs. As for the house, Julie amazed me by offering to buy me out in cash; how she managed that I still don't know.

There was never mention of alimony; I knew there wouldn't be. Julie, proud of her independence, had been working as a registered nurse for years. The thought of her needing me to help support her would have been offensive. The triplets would reach eighteen by the time we went before a judge and so all our children were considered by law to be adults, eliminating the requirement for child support. I agreed to cover the cost of college for them, as I always had. She would pay expenses when they were home. It was all very civil.

While the atmosphere between the two of us over the remaining nineteen months of our living together was colder than before, there was a peace that often accompanies the resolution of a complicated and stressful situation. I think we both felt it. But with that relief also came one big question for me, as in what am I going to do now? Where do I go?

My first thought was my apartment at 336. My time on the Cape had not worked out as well as I envisioned, especially as I continued to compare it with the many attractions

of New York. And there was a stigma to being divorced in this land of couples that upset me; I just wanted to flee.

But the more I considered the plan, the more it showed flaws. While all four children were well on their way to adulthood, the Cape would still be their home, their base for the foreseeable future. If I had gone through such extremes to hold the family together through ten trying years, did I now want to pick up and abandon whatever was left of the family structure?

At the same time I felt my relationship with the city changing, an evolutionary process taking place somewhere in the back of my mind.

It had started slowly and with the most minor of irritants. I found myself growing impatient with the crush of what appeared to be tourists, more than ever before, roving packs of them materializing everywhere, from Times Square to the elevated promenade on the Brooklyn Bridge. I was annoyed at the car alarm that woke me at two in the morning, frustrated with the subway that suddenly and en route switched from being a local to an express, ending me four stations beyond my intended destination. I didn't much like the smell of urine in the subways, either, or the garbage on the tracks.

More upsetting was the new commercial profile of my neighborhood. Walking through the streets near my apartment, I became aware of vanishing laundromats and hardware stores, shoe repair shops and those little key-making cubicles crammed into slivers of space—low-profit, utilitarian

businesses that nonetheless made the area more livable. In their place were endless outlets selling overpriced confections, more opportunities to buy ice cream and cookies than anybody needed.

The odd part of my negative reaction was that none of these irritants were new. Noise, filth, crowds, and inconvenience were the essence of city life. When out-of-towners complained, I attacked them. This is New York, I'd say; embrace it or go back where you came from. As for those basic service providers that were gone, that reflected the planned alteration of the Upper West Side, primarily that patch just north of Columbus Circle, roughly the area known as Lincoln Square. Saving New York, some people called it.

While much of the region showed a classy residential flair from the late 1800s on, with stately apartment buildings and fashionable town houses, in contrast were tenements, warehouses, inexpensive hotels, cheap shops, and markets. City powerbrokers turned to developer Robert Moses, best known at that point for building highways, bridges, and other public works projects, most notably the Triborough Bridge linking Manhattan, the Bronx, and Queens. In 1956 he took on his biggest challenge, the Lincoln Square Urban Renewal Project.

Gutting what Moses called a "blighted slum" made room for the hugely ambitious Lincoln Center for the Performing Arts, which debuted in 1962, and the twenty-acre, six high-rise apartment complex of Lincoln Towers. Together they marked the beginning of the gentrification

of the Upper West Side. By the time I moved to 336 in 1965, that dramatic metamorphosis had begun but barely crept as far north as 72nd Street. Its rate of progress was so slow that we were hardly aware it was happening and so had no fear that our neighborhood was being transformed, for better and for worse.

Then came the 1970s. Change was more intrusive, harder to ignore. Midway through the decade we lost Gitlitz, two blocks from 336 on Broadway and a frequent stop of mine for a kosher hotdog, and then the Tip Top Inn on 86th Street and Broadway, not accommodating overnight guests as its name suggested but satisfying hungry customers with its bakery, delicatessen, restaurant, and catering service.

Most dramatic was the impact on Columbus Avenue. Longtime favorites vanished. LaRochelle Pharmacy at 76th Street closed in 1978, followed a year later by the neighboring Parkwest Stationers. Soon the family-run King Cole Supermarket at 75th Street went out of business. Victor's Café at 71st Street, popular among the Lincoln Center crowd and Cuban expatriates for nearly twenty years, closed in 1980.

Early in 1984 the *Washington Post* commissioned me to write about the transformation. At this time the avenue was still home to a quirky collection of distinctive shops. One Woman sold antique clothing; Jerry Jares, antique lamps. As Times Go By concentrated on Art Deco items, Fiestaware, and Depression glass. Mythology's spark-shooting ray guns and hopping chickens rivaled the mechanical toys of Last Wound Up, but New York provided customers for both.

As the '80s picked up speed, "quirky" became a pejorative. Unique little shops were threatened even in New York's diverse and healthy commercial environment, known for having a consumer for every kind of product, a diner for every cuisine. By then the holdovers competed with glitzy new arrivals, specialty clothing stores and fancy restaurants fighting to claim the title of the next "place to be" on the new Columbus Avenue. The two leading pretenders to that crown when my article ran in February were Café Central and Ruelles, both jammed nightly while older, less fashionable restaurants died a not-so-slow death.

Don't bother looking for any of these on your next trip to New York. All are long gone. In their place are ever more upscale boutiques selling designer hats and clothes and shoes to adults and children, bistros featuring quiche and pasta primavera, some with gardens in back, glass-enclosed terraces in front, or both.

Researching the *Post* article revealed the power of higher rents as a force of change. Dorothy Friedman opened her antique store Portobello Road in 1977. At first she saw the local revitalization as good for business, but then she was hit with the hard reality. "I knew the rent was going up, but I had no idea it would be so much," she said. "I was paying twelve hundred a month; he wants sixty-five hundred." She shrugged as if it were a million. "I'll be closing this summer." Two blocks away, where Lilit Goodman had been selling antiques at Eclectriques since 1973, rent was jumping from $750 to $5,000; she was closing at the end

of that February. (Commercial rents in 2018 along that same stretch were about $400 per square foot, or $60,000 a month for a typical 1,500-square-foot shop, according to real estate sources.)

Maybe these changes were so gradual while I lived in the city that I didn't see them as epidemic. Moving to Cape Cod afforded me a new perspective. Every trip back to 77th Street made me more aware of the latest victims, that familiar old names were gone.

It was impossible not to notice. More than bricks and mortar, they were part of our daily lives. Eeyore's Books for Children, at Broadway near 79th before it closed in 1993, offered me guidance for young readers, first for friends' kids and then for Rebecca and the triplets. The Broadway Nut Shop, across from Zabar's, a destination for sweets aficionados throughout the region, closed in 2002.

Shakespeare & Company, the Broadway and 80th Street branch of that independent New York chain that closed in 1996, not only sold books and hard-to-find literary magazines but offered patrons an opportunity to hear authors such as Toni Morrison read their work. Éclair Bakery and its restaurant on 72nd Street between Columbus and Amsterdam offered transplanted Europeans the taste and feel of home; it limped along after originator Alexander Selinger sold it in 1993 then closed.

I desperately did not want to be bothered by their passing. This was still my part of the city, I told myself, the place where at least a piece of me belonged. But clearly I was troubled.

Viewing all this with the advantage of time, I realize that two forces were at play simultaneously. Most obvious were all those stores and restaurants going out of business, longtime favorites that I had grown to rely on. Less clear, and more difficult to grasp, was my shrinking patience with these changes. Together they were impossible to ignore.

By 2005 that process of change was in high gear. Instead of just a neighborhood, we had become a destination, like SoHo (south of Houston Street), Tribeca (the Triangle Below Canal Street), NoHo (north of Houston), NoLIta (north of Little Italy), and the very specific Dumbo (Down Under the Manhattan Bridge Overpass). It even had its own acronym: UWS.

The forces behind urban renewal had my old neighborhood right where they wanted it, and they were delighted. I was the one who didn't fit. It took me till then to realize how much I had grown away from the twenty-four-year-old who moved to the city—even the forty-nine-year-old who left there in 1991. He would not have been bothered by the vanishing stores, not just the little nearby regulars but famous retail establishments like B. Altman's and Gimbels, all by then gone. He would have applauded the evolution. What could better symbolize today's New York than to reject sentimentality and charge on toward the future? Out with the old and in with the new!

I, however, missed them, these symbols of New York and of its stability, its resistance to change. I missed Lüchow's on 14th Street, the Camel billboard sending huge smoke rings

out over Times Square, and Checker cabs with room for your legs. Not that they were part of my everyday life, but knowing they were still there gave me a feeling of stability about the city, a permanence that in my mind linked it with the city of those old black-and-white movies, with the New York of Damon Runyon and Fiorello La Guardia, of George Gershwin and James Cagney, figures forever fixed in the city's history.

Rome may be the Eternal City in terms of western civilization, but for me classic New York is the model for the New World. At least it was, until they bulldozed all those emotional landmarks that we could visit and reconnect with that past, leaving us with books and movies. It was the loss of those connections that I missed, and the city's refusal to honor them.

Perhaps it didn't bother me at twenty-five or thirty; at sixty-four, it did. I had come to realize the difference between these two people, the me of then and the me of forty years before. It wasn't that I was no longer attracted to New York's energy and culture, its abundance of stimulating people, to restaurants serving the most exotic of cuisines and theaters showing movies so obscure you can find them in few other cities. At the same time, something else was happening.

As much as I embraced the wonder of the city, I found the sense of community exhibited on Cape Cod very appealing. Some of this had personal origins. After one of Jake's performances in a high school play, a member of the audience introduced himself to me as the cook at Cranberry Point,

the nursing home where my mother spent her final years. "Is he one of the triplets who used to come into the kitchen looking for cookies?" he asked, pointing to the stage, by then nearly empty. I nodded in response. We both smiled at the ten-year-old memory.

Other events were notable for their lack of identity, as with random encounters on the street that generate a friendly wave of acknowledgement, or a quick greeting to the cashier whose name may be a mystery but whose face you get to know over time.

These seemingly innocuous experiences occasionally lead to surprising acts of kindness. A butcher at the local Stop & Shop, accustomed to seeing me in the quiet off-season, once shared with me the bounty of his fishing efforts. "This striped bass was swimming in the Atlantic at five o'clock this morning," he said, passing along his gift. The smaller Friends Market has a wine manager with an eye for bargain French reds. One evening when there were none of these, I considered a California Zinfandel. "Not for you," said the manager with surprising confidence and directed me to a Bordeaux packaged for the 2016 Ryder Cup. The caddy and golf bag image on the bottle put off customers, he explained, resulting in the market reducing the twenty-dollar wine to five dollars. I tried one and returned the next day for a case.

These minor episodes are seductive. They foster a sense of shared space that reinforces a person's feeling of belonging. Of course this can happen in a big city but not so easily, and it is this ease that is so appealing. When added to the other

everyday activities that small-town residents take for granted, life there is suddenly viewed in an inordinately positive light.

I think this happens to many of us adopted New Yorkers. Our ability to embrace the city's remarkable qualities finally gives way to the difficulty of coping with its inconvenience. (In 2003 the city opened the NYC311 call center for help with nonemergency governmental services and to register complaints. Of the 2.8 million entries logged in 2016, the top category was noise—calls more than doubling in six years—followed by apartment issues, illegal parking, and blocked driveways.)

As we get older and raise a family, our priorities shift. And while we move away for undeniably practical and obvious reasons—among them more space and good public schools, and of course jobs—we are beguiled by wide aisles in grocery stores, by patios and decks, sunsets that fill the sky with vivid reds and purples, by nights so quiet you can hear the ocean's waves lapping at the shore. And yes, by the ability to park anywhere without the fear of having your car towed, vandalized, or stolen.

I reflected on all this while deciding where to settle, and then the momentum of my internal discourse carried me beyond the practical attractions of the Cape, past free parking and clean air, back to my children. They liked the city and treasured their time there, but Cape Cod was home. Without polling each of them, I felt confident that wherever adult situations carried them, they would always consider their roots to be there. My positioning myself on the Cape

would facilitate this and in the process improve my chances of remaining part of their lives, a consideration that showed itself to be important to me, reinforced during this period.

For all of my early failings at balancing the responsibilities of being a father to four children with being a writer, I like to think that I improved later on. I am not sure how this happened. I suspect it had something to do with my taking pride in the teenagers and young adults they were becoming. They gave every indication that this would continue, and I gained joy from watching it happen.

Part of this is normal to parenting, but part comes from being a writer. We like to think we are creating something that lives on. Rarely is this true, certainly for most of us. Parents get that chance if they are lucky, and about this time I was feeling very lucky.

The forces pushing me in one direction were mounting. For all the changes in the city and the changes in me, committing to the Cape was the right thing to do. The apartment on 77th Street sealed it; as long as I had it, I could have the best of both worlds. The relief was enormous and made moving ahead easier.

During the Christmas holiday that year, with all the children home, Julie and I gathered everyone together in the family room and broke the news that we were divorcing. We tried easing the shock by citing the things that would remain the same: They would continue to live in their old house with their mother, and I would find a house not far away; they could even help me look. And we would still have the

apartment on West 77th, available whenever they wanted to visit the city; I presented each of them a key. Some changes, but lots the same.

Rebecca pretty much expected it and remained calm. The triplets seemed shocked. Their blank expressions were the indicator, along with the dead air that filled the room.

I asked if anyone had anything to say. The room remained quiet. Then Matthew had a question. "If you two are so unhappy together, why have you waited this long?" More quiet, which I took as a sign that it was my place to answer.

"We love being your parents," I said, addressing all of them. Julie nodded her agreement. "We just don't like being married anymore. And since you're soon all going to be in college, there is little reason for us to remain together."

Nobody said anything more. That quickly, it was done. By the time Julie and I went before a judge, the official end to our marriage was anticlimactic. Sad but almost mechanical, as if it had happened already, which I guess it had.

Transitions

What followed with the children appeared to be easy. I say appeared to be because I don't know what was really in their minds; they seemed OK.

The rest of the school term sped by for the triplets, like most senior years, and we held together as if we were a normal, happy family. The great event was graduation. My soon-to-be-ex-mother-in-law, Mona, Julie, and I sat together, filled with that special pride that comes with the success of your children—or in Mona's case, grandchildren. Rebecca drove in from Poughkeepsie. Three Rozins graduating made for a joyful scene.

The other activity of that summer was my looking for a house. Or more accurately, our looking; the kids took an active part.

Having them along was an enormous boost. Their support, that lively enthusiasm, was an antidote to what would could have been very depressing, my looking for a house that I would live in alone, so different from the excitement that surrounded our house hunting in Orleans.

Late in August we found the perfect choice one town away in Harwich, just six miles from our old location. With three bedrooms and two and a half bathrooms, there was plenty of room for visiting children, pushing the focus forward to the future. Everybody approved. Alex, who would go on to study biology, liked the fish pond and surrounding garden, complete with a wisteria-covered pergola; the boys took one look at the finished basement that had walkout access to the back yard and broke into celebration mode. "Par-tay, par-tay" went the accompanying lyrics. Rebecca claimed the larger of the two spare bedrooms for the girls; I think the big closet attracted her.

The end of summer 2006 brought the triplet exodus. Julie and I used the van to take Jake to Northeastern in Boston and Matt to UMass in Amherst; I flew with Alex to Sarasota and got her settled at New College. Seeing them off had a melancholy feel for me, the end of my time as a member of this complete family. I know, maudlin, but that's how I felt.

And I was wrong; it wasn't the last, not yet. The kids came home for the summer and Christmas breaks, and Julie always invited me for special family events, lighting Chanukah candles, Christmas dinners, and early on to open presents on Christmas morning.

This also began their forming their own relationships with the apartment. It had started with Rebecca, who took time off from Vassar between her sophomore and junior years, September 2005 to May 2006. She landed an internship with the Manhattan Theatre Club, designing and fabricating

props for their one Broadway theater, the Biltmore, and two off-Broadway stages at City Center. To buttress her income she worked at Saks Fifth Avenue's British chocolate shop, Charbonnel et Walker, and designed the short-lived women's line for a fashion label called Rogues Gallery. Even juggling three jobs, she could not have managed if she didn't have a free apartment.

That was a great nine months for her and me, the first time the two of us had spent an extended amount of time together. We had dinner with my friends and I could show her off—what a treat to sit back and witness my very adult daughter being charming and intelligent. But the best times were just us together, cooking dinner at 336, going out to Coppola's on 79th Street, or bringing in pizza from Big Nick's or Cuban and Cantonese from La Caridad up on Broadway.

My favorite memory was the day I took Amtrak's 4:01 local out of Providence; the full 269-mile drive had gotten tedious and with a little advanced planning, the round trip to Penn Station came to $96. We were to have dinner at the apartment and I tried calling to tell her I was running late but couldn't get a cell phone signal from the subway. I called her cell as I emerged from the 79th Street stop. One ring, two rings, and she answered. "Dad," she said in recognition.

"Rebecca, I'm a little late but I'm almost home," I said.

"I know," she said, "turn around." And there she was, right behind me, on Broadway in the middle of Manhattan, my daughter. It was a New York moment.

She returned to Vassar in the fall of 2006 to finish her degree but was back in the apartment three days a week early in 2008, working on an internship at Marc Jacobs. She loved the work and gained a textured feel for being a commuter, as indicated by this email from her:

"I took the metro North train from the Poughkeepsie station into Grand Central every Wednesday night to work in the city Thursday and Friday, and took it back to Poughkeepsie on Friday afternoon, with the commuters and construction workers with hard plastic lunch box coolers, drinking beer out of large cans in paper bags in the last car."

Rebecca graduated in May then headed into the city to work fulltime for Marc Jacobs, again living at 336. That lasted six months until the economy slowed down and they let her go. I accused them of being scum; Rebecca said they weren't. "It was in the wrong place at the wrong time," she said.

As the oldest, it was appropriate for her to be the first to forge her own relation with the city and the apartment. Jake was not far behind. After enrolling at Northeastern, he occasionally got to the city, at first revisiting family favorites like Fairway, Zabar's, Central Park, the Natural History and Metropolitan museums, then making his own connections: seeing *South Pacific* at Lincoln Center, and with his then girlfriend walking across the Brooklyn Bridge and stopping at Grimaldi's for a coal-brick oven pizza. When he rode with the Northeastern bike team, he stayed at 336 during a race at Columbia; I don't know where the other guys slept.

Alex never attended school in the Northeast. She started at New College, and when she ran through their biology courses spent a year at the University of Guam then moved on to the University of Florida in Gainesville for her bachelor's and master's degrees. Her experience using the apartment included a couple days in June 2007 while heading to Tanzania for a summer job working in a rural maternity clinic and once in 2011, passing through from Gainesville to Boston for Jake's graduation.

Matthew took up the slack. He was the closest—Matt boasted he could make the 160-mile trip in three hours—and devised his own itinerary for the commute. I felt a pang of nostalgia when he relayed some of the details to me. "My agenda followed a time-honored ritual, closely following the traditions I had learned from countless trips to the city from years' worth of family holidays," he wrote. In other words, he left at night, arriving sometime after midnight, just as we had.

He repeated the pattern often and over that time formed his own close attachment to 336. The following is from one of his emails.

"Getting into the apartment was always one of the greatest moments of my weekend get-away. I felt at home. Once I enter the building, the ground-floor hallway has that familiar smell of decades-old linoleum glue. Stale cigarette smoke lingers from a time when you could still smoke indoors.

"The first thing I'd do once I get through the door is turn on the buzzing fluorescent kitchen light and crank on the old steam-heat radiator. Next I'd begin the ritual of

carefully investigating each and every room in the apartment, comparing what I saw to the trove of countless memories of how the apartments looked throughout the years. I would make a game of guessing which of us was the last occupant."

Their time in Apartment Four was important not only for the opportunity it provided to interact with New York but for the contrast it offered to their lives on Cape Cod, one close to being ideal.

People in small towns take care of one another, especially the children. Orleans Elementary School understood why Julie wanted the triplets in separate classes; the bus driver came down to the end of our cul-de-sac, literally door-to-door service.

And in such a popular resort there was plenty of summer work, appropriately safe for youngsters. It started with their lemonade stand and grew during their teenage years into real jobs: Alex cleaned rooms at the Parsonage Inn, a popular bed-and-breakfast, and later worked at Thayer's flower shop in town; both boys caddied at Cape Cod National Golf Club in nearby Brewster. Jake, our vegetarian son, cooked fried clam fritters at Liam's, the food shack at Nauset Beach. Matthew conducted field inspections for the Coastal Engineering Company. Rebecca performed ballet and tap at the Academy of Performing Arts, the Orleans theater, and entertained little kids at Town Cove in the Pirate Adventure.

More important were the educational opportunities, especially at Nauset Regional High School. Nauset sought to

address every student's needs, offering advanced placement classes for the smart kids, remedial classes for slower students, and lots of tutoring for those in between who wanted to move up. The triplets were ill prepared for high school math; tutorial classes the summer before they entered helped make them ready. Fill-in lessons helped many students. The year the triplets graduated (2004–2005), 68.8 percent of Nauset graduates went on to college or university, according to the Massachusetts Department of Elementary and Secondary Education (ESE).

But socially our piece of Cape Cod was artificial by national standards: affluent, pristine, and highly monochromatic. The academic year before the triplets graduated from high school, 2003–2004—the first year for which racial figures are available from the ESE—the enrollment of 1,037 students was 96.1 percent white, followed by Hispanics at 1.5 percent and Asians at 1.2 percent. Blacks came in second to last at .8 percent, ahead of Native Americans at .4 percent, perhaps one reason it took the school until 2008 to discontinue use of its "Indian" logo.

New York offered a more realistic version of the world. Grittier, louder, accommodating different kinds of people who not only looked different but held different views, it was the kind of place that would better prepare them for seeking their own way. Part of that was learning to deal with everyday urban risk, parking your car on the street or riding the subway late at night, the potentially intimidating prospects of visiting friends in far-off Queens and Brooklyn,

learning to exhibit caution while not letting danger inhibit getting around.

The city offered all that, and the apartment on West 77th Street gave them the opportunity to experience it, not just occasionally as a tourist staying three nights at a Midtown hotel might but with that sense of familiarity that comes with returning over and over, granting that comfort level usually earned only by natives.

Toward the end of Jake's final year at Northeastern, he brought a classmate to the apartment who had just accepted a job on Wall Street but was new to the city. They toured the Upper West Side as far north as Columbia University on 116th Street, went to Zabar's and Fairway, and met a friend of mine who showed them the South Street Seaport and then over to Brooklyn. Jake's friend liked jazz, so they went to the Blue Note in Greenwich Village, heard The Bad Plus, and went for pizza.

"It was nice to realize that I had a working knowledge of the city, to discover as an adult what I had as a child," Jake told me later. "After all those years of you and Mom taking us to Chinatown and the Village, to museums and the Garment District for beads, now I felt comfortable introducing it as a New Yorker."

That is a gift, a little something extra that Apartment Four could grant to improve the quality of their lives.

Oh shit!

The first indication that the status of my building might change came in 2010, when one of my landlords let slip that there was some thought that 336 might be sold. Nothing certain, he said, just a thought—something about needing cash.

Did I interpret this brief conversation as a warning to me, personally? No, mostly because I didn't believe the boys were going to sell. They had said it wasn't a sure thing; that was good enough for me. Besides, why would anybody in their position sell? My original landlord, the eccentric and aging Florence Lescot, eased herself out of the real estate business one brownstone at a time, presumably to help fund her senior years. Our landlords, and their father and grandfather, were in the business of acquiring buildings, not selling them. So this whole thing wasn't a real threat, I decided. That conversation was just friendly landlord-to-tenant banter, letting me know what might happen, someday, as in the future.

That's how I treated it, a someday thing. Meanwhile I continued my normal routine, coming and going from the Cape to the city as needed for work or just as I desired.

Sometimes I had a hankering to see friends or just to walk around and absorb some of that Manhattan ambiance. I could come and go as I chose, having my own apartment as I did.

Then in the spring of 2011 came a second conversation about the building's future. It wasn't so different from the first but instead of the subject being casually introduced, it now came with a tinge of urgency. "There's a good chance the building might be sold," one of the boys said. Hardly a seismic shift, I told myself, but then came the killer line about the potential new owner: "We've let you stay here . . . but the new guy's all business."

I sped right by the implication that they knew I was not a legal tenant and concentrated on other logic, on tangible if irrelevant evidence of my residency like my presence in the Manhattan telephone directory, my library card, and Con Edison electric and gas accounts. Surely all this gave me standing as an official resident, didn't it? I was good, wasn't I?

My resolve weakened late in June when I came into the city and found a letter from my landlords on the wall of the foyer. "Dear Tenants and All Others Concerned," it began. "Please know that the owner of 336 West 77th Street has this day conveyed title to the premises to . . ."

The words of the letter faded from my eyes at that point, but the meaning was clear: everything that was firm and reliable before that point was now in question. Or was it?

So, sold! Maybe no big deal. Instead of visiting with the boys and handing over my $330 in cash, rent paying will be more formal. I'll get a money order from the post office and

mail it to the new owner, return receipt requested to secure proof of payment. Not as friendly but prudent; it was time to cover my bases.

I was back in the city in July when there was a knock at the door. *Strange*, I thought. I no longer had old friends in the building who might just drop in. Apprehension describes my state of mind as I went to the door. "Hi," said the middle-aged, neatly dressed man standing there, a little boy hiding behind his left leg. He introduced himself as the man who just bought the building and asked if he could come in. I said yes.

The visit was brief and not unpleasant. I showed him around, pointing out with pride my two lofts and eased the conversation into my work, purposely adding how often I had to travel. I hoped for some connection—maybe he'd be my new quasi-friend—but there was none. No "So you're a writer. What do you write?" Or maybe "What an interesting use of space!" Nothing.

Midway through August, trying to work in my basement office on the Cape, I was distracted by thoughts of 336. What was happening? What horrendous news was contained in envelopes waiting in my mailbox? I sent copies of my apartment keys to a New York friend and asked that he stop by and check things out; I hate surprises. Two weeks later he called to inform me that my key no longer opened the outer door.

Of course it didn't; the new owner had changed the front door lock. The boys had been right; this guy was a serious businessman. I was desperate. I contacted one of the few people I knew still in the building and asked that he make

a copy of the new front door key and send it to me. While we were not close, the threat of the new landlord created a bonding atmosphere and he agreed. Come September, I was back in 336.

Strong and secure as my position once seemed, its foundation was now shaky. It would be easy to discover that I had a house on Cape Cod and that Apartment Four was not my primary residence and therefore I had no legal right to it. My real estate brain trust, lawyers representing tenants as opposed to those who helped me avoid Vietnam, informed me that while I had not a leg to stand on legally, practically I was in good shape. I could fight this—if not to win, at least drag it out. It was divorce all over again.

Then came that Wednesday evening in October. It was seven thirty when I reached the apartment and hauled my suitcase up to the second floor. There they were, taped to my door: not one or two but three copies of a very official-looking document. My knees weakened as I read to myself the bold, all-caps type centered at the top of the first page.

30 DAY NOTICE OF TERMINATION OF RENT CONTROLLED TENANCY AND INTENTION PURSUANT TO NEW YORK CITY RENT AND EVICTION REGULATIONS SECTION 2200.2 (f) (18) TO COMMENCE COURT PROCEEDINGS TO REMOVE YOU FROM THE PREMISES FOR FAILURE TO MAINTAIN SAME AS PRIMARY RESIDENCE

My initial reaction was simple: Oh shit! That quickly morphed into waves first of disbelief—this can't be happening—and then agita, that rocking feeling in the stomach.

Once inside the apartment, the door securely locked, I read the entire document. It was addressed to Louis E. Rozin—my legal name—and "a/k/a Skip Rozin." Also to John Doe and Jane Doe as undertenants (I later learned this meant the tenant of a tenant, or someone living in the apartment under a sublet agreement), then four pages of legalese, dated October 25, 2011, with a copy sent to my address on the Cape.

Obviously, the new owner had been through this before. He and his team had done their detective work and knew all of my names and all of my addresses, what few rights I had, and how many he had. If I didn't know it before, I knew it then: somebody was going to take away my apartment.

You must be thinking, what did you expect? Evidence that this was coming had been building for months! Honestly, I didn't expect anything; losing the apartment would have countered something I had grown to think of as my "forever clause." It may sound crazy but I viewed every major life choice as permanent, no matter how many times I was confronted with evidence to the contrary. I thought my marriage would last forever, that we would live in Lincoln Towers forever. I was really certain that moving to High Street in Orleans would be my last move; I even envisioned our children getting married there.

Nothing better exemplified that belief in the concept of perpetuity than Apartment Four in 336, especially by the time I was halfway through my fifth decade there. Lucky, you say, to which I say of course, but it was so easy to take that luck for granted, assume that it would go on, and on, which is exactly what I did.

Over those years that little one-bedroom apartment was the most stable factor in my life. Friends and lovers came and went, parents got sick and died, books and articles and stories were written there; word of their rejection and acceptance reached me there. I was single, then married and single again.

I became thirty, then forty and fifty and sixty, all seen through the prism of that apartment. From inside I had watched the city suffer through two power failures, four garbage strikes, three transit strikes, and four terrorist attacks. I assumed that a parade of events would continue and I would remain there to witness it. As for those signs to the contrary, I ignored them, until that moment in my hallway. In short, Apartment Four represented home more than any other place I'd ever known, with all the good feelings associated with home: comfort and security.

Briefly I considered fighting the new landlord. "It can take him years to get you out," one veteran of the real estate wars urged. But this was nothing more than a delaying action. In the end I would lose and in the interim be filled with anxiety as one legal maneuver after another failed. I was not up to buying a few months at that price; unlike with my divorce, there was nothing to be gained.

Timing for separation was not so bad, I reasoned. Our triplet sons had moved to California, one for work and the other for graduate school; their triplet sister was in graduate school at the University of Florida. That left our elder daughter, Rebecca, and me; we would have to cope.

This proved not so easy. My days in the apartment became filled with thoughts of times passed, the rooms strewn with an odd assortment of random stuff, items with no intrinsic value other than their meaning to me. There was the iron dog doorstop that I bought for Julie when we were dating, the shelf of phone books brought back from assignments in Greenland, the Kewanee Peninsula, and Letcher County, Kentucky—collections of names and businesses for some future writing project—and the bowl of matches from favorite restaurants long closed: Marta in Greenwich Village, Café St. Denis in Midtown.

Too much nostalgia; too much sentiment! I needed one of those slaps in the face from a celluloid hero, administered to an hysterical co-star along with a strong "Get ahold of yourself." It was time to let go.

A month later I rented a van, filled it with empty wine boxes, and drove into the city. On a cold and wet day, a trip I regularly completed in four and a half hours took close to six. As I had done so many times before, I double-parked in front of my building to unload before seeking a parking place.

It was after my third trip up and down the stairs that I saw the traffic agent placing a ticket under my windshield

wiper. "What are you doing?" I demanded. "I'm just unloading."

She pointed to the street, where for the first time I saw the newly painted parallel white lines, about three feet wide, one of those New York changes I had failed to notice. "Not in a bike lane you're not," she said.

"Bike lane? There was never a bike lane here."

"Well, there is now."

"So where am I supposed to stop while I unload?"

"In a legal space!"

I found one a block away and returned to the apartment, boxes covering the floor, and addressed the task at hand. But as much as I tried to concentrate on packing, nearly every item urged me to indulge a trip back in time, to reconnect with the people and the events that had come and gone while those rooms remained the one constant. Suddenly my attention caught on the large mirror on the living room wall.

There I was, again standing at the juncture of my present and my past. The image before me was not the man who interacted with all those people and collected those things, who lived through events that made these inanimate objects special, who in his forties sported a full head of curly dark-brown hair. This was a man just turned seventy; what hair remained was thin and white. As for those things, they were, well, just things. That image in the mirror was even more proof that I was no longer the man of my youth. Life changes, ready or not.

I packed up as much as I could—mostly requests from my children—performed a cursory last cleaning, and left. Fled actually, and while driving north I thought of all the items I had wanted to take for me, pieces of my past but left behind. I nearly turned around, but fought to stay on course. Things, I reminded myself, just things, and too many of them.

Days later, with the help of Verizon, I did reclaim one thing: my New York number for my cell phone. Those years on West 77th, tied up in ten digits. It would have to be enough to satisfy my forever clause.

Reckoning

A month passed before I returned to the city, and then it was a quick trip. In previous years I had ventured in during the Thanksgiving holiday to see a boyhood friend who moved to Israel and travels to the States to attend an annual dental convention. Coming in was easy for me; the apartment was always there.

But not by Thanksgiving of 2011, and I could not bring myself to check into a hotel. I still thought of myself as a New Yorker, not a tourist. So I rode the train in, had lunch with my friend at Tracks—Penn Station's lesser version of Grand Central's Oyster Bar—took an afternoon train back to Providence, and drove home to the Cape. I could not stay any longer. Having lunch amongst other travelers was doable; walking those streets that had been home for forty-six years was not.

About then I received a notice from the State of New York's Division of Housing and Community Renewal informing me that my old apartment had been rented for $2,800 a month. My apartment, for $2,800? Really!

Probably not my exact apartment—renovated, I was certain, with a new kitchen and bathroom and probably without my wonderful lofts, but this last is a guess.

Still, it was essentially Apartment Four, second floor front in 336 West 77th Street, renting for $2,800 a month. It was a sobering number, even stunning. Not that there was an increase; $330 was ridiculous in that market. It was the concept that my old apartment was renting for close to $3,000 every month, my little one-bedroom in a brownstone without a doorman, an elevator, or air-conditioning. And even if the kitchen had new appliances, it could not have grown in size, could not accommodate more than one person at a time, two if they were friendly.

Receiving that notice emphasized how unusual my situation had been and how fortunate I was to have enjoyed it for so long. I always knew; all of us with rent controlled apartments know. But did we really know, feel the economic absurdity? I didn't, not till that moment. Being confronted with the number drove home the point and testified as to how out of touch I had let myself become with the world around me.

I did not make it into the city at all in 2012, less a conscious decision than a better choice getting in the way: Thanksgiving with Alexandra in Gainesville.

This brings us to 2013, two years after giving up the apartment. With more than a little trepidation I took the train from Providence to Penn Station on the last Thursday in November, staying with a friend near the South Street Seaport and determined to hit the old neighborhood.

I expected changes; every trip in since we had moved to the Cape revealed more. And I had been kept informed through friends and the press. I knew that two of my Midtown favorites were gone: Colony Records, one of the last sources of vinyl, and the Stage Deli, famous for competing with the nearby Carnegie Deli for the best—and most over-stuffed—pastrami sandwich. Still, the local carnage was shocking. H&H Bagels, on the corner of Broadway and 80th Street since 1972, was closed—disheartening, though the cost of a single bagel had ballooned from nine cents to an absurd $1.40. A greater loss was Big Nick's Burger Joint and Pizza on Broadway at 77th. Owner Nick Imirziades beat me to the neighborhood by three years. Now we were both gone. Perhaps most upsetting was news that the Collegiate School, nomadic early in its 385-year history but on 77th and West End since 1892, was moving to 62nd Street.

Mourning the changes in New York's commercial and residential profile—everyday businesses closed and torn down, along with vanishing apartment buildings, town houses, and unique structures from subway station entrances to amusement park rides—has become a cause célèbre since, well, soon after they began disappearing in numbers but especially in the second half of the twentieth century, when post–World War II prosperity allowed nostalgia to enter the psyche of those sensitive to this kind of loss.

For me it began with the publication of Nathan Silver's classic, *Lost New York*, in 1968. Pouring over black-and-white

photographs of some of the city's most prized architecture, I became an instant fan of the Hippodrome Theatre, the steeplechase mechanical horse ride at Coney Island, the New York World Building, and the Charles M. Schwab House, none of which I had ever seen in person, all razed by then. The destruction continued as I settled into city life. Within the first three years of my arrival, demolition crews claimed the original Ziegfeld Theatre in 1966, the Hotel Astor in 1967, and the Singer Building in 1968.

These days the escalation is closely monitored. The *West Side Rag*, an online newspaper/blog reporting on art, news, and activities of the Upper West Side, devotes a regular column appropriately called Open/Closed. *Jeremiah's Vanishing New York* is a blog covering nothing else. Creator Jeremiah Moss—he admits it's not his real name; apparently it is Griffin Hansbury—calls his publication "a bitterly nostalgic look at a city in the process of going extinct." His 2001–2013 master list marked 163 losses. (In January 2019 the blog announced that it, too, would soon be discontinuing, adding itself to that painful list.)

The most common reasons, according to Jeremiah, are rent increases, declining business, and the rush to erect luxury condos, apartments, and boutiques, which I had come to gather differed from regular stores in that what they sold was more expensive. These forces constitute an assault on the city's already threatened middle class, not only driving up their rents but denying them reasonable places to shop, a trend that has seen bargain stores like Korvettes and S. Klein

close while pricier Bloomingdale's, Bergdorf Goodman, and Saks Fifth Avenue flourish.

The Upper West Side was ripe for this revolution in the new millennium, with an added element of vulnerability seemingly related to an elevation in modern taste, in some cases literally. Williams Bar-B-Q, on Broadway near the uptown subway stop on 86th Street, closed in 2005 after selling some of the best chicken and duck hot off the spit for fifty-three years. The culprit was changing attitudes toward barbecue, according to owner Noah Pesso. "People look at it as greasy and fatty," he told the *New York Times*.

Few stores have prospered from the public's accelerated epicurean obsession more than Zabar's. A modest presence when I arrived in 1965, it now occupies the space of four stores, selling cheeses and fresh-roasted coffee, smoked fish, prepared foods, and fresh beef, fish, and poultry. Its café on the corner of Broadway and 80th offers freshly made coffees and teas, smoothies, sandwiches, and desserts. Above all of these is a second floor mezzanine totally dedicated to culinary merchandise, from compressed sponges from France that expand when wet and cost $1.49 each to a one-touch cappuccino maker from Italy for $2,999.

I stop in occasionally, less to shop and more to revisit its sights, sounds, and smells. The place was packed at two o'clock on that Friday after Thanksgiving, and with a particular breed of New Yorker, well dressed and self-assured. I offered help to a sixtyish woman stretching for a box of organic wheat crackers on a high shelf; she shook me off. "No,

we're good," she said in that clipped New York manner that often employs the royal "we." From a man ordering coffee: "A pound of decaf, espresso, ground for Number Four." And another ordering sturgeon: "Not that piece; I don't want that piece. Good, I like that one."

These were, admittedly, not typical New Yorkers, yet were definitely part of Manhattan's demographic; many, I suspect, came into town from Greenwich or Scarsdale to shop and attend opera and theater. Nearly all were white, in contrast to the group of riders on the Seventh Avenue subway I had taken uptown, best described as multiethnic.

Zabar's clientele were also financially comfortable, a conclusion I derived from their purchases. They bought prepared grilled shrimp at $25.99 a pound, smoked salmon—mostly plain but at least one patron ordered double smoked and Scotch cured—at $39 a pound, cooked and ready-to-eat vegetables including winter roasted kale at $9.99 and cauliflower with hazelnuts at $6.99, cheese blintzes at $2.25 each, and latkes at $8.99. Also available were duck foie gras at $99 a pound, sable at $49, and a whole white fish fillet—about three pounds before filleting—for $70.

It was easy, having just left the subway, to view this opulence against the backdrop of panhandlers and at-risk individuals who searched trash containers for edible ends of discarded meals and empty drink cans worth five cents each. They may not have been any more typical of New York's population than those buying pâté, and yet the city

does set homeless records every year, with more than sixty thousand people arriving at shelters each night.

That the distance between these divergent groups is growing is part of the city's new dynamics, as is the trend of big chain stores replacing smaller, individually owned shops. That November I found a string of small shops on the east side of Broadway from 77th to 78th replaced by a giant CVS and an equally big Marshalls—one city block taken over by two stores. Both were busy.

This new paradigm appeared to be good for the new Upper West Side. The neighborhood was obviously thriving, a clear victory for the forces that pushed hard for urban renewal. Space was in such demand that the garage at 210 West 77th Street, that for decades accommodated Hertz car rental, ended up in a month-long bidding war in 2013; its market value jumped from $10 million to $55 million. A 2015 *New York Times* article would say the new space was destined for apartments "ranging in size from two to five bedrooms and priced from $4 million to about $22 million for the penthouses." By then what was once Big Nick's would be taken over by the Mille-Feuille Bakery Café, where a box of twenty-one French macarons—not macaroons, the coconut-based cookie popular during Passover, but a pastry made with different fillings—sold for $44.90.

These new economics apparently fit the tenant now paying $2,800 for my former apartment and those paying twice that for a similar one-bedroom in a doorman building. Who they do not fit was me.

I miss the old Upper West Side, the smaller businesses run by people I knew and who knew me, businesses that served a residential community that might occasionally purchase a quarter-pound of thinly sliced Nova but were more likely to show up near closing for discounted smoked salmon ends and would rely on getting their shoes resoled instead of replaced—or would if they could still locate a cobbler. And while I find sightseeing at Zabar's entertaining, I cringe at the prospect of its continuing to devour small shops on its block, drawing even more limousines to double-park out front, and what all this represents.

Early on in this transformation, when I still had the apartment and these new attitudes were first surfacing, I sought out an old colleague for whom I had written when he was staff editor on a major publication; by this time he was semiretired, picking up occasional work as a freelance journalist. Ours was one of those hybrid relationships that often develops, or at least did during my earlier days in New York, primarily professional but also friendly. I wrote for him in his various positions and we also socialized, often discussing his jobs and mine, projects that had nothing to do with our work together. So when I had an idea for a magazine article and needed a sharp editorial eye to test its merits, I felt comfortable seeking him out—a little conversation over coffee, along with some guidance. I had engaged others in the same capacity in the past and offered similar assistance to other writers.

At first it went well. He listened and offered cogent views. But when I asked him to explain how I might implement one of his suggestions, he did not respond. Instead came, "You know, I get paid for this now." No talk about a fee followed. The moment had passed and our editorial coffee was over. We have not spoken since.

Perhaps it is harsh of me to suggest that my former colleague had become less generous. I appreciate the pres sure to squeeze out a living in hard economic times and maybe he was financially pressed, but I admit to being surprised; the switch in his tone was abrupt. It may also be simplistic of me to take one encounter and turn it into a trend. If so, call my reasoning superficial. But I don't think that same exchange would have happened in the New York that I found in the 1960s and '70s.

And while many of the changes in the face of businesses on the Upper West Side are the product of escalating rents and aging owners whose children would rather become business executives than shopkeepers, I think my old neighborhood—and maybe the entire city—has changed in ways both obvious and profound, more noise and crowds, as well as reduced generosity. It is still smart and charged with creative energy but more buttoned up and less accessible than it once was; still strong but less easy as the new economics impact everyone's behavior.

My reaction to this evolution is not unique; previous generations have had their own versions. They mourn the passing of Schrafft's restaurants, the Third Avenue El, and

the Polo Grounds. They insist that Louis Hardin, the blind poet and composer known as Moondog, who in his horned headpiece and robe haunted city streets day and night from the 1940s till the 1970s, represented a kind of free spirit no longer welcome.

Their objections are frequently not specific, referring to a good feeling now gone. In his 1948 essay "Here is New York" for *Holiday*, E. B. White complained, "By comparison with other less hectic days, the city is uncomfortable and inconvenient." Visiting from North Brooklin, Maine, White separated himself from residents of his former home, as so many of us do. "But New Yorkers temperamentally do not crave comfort and convenience—if they did they would live elsewhere."

Still, like the line from the 1970s advertising campaign and the song of the same name, I love New York. I really do. I am filled with affection when I reflect back on my time living there and feel strong admiration when I return. When others criticize it, I rush to its defense. At a recent gathering on the Cape, I challenged a woman who praised Washington's subway—so new and clean—in comparison to New York's. I pointed out that DC's system covers less of its city than New York's and shuts down at midnight on weekdays, when working people need it most; New York's subway—not so new or clean, always in need of repair and much maligned for that—operates twenty-four hours a day. I'm afraid I suggested that her view of the primary mission of urban public transportation systems was skewed, even a tad elitist.

I recognize that this duality, embracing New York while accepting that it and I no longer find ourselves in the harmony that once characterized our relationship, is at least partly my adjustment to a situation I cannot change, my forty-six-year connection with New York being severed. And while I accept that my return visits—joyous as they are—are now only as a visitor, I am left with a hole I cannot fill.

Now that I am committing myself to Cape Cod, how do I make a good life there without the grit, stimulation, and wonder of New York to balance all that pastoral beauty and clean air? Civil, loaded with charm, and accommodating to the needs of its population as the Cape is, my time there is now being forced into the shadow of a place I cannot stop thinking of as The City.

It remains for me not Manhattan or New York but THE CITY, the destination of all those international visitors flying into JFK for business or pleasure and teenagers who take the 59th Street Bridge from Queens, who are, in the words of Paul Simon and Art Garfunkel, "Feelin' groovy."

Legacy

Coping with the winter of 2013–2014 on Cape Cod replaced my obsessing over the quality of life in one great place or another, at least temporarily.

That season inspired the *Cape Cod Times* to lead a mid-March article with the following: "Another frigid morning. You slip and slide out to the car. The ice-frosted windshield mocks you. The door handle is frozen. You put your coffee cup down on the hood and it slides off. It begins snowing. You sob. Tears roll off your cheeks, turn into ice cubes and fall inside your boots." All of this was in preparation for the paper's essential point, that it was the worst of Cape winters.

Or maybe not. It was bad but not that historically bad by New England standards—but it sure felt bad. We suffered through brutally cold temperatures and lots of snow, as much as eighty inches, prompting two prolonged power outages. Julie by now had remarried, and her new husband supported her long-held passion for California and its milder climate. They moved to an unincorporated community in

western Sonoma County—seriously rural, off the power grid, requiring solar panels for electricity and cell phones for communication with the world outside, and drawing water from their own well. Mail was delivered to a box at the bottom of the steep hill that they shared with four other houses, a fifteen-minute drive each way, switchback after switchback, down and then up. But it was still California and so warm, except during the rainy season, when it was cold and wet. But it was never cold like Cape Cod, and no snow.

They were thrilled with their decision, filled with enthusiasm about the future. The children were surprised and quietly supportive until the reality filtered down that the plan involved selling the house on High Street where they grew up, the one place they all called home. They were accepting but not so happy.

Their mood worsened when they were told to clear out their belongings, everything saved from childhood, from elementary school and middle school, high school and college, books and clothes and papers, tangible pieces of memory collected from their time on the Cape, dating from when Rebecca was nearly six and the triplets almost three. That was twenty-three years times four children: a total of ninety-two years of accumulation. And not gather it someday but right then. Julie and husband, Rick, were renting out the house for the summer with tenants due the first of July.

However emotionally wrenched the children felt, more pressing was what to do with their possessions. The choices were to throw them out or store them at my place. I came

down on my side. If our children stored their worldly goods at my house, this was one more reason for me to remain an active part of their lives. I welcomed whatever they had.

The deadline was the first week in June 2014. All four children flew in; Rebecca from DC, Matt from San Diego, Jake from San Francisco, and Alex from Gainesville. Since they all lived in small apartments, there was little they could personally claim. What to take, what to store, and what to deposit at the town dump made for a tension-filled four days. Nights were worse. While the house by then had a bedroom for each child, some rooms were bigger than others, and so they had rotated every few years. Now last-night choices were the issue; each of them wanted to sleep in his or her favorite room one last time. There were some harsh words and tears, but they all managed to behave for the final family dinner at 12 High Street.

By Sunday they were all gone, soon to be replaced by summer renters and eventually new residents. The children headed to Boston's Logan Airport; Julie and Rick temporarily remained local. They spent the summer with friends, cleaned up after the last tenants left, then turned the house over to realtors for sale. On September 18, having shipped most of their belongings to Sonoma County, they crowded our Luna and Rick's dog, Dude—the product of a romantic moment between a golden retriever and a husky—into their eight-year-old subcompact and headed west.

The only one of us remaining on the Cape was me, a result long in the making and yet surprisingly unsettling. You would think I'd have been perfectly comfortable; I had courted a life

alone since I was old enough to influence my own existence. All of those years traveling for work were alone; all that time spent writing, tens of thousands of hours, all of them alone. Even through marriage and parenthood I managed to block out time for myself—a lot of time, apparently. Julie made this clear when ending our marriage.

Would it have made a difference to her if I had been off reporting on war, famine, or pandemic, forced by circumstance and professional responsibility to cover a story, wherever it was and however long it lasted? Perhaps, but I wasn't. My assignments were by comparison inglorious. But I suspect the issue was less the nature of my work and more the fact that it lasted as long as it did, and this by my own choice: a few more days in the field to get the facts straight, or at least straighter. Probably worse were the hours of writing, days and often nights of them, indulging my pursuit of the best possible version of a sentence or a paragraph, all of this while home—just next door—but alone, leaving Julie the only parent with four children.

I understood all of this, and I knew that this day was coming. By that summer I had nearly twenty years to digest the eventual dissolution of our family unit and the prospects of being alone, and I never totally abandoned my attitude toward that condition. Even my attempts at subsequent relationships failed, at least partly because of my preference to be alone. Good as the companionship was—and it often was very good—I invariably found myself eager to end it. Hours of closeness were good, even days strung together,

but hardly ever longer. Obviously, being apart from other people was my choice.

But this was different. This time my preference took on an absolute quality and a sense of finality, something I had not experienced before or, more accurately, not fully grasped. In truth, the realization of what lay ahead had been coming on me for years, lingered around the edge of my consciousness. It built from the time our marriage began to fragment and divorce seemed inevitable, and it became most evident with the milestone events of 2006—the actual divorce, the High Street house being empty of children, and then my moving out. It was toward the end of this noteworthy series that the full impact presented itself to me. One occasion that fall brought the point home.

In October 2006 I accompanied my brother to Miami to deal with the affairs of Sadie Avin, his ninety-eight-year-old mother-in-law, who had just died, having outlived her husband and daughter; Lee's wife, Judy, died of cancer in 2003. We cleaned out Sadie's apartment and settled her bill at the nursing home.

Our final task was to attend her graveside service. It was eleven thirty on a hot morning, the sun beating down on the large tent that was set up to shade the mourners; I counted forty-five folding chairs. Only two were occupied: one for Lee and one for me. As the rabbi recited the Kaddish, the Jewish prayer for the dead, I pondered if this were not an advanced version of my own funeral, alone, proceeded by years of growing old, alone.

It was a morbid thought and probably not based in reality. I did have four children, and when I relayed this story to Jake, he guaranteed that for me "the tent will be full." I nonetheless found the image impossible to ignore, with all those symbols of a life shared dropping away, one after another. Now, eight years later, the process had been pushed much further along. The family home and the marriage were elements in our past, and the children were well on their way to creating new lives elsewhere. Even Julie, with whom I was still friendly, was a continent away, and with our dog. I remained on the Cape, along with the only tangible reminders of my family: old photographs, notes from my children attached to my refrigerator, and forty-eight plastic bins containing their stuff.

Alone was no longer just an idea, a now-and-then ideal in response to my designing my own life with all the peace and quiet time to write. This was real and complete, the ultimate "be careful what you wish for" scenario. And this was not happening in New York, a place that so perfectly accommodates people on their own, but on Cape Cod, better suited for couples.

I have been alone for days and weeks at a time in London and Madrid, for months on the Costa del Sol and in Paris, and gotten along nicely, but I have been alone best in New York. Most aspects of New York life, while easily enjoyed as part of a couple, adapted perfectly to being single. Window shopping along Fifth Avenue or people watching in Greenwich Village may have been good social activities, prompting conversation filled with shared observations, but I maintain

that they were just as good—and in some cases better—alone, elevated as an intellectual exercise when one person takes quiet time to reflect on what is being observed.

This was especially true in museums, where Siqueiros's *Echo of a Scream* at the Modern or the Egyptian Temple of Dendur at the Metropolitan will hold one person's attention for twenty or thirty minutes while someone else prefers to pass them by. Accommodating another's taste may be prudent—even important for being a good companion—but it is contrary to the value of the museum experience, not only to look but to see and think.

My favorite example of what was better alone was attending the movies, dating back to my early days in New York. Taking myself to a movie, particularly in a near-empty theater in the afternoon—my favorite situation—was a mini vacation from the confines of my office and the pressure of work and life, and yet so easy, with six theaters on Broadway between 72nd and 96th Streets. Each viewing was a sensory extravaganza, seated in my preferred location in the middle of the second row, engulfed by the giant screen and stereo sound while enjoying the sandwich and wine that I'd smuggled in.

Even walking alone in New York is worthwhile. In addition to those visual treats that the city provides, I have this sense of liberation—no one to hasten my pace or deter me from stopping at a shop on a whim, no one to disappoint or embarrass or bore with the wrong comment. All the while, if I feel moved to interact with someone else who is also alone, I can—impossible if I am walking with a partner.

Do I think I'm describing a particularly healthy lifestyle, one I am suggesting for anyone else? No. But I have been seduced by the ability to follow my own schedule for eating, working, sleeping, and recreating, along with exactly how I pursue these activities, all without negotiating or being judged. If I work till midnight and then cook a full meal, there is no one to criticize me; a nap between particularly difficult paragraphs will not elicit a charge of my being lazy. If I find myself awake at three o'clock in the morning, there is no one to disturb if I switch on the light to read until I'm sleepy.

And while this freedom occasionally leaves me lonely, that is the price for fully indulging these choices, behavior so common today that it sparks academic research and thoughtful essays in the press and online, complete with warnings about its dangers and suggestions for how to more successfully manage the solitary life.

This is not to negate the value of socializing, and I propose that the city is also a great place for connecting. It creates many opportunities for good conversation, not just as gateway events, possible grounds for long-time friendships, but as singular entities in themselves, exchanges to satisfy the need for human interaction. Encounters at The Coffee House, *Audubon*, and the other venues in my limited world rarely led to bonding; mostly they were good, one-off conversations. There were exceptions. An *Audubon* editor and I formed a close relationship that has lasted forty-five years; the designer of my AKC newspaper is to this day

a dear friend. But this was never the goal; stimulating communication was, along with a little personal contact.

Time in New York taught me to understand my need to be alone and my need for company and how to effectively seek both to achieve a measure of personal harmony. Once these lessons were learned and thoroughly tested in the streets, the bars, parks, and museums of New York—and mostly in Apartment Four of 336—I developed a set of canons to live by: even in the most positive of situations, vacationing with friends or visiting my children, I needed to mix in a little alone time with all that good social interaction; even when working well for two or three days alone, I needed a few hours' worth of conversation with another person.

Now, more alone than ever before, came the ultimate test: Could I make these truths transferable enough to create a new life on Cape Cod? This was different from when I first moved to the Cape, fresh from New York, bolstered by my family and filled with optimism and naiveté about how smooth my transition would be. I now knew better and had years of trial and error to guide me.

As most of my time was spent sitting in a chair, reading or working but always sedentary, I had been going to a gymnasium since moving to the Cape; an hour of exercise four or five times a week after work and before dinner. I soon found it also provided entertainment, mostly voyeuristic. Gyms are filled with attractive men and women wearing reduced amounts of clothing, their well-developed and toned bodies inviting observation that is tolerated if it does not cross the

line to ogling. (Not all of these experiences are positive. I happened upon a naked, overweight man in the locker room, freshly showered, legs spread apart and bending forward to apply a blow dryer to his genitals, a disturbing image I remain unable to wipe from my memory.)

And because they attract people who share a commitment to physical exercise, gyms are their own little communities, offering opportunities for interaction for those who wish it. Members say hello and good-bye, wish each other a good day, inquire as to why several sessions have been missed, and are quick to compliment new gear or even a recent trip to the barber. And there is often shared banter about working out. One evening when I was struggling to finish my twenty minutes on the treadmill, a little old lady—probably in her eighties—jogged past me on her way to the locker and commented, "Faster, sonny, faster." Simple, pleasant ribbing, and oddly satisfying.

Over time I noticed an unusual level of personal information disclosed in casual circumstances. A Vietnam vet with an obvious limp freely volunteered that after a mortar round riddled both his legs with shrapnel, thirteen operations were required to allow him to hobble as well as he did. "I told the surgeon before that last operation that if he couldn't get it right this time to cut them both off," he said; no update was necessary.

Some of these conversations were surprisingly intimate. "You probably noticed I haven't been in for a while," said a man my age whom I hardly knew; I hadn't noticed. "My wife

died—ovarian cancer. They operated in April and said she might have six months. She died in four." I said that had to be depressing. "No," he said, "my mind doesn't go there, but I have been very sad."

I never tried extending any of these interactions beyond the gym; I didn't feel the need. I had a wife and four children and the associations they engendered. Even later, after getting divorced, I traveled regularly to New York and saw the kids when they came home, creating what I felt was enough of a social life.

But by the fall of 2014 my situation was radically different and I recognized a need to pursue more human contact. The gym proved to be a convenient source, made easier by people's pattern of keeping to set schedules, one that I shared. I met a contractor, hired him for repair work on my house, and found we liked talking. A teacher newly retired from a college-preparatory school in Western Massachusetts was also on my schedule; working at adjacent elliptical machines, we discovered we had similar taste in writing. Some of these encounters led to time spent together outside the gym, others just expanded our dialogue while exercising, but they all provided a sense of community.

Since getting divorced, I began taking in occasional nights of music. There were plenty of choices. The Barley Neck Inn near our old house in East Orleans offered rock and roll, the Harvest Gallery Wine Bar in neighboring Dennis had pop and jazz, and house concerts turned local residences into music halls, where as many as fifty or sixty

people kick in twenty dollars each to hear live, professionally performed music; a contribution of wine and snacks was not required but always materialized, social lubricants to facilitate conversation.

At first I went just for the music, but once the current and former members of my family departed and I lost the apartment, I needed to invoke that brand of linkage once found at Jay's and the Limelight in New York. And it worked. I met a singer and her bass-playing husband. I met a keyboardist and then an events producer. Suddenly there was a new group of people to share conversation between sets and even go out for an occasional drink when no performance was scheduled.

Together with the people from the gym and a few holdovers from my marriage days, they formed the core of a friendship group that satisfied my meager requirements for human interaction. These were lessons learned in New York, necessary for the solitary life without the social structure of a job: seek out various populations in search of individuals willing to engage in an occasional evening of conversation.

This has not been as easy as in New York, a place filled with interesting people eager for lively debate and conversation that serves as entertainment. New Yorkers tend to look for new opportunities to interact; full-time Cape Codders— essentially New Englanders—are more likely to be satisfied with the friends they have and have had for years.

But the Cape offers a wide breadth of personalities, people with a variety of human experience in their histories. The trick is to find them. As it is nonurban, there isn't that automatic

flow into public spaces and so people must be sought out and on their schedule. But because it is such a small population in a limited physical area, the choices are well known, drawing people whose familiarity with each other, over time and with a little extra effort, creates a congenial atmosphere. The result is that serendipitous happenings occur that may be harder to duplicate in the rush and pressure of a metropolis.

In the summer of 2015, about a year after my family's official exit from High Street, my musician friends invited me to a small house concert, one with a more narrow focus than most. This evening a dozen of us gathered to hear a young local singer-songwriter, Jordan Renzi. I think no money changed hands, but there was wine, something to eat, and an eagerness to hear a bright, new talent.

While getting acquainted, I was introduced to our host's sister, visiting from Goshen, New York. Always looking for something unfoolish to break the ice, I said that a New York friend had relocated to Goshen. She was surprised, Goshen having a population of fewer than five thousand. I explained that my friend was Joan Goldberg and relayed the story of lawyer Goldberg's intervening with my being sent to Vietnam in 1968, and in doing so, I was convinced, saving my life—a shorter version of the story I told you in Chapter Four.

It was one of those little coincidences, and we all laughed. I asked her to say hello to Joan for me. She promised she would, and we moved on. We drank wine and snacked on chips and salsa while waiting for Jordan to tune her guitar and sing.

That was it, or so I thought, until mid-November when I received an email from our host that evening. "I am sending you Jordan's song that she just recorded," read the email. "Please don't share as it is a demo, but she wanted you to hear it." I had no idea what she was talking about. Then I played the song.

"Please say hello to a lady up north who told them to pass me by. Her name is Joan Goldberg, a lawyer from New York, she gave the orders to save my life," it began and went on to tell Jordan's version of my adventure with the army.

Listening to the song, I thought of the chain of events that took me to Joan's office in 1968, that led to Jordan in 2015, and of all that came between. When the lyrics described a scene when the war is history and I am sitting "across from my wife, our daughter just turned sixteen," I became misty, touched by an image personal to me but configured in another writer's mind. (Jordan has since released the song on a CD. Listen to it at skiprozin.com under the section about this book.)

Julie and the marriage were gone from my life, but Rebecca and the triplets were ever present, a connection forti-fied for me by simple check-in phone calls, the occasional note sent for no reason, and some special instances with powerful resonance. On a recent birthday I received a series of five photographs. The first was of a twenty-year-old me, wearing sunglasses and sitting on the roof of the old *Miami Herald*, one of the outtakes for the article I wrote about the city jail that years later helped stall my induction into the

army. The photo had become for the kids part of family lore: "Dad released from the joint." The other photos were of each of my children, posed for the occasion just as I had been in that shot in 1962, complete with sunglasses. (See page 199.)

The importance of these gestures is their power to remind me that for all the twists and turns that appear to leave me mostly alone, I am in fact not. With none of my children living on Cape Cod and their only physical presence represented by storage bins and refrigerator art, they are never far away, a reality that they reinforce with frequency, in person and through various forms of long-distance communication. And while they never use these words, I interpret this to mean that they do not consider me to be a bad father and that something about our time together was positive enough for them to want to save and take with them into their futures.

I continue to love New York; I go in three or four times a year. And while I miss living there, what I really miss is living there in those years between 1965 and 1991, a time—and to a certain extent a place—that no longer exists. But even then, good as it was, I never inspired anybody there to write a song.

Still, without New York I would never have met Jim Brown, who before I had sold a single story or article took me on as a client, or the string of other people who helped me continue to write and publish in the most high-risk center of a profession already fraught with rejection. I would never have met Joan Goldberg who saved me from going to Vietnam, never have met Julie and had these four kids; perhaps other children but not these, and that is what matters most.

This book is about all that, about how many of us are drawn to New York at a point in our lives and, while most of us eventually leave, we are profoundly changed by our time there—and, I maintain, made better by the experience.

And so what this book is really about is change, how we resist it and accept it, and how it shapes our lives. For me that change was viewed from one small apartment on West 77th Street, second floor front, the point of convergence for forces major and minor for forty-six years.

I am officially gone from the city, but those changes continue to impact the quality of my life.

Acknowledgments

This book would not exist if I hadn't been evicted from Apartment Four at 336 West 77th Street, my connection to all that is New York from 1965 until 2011. I have no hard feelings toward the landlord who ousted me, but neither am I about to thank him for inspiring my work.

The people I do thank are those who helped me turn the forty-six-year relationship between my apartment and me into a book. Most prominent among them is Ned Crabb, who believed from the beginning and was passionately supportive as I moved from an idea discussed over drinks to a completed manuscript. Sadly, Ned died in 2017 but remains in my thoughts.

Since the book details a writer's hit-and-miss efforts to remain viable, I thank those who extended whatever connections they had to gain me work. While I cannot possibly list them all, in addition to those mentioned in the text, I single out Melanie Radley, Sheldon Cotler, Ann Guilfoyle, and of course, Ned Crabb. All were part of that chain of New York connectivity, friends of friends.

Not every act of friendship during my New York years was work related; the city was good to me in innumerable ways. If I were to describe the many instances that I was aided by the legal and ethical guidance of Hanno Mott, I would lose track of my primary narrative.

No individual bridges the gap between jobs, friendship, and this book better than Tom Carling. He has never failed to share access to work and his New York apartment, once I lost mine. His generosity extends to the cover design of this book and the building of a website.

Finally, I thank Julie, for accepting my airing the intimacies of our life together, for fact-checking the manuscript, and most important, for permitting the prolonging of our marriage under circumstances often less than comfortable. I cannot speak for anyone else, but I prospered from that in profound ways.

CPSIA information can be obtained
at www.ICGtesting.com
Printed in the USA
JSHW022337130819
1083JS00001B/6